Influence Mar

How to Create, Manage, and
Influencers in Social Media Marketing

DANNY BROWN
SAM FIORELLA

800 East 96th Street
Indianapolis, Indiana 46240 USA

Influence Marketing

ISBN-13: 978-0-7897-5104-1
ISBN-10: 0-7897-5104-6

Library of Congress Cataloging-in-Publication Data is on file.

Printed in the United States of America

First Printing: May 2013

Trademarks

Warning and Disclaimer

Bulk Sales

Que Publishing offers excellent discounts on this book when ordered in quantity for bulk purchases or special sales. For more information, please contact

> U.S. Corporate and Government Sales
> 1-800-382-3419
> corpsales@pearsontechgroup.com

For sales outside of the U.S., please contact

> International Sales
> international@pearson.com

Editor-in-Chief
Greg Wiegand

Sr. Acquisitions Editor
Katherine Bull

Peer Reviewer
Tonia Ries

Development Editor
Karen E. Klein

Managing Editor
Kristy Hart

Project Editor
Andy Beaster

Copy Editor
Geneil Breeze

Indexer
Heather McNeill

Proofreader
Sheri Replin

Publishing Coordinator
Cindy Teeters

Cover Designer
Anne Jones

Compositor
Nonie Ratcliff

Que Biz-Tech Editorial Board
Michael Brito
Jason Falls
Rebecca Lieb
Simon Salt
Peter Shankman

CONTENTS AT A GLANCE

TABLE OF CONTENTS

4 The Current Influence Model and Social Scoring 55

5 Situational Influence: A New Model for a New Era 73

About the Authors

Danny Brown is Chief Technologist at ArCompany, a business intelligence consultancy helping organizations adapt to the changing communications landscape, allowing for more meaningful dialogue with customers and stakeholders. He is a multiple award-winning marketer, who has worked with leading consumer, technology, and digital companies including IBM, LG, FedEx, Ford Canada, Microsoft Canada, Scotiabank, Vodafone, Dell, BT, Orange, and BlackBerry. He has spoken at TEDx as well as numerous business conferences, and his blog is recognized as the #1 marketing blog in the world by HubSpot.

Sam Fiorella is Partner at Sensei Marketing, a customer experience consultancy based in Toronto and New York. Over the past 20 years, Sam has developed the strategy and led the execution on over 1800 Web projects for clients and marketing agencies around the world including Morgan Stanley, AOL, Snyder's of Hanover, Deutsche Bank, Hyatt Gaming Management, and Intrawest Resorts. These experiences—and the proven results—have made Sam a highly sought-after strategist and public speaker on the importance of customer experience and measurement in social media marketing.

Dedication

For all those who refuse to be defined by a score.

Acknowledgments

The ideas, strategies, and methodologies shared in this book were born from years of dialogue, debate, and professional work with a very large community. As such, there's no way we could mention everyone by name; however, a few people must be given special mention.

From Danny:

To my amazing wife, Jacki, and my awesome kids, Ewan and Salem—you are the true influencers of me every single day. Thank you for putting up with me more than usual for the last 12 months. I love you.

To my wife's mother, Traci, for your support and belief in Jacki and me from the very first day. I know we couldn't have done half the things we have without you. Thank you.

To Hessie Jones, Amy Tobin, and Andrew Jenkins of ArCompany, for allowing me to be around your smarts each day and showing that integrity and honesty in business aren't just a sound bite, and for shouldering my work while I was buried in book edits. Dinner is on me.

To Faheem Rauf, an influencer of the truest kind when it comes to the definition of leading by example and staying true to your morals. You inspire me.

Huge thanks to the PVSM Punks. From an idea borne out of frustration, our little group has become an area where I know I can go to laugh, cry, cheer, and be amazed, all at the same time. I'm indebted to you for letting me be part of such an amazing collective.

To the community I've been incredibly fortunate to grow with around my blog and across social media, thank you for taking the time out of your day to visit my little part of the Web. My online adventures would be very mundane without you.

And to my coauthor, Sam, a special thank you. I can't think of another person I'd rather have written this book with, and your support when the words wouldn't quite flow helped more than you could know. You're a good man and someone I'm proud to call friend.

From Sam:

To Susan, Lucas, and Vanessa, thank you for your patience, understanding, and support during the past year as I dedicated every free moment to planning and writing this book. I appreciate your sacrifices, love, and encouragement.

To my team at Sensei Marketing and clients like Nick and Peter Grande at MV-1 Canada, many thanks for your willingness to take this ride with me and for your roles in testing various influence marketing campaigns.

Thanks to Ric Dragon, Jure Klepic, Fred McClimans, Alan Berkson, Steve Woodruff, Lee Bogner, Dr. Natalie Petouhoff, Rebel Brown, and Judi Samuels for debating the issue of influence marketing with me over the past few years. Thanks also to all those who have exchanged ideas on this subject during my weekly #biz-forum debates on Twitter. You pushed me to not accept the status quo and to envision what's possible.

My section of this book was written almost entirely at the Starbucks located at the intersection of Dundas and Trafalgar in Oakville, Ontario. Gratitude to the entire team there including Erika, "the smitten kitten" barista who kept me well caffeinated and alert!

Finally, thanks to my coauthor, Danny Brown, who, between the laughs, beers, jabs, and brainstorming, turned out to be the perfect writing partner in this endeavor and an even better friend.

From both of us:

Many companies engaged in influence marketing were generous with their time and insights through the many interviews and work sessions we conducted during the writing of this book work. We want to thank each of them: Eric Weissman from oneQube, Robert Moore from Internet Media Labs, Andrew Grill from Kred, Azeem Azhar and Ferenc Huszar from PeerIndex, Pierre-Loic Assayag and Evyenia Wilkins from Traackr, Larry Levy and Dave Fausel from Appinions, Jason Weaver from Shoutlet, Jon Ferrara from Nimble, Susan Emerick from IBM, Mark Fidelman from Evolve!, Brian Vickery from Mantis Technology Group, Matt Hixson from Tellagence, Mark Zohar from TrendSpottr, Jen Evans from Squeeze, Johnny Miller from Manumatix and Yoram Greener from Salorix.

Their support and feedback were invaluable.

To our peer editor Tonia Ries and development editor Karen E. Klein, for taking our raw words and actually making them sound smart. We hope we left some of your sanity intact!

To our amazing production team at Que—Andy Beaster, our production editor, our copy editor, Geneil Breeze, our proofreader, Sheri Replin, and our cover designer, Alan Clements. Thank you all for helping us through the scary process of authoring a book for the first time. We couldn't have done it without you.

Finally, a special thank you to Katherine Bull, our acquisitions editor. You believed in the book we wanted to write and kept us sane when the real work began. Thank you.

Online Files

Additional online resources can be found at www.influencemarketingbook.com.

We Want to Hear from You!

As the reader of this book, *you* are our most important critic and commentator. We value your opinion and want to know what we're doing right, what we could do better, what areas you'd like to see us publish in, and any other words of wisdom you're willing to pass our way.

As an associate publisher for Que Publishing, I welcome your comments. You can email or write me directly to let me know what you did or didn't like about this book—as well as what we can do to make our books better.

Please note that I cannot help you with technical problems related to the topic of this book. We do have a User Services group, however, where I will forward specific technical questions related to the book.

When you write, please be sure to include this book's title and author as well as your name, email address, and phone number. I will carefully review your comments and share them with the author and editors who worked on the book.

Email: feedback@quepublishing.com

Mail: Greg Wiegand
Editor-in-Chief
Que Publishing
800 East 96th Street
Indianapolis, IN 46240 USA

Reader Services

Visit our website and register this book at quepublishing.com/register for convenient access to any updates, downloads, or errata that might be available for this book.

1

Logic and Reason (or How We Learned to Love Influence Marketing)

Influencer marketing, (also Influence Marketing) is a form of marketing that has emerged from a variety of recent practices and studies, in which focus is placed on specific key individuals (or types of individual) rather than the target market as a whole. It identifies the individuals that have influence over potential buyers, and orients marketing activities around these influencers.
—Wikipedia

Influence is a complex and misused term in our world today. At its core, influence is a force created by one person or entity that causes a reaction in or by another. In plain language this could be a parent influencing the behavior of a child, a fashion designer influencing retail trends, or a religion influencing the beliefs and actions of its members.

Simple, right? Well, it might be if we lived in relative isolation. The reality is that we live in a hyperconnected world with an overabundance of data from news to advertisements to opinion. The Internet and social media channels have created a world where everyone can be a news source, a thought leader, and a potential influencer. When everyone adds his or her voice to the collective conversation, have we created clarity or generated noise? Ironically, information overload, the hallmark of our digital age, has simultaneously increased our desire for more knowledge and decreased our patience for it. We seek more information and have faster access across multiple devices, yet the length of time we spend on websites and our willingness to look past the first page of search engine results are decreasing.[1]

Exerting influence over customers has always been one of the key roles of marketing professionals, including influencing desires and purchase decisions. Brand marketers infuse everything from love, humor, guilt, and sex into emotionally charged advertisements across every media channel to persuade consumers to buy or talk about their products. Another oft-used technique, especially during the 1980s and 1990s, is word-of-mouth marketing, which encourages customers to recommend the products and businesses they love to their family and friends. Marketers quickly learned the power of word-of-mouth marketing when studies showed that such messages were seen as more credible by the public—and thus more likely to be acted upon—because the referrer had no stake in the product being recommended. The recommendation was seen as an authentic declaration of support, not spin created by savvy marketers. And so influence marketing, the orientation of marketing tactics around people identified as having influence over others, was solidified.

As with influence, the practice of influence marketing was relatively simple and straightforward; that is, until the Internet and social media disrupted the direct communication path between the brand, its influencers, and their followers. The implied trust that was critical to the success of word-of-mouth marketing campaigns was challenged when so many different voices and sources of information began to weave their way into the decision-making process of consumers. With social technologies empowering people to share their opinions and views with the world, everyone has become an influencer, and when everyone is an influencer, how do marketers identify influential people to execute their word-of-mouth campaigns?

In 2010, social influence scoring platforms began to emerge in an attempt to sort and rank individuals by their perceived influence based on the content they shared on social networks, the frequency at which they shared that content and the size of their audience. Marketers, desperate to regain the power of word-of-mouth marketing, and in the absence of other options to adequately identify influencers, quickly embraced these platforms with mixed results. The resulting level of heated public debate over the accuracy of social influencer scores, their effectiveness in word-of-mouth marketing efforts, and their impact on the authenticity of social conversations is proof that the desire to identify and leverage influencers for brand marketing efforts is still high.

We're no exception. As brand marketers and consultants, we've sought digital solutions to once again leverage the power of word-of-mouth marketing for our clients, including the use of these social scoring platforms. Based on the lack of measurable results, inconsistent algorithms, and digital security concerns—among other factors—we understood more study and experimentation were required. Retaining the principles of effective word-of-mouth marketing, we decided to experiment with different methodologies in the new digital world. This book is the result of that experimentation. We share our successes and failures and outline the resulting methodology based on our lessons learned.

So let's begin. Please allow us to tell you the story of a client's business that was the genesis of our influence marketing methodology and what inspired us to write this book. It's the story of a venture that took a company with a great product, no distribution channel, and seemingly insurmountable obstacles to a company with that same great product but also national exposure and profitable sales after successfully implementing an influence marketing strategy. The rest of this chapter takes you on that journey with us, where we share with you the two failed attempts to markedly improve sales and how those failures led us to the discovery of a new model that anyone can use to achieve similar results.

Introducing MV-1 Canada

The experiences of brothers Nick and Peter Grande, CEO and president of Grande National Leasing, respectively, one of Canada's oldest independent auto leasing firms, highlighted the lack of accessible transportation options for people challenged with physical disabilities. "The requests for accessible vehicle leases by consumers and transit authorities alike were on the rise," shares Nick Grande. "We grew frustrated by the lack of options we had to supply the demand."

The savvy duo understood the business opportunity in supporting this underserviced market yet also understood the financial and operational obstacles. In the end, their personal commitment to this community emboldened them to accept the challenge. They refocused their core business operations from auto leasing to sourcing innovative products and services for people living with disabilities and their families. They began investing in all areas of the industry including retail outlets that provided accessibility supplies and accessible conversions for automobiles and homes.

Their business continued to expand when in 2006 Nick Grande was approached by the Toronto Transit Commission with a request to supply an accessible transit vehicle that was more sturdy and durable than that currently available. This led to the discovery of a new, purpose-built accessibility vehicle—the MV-1—that was being tested in Chicago, Illinois, by Patton Corrigan, owner of a large fleet of taxis there. Corrigan conceived and built a prototype of the MV-1 in response to a similar request received by the City of Chicago for more accessible taxis.

As a result of the demand and positive feedback, the new vehicle is now a factory-built, commercially available accessible vehicle for consumers, public transit, and private limousine companies across North America. Soon after meeting with Corrigan in Chicago, Nick and Peter Grande formed MV-1 Canada and penned an agreement to be the exclusive importer and marketer of the MV-1 to the Canadian marketplace. As shown in Figure 1.1, this new car features an industry leading powered telescoping ramp that disappears beneath the floor but above the frame to ensure it is protected from the elements. With a cavernous door opening, the MV-1 easily accommodates any size of wheelchair or scooter while the large internal cabin allows easy maneuverability inside the vehicle. In fact, it has no "shotgun seat" so that family members in wheelchairs can sit up front or easily transfer from their wheelchair into the driver's seat. Inside and out, the vehicle is truly revolutionary for people with disabilities, caregivers, and the transportation businesses that serve them.

Figure 1.1   *The MV-1 is the first purpose-built vehicle for people with disabilities and their families.*

Before the introduction of the MV-1, people who required transportation to accommodate wheelchairs often struggled to use standard vehicles or relied on accessible public transit (where available). For greater freedom and independence, some chose to have a third-party retrofit a standard minivan, which often required cutting out and lowering the vehicle's floor, adding a retractable ramp, or reconfiguring various user controls. Unfortunately, the costs of converting a standard vehicle, on top of its purchase price, are shockingly high. For example, a converted minivan averages US$20,000 more than the MV-1. Further, the conversions necessary to accommodate wheelchair passengers often void the manufacturer's warranty because it could compromise the vehicle's structural integrity and safety features.

On the commercial side, with no other options, transit companies favored similarly retrofitted vans or custom-built mass transportation vehicles. And as with individual consumers, the costs to purchase and maintain customized or retrofitted vehicles is high, leading most to subcontract the service out to specialty businesses. In turn, they pass the costs on to consumers and taxpayers.

By building in the accessibility features at the factory instead of converting a standard vehicle, the MV-1 provides a more stable and safe automobile that saves consumers and businesses substantial costs in the short and long term. Yet, however well intentioned, innovative, or cost-effective, introducing a new vehicle into any marketplace is an uphill battle.

Driving the Mission

Conceiving and building a vehicle to address this growing need in the marketplace is one thing; getting consumers to embrace and purchase it is another. Successfully marketing and selling vehicles has traditionally required brick and mortar dealers with trained personnel across the country as well as national media and PR support, all of which require time, infrastructure, and money—lots and lots of money.

Time and money are things few startups enjoy, and MV-1 Canada was no exception. Soon after negotiating the contract to become the official importer and marketer of the MV-1 in Canada, the company spent most of its working capital on business startup expenses, operational software, government regulatory compliance, staffing, and procuring the necessary inventory to meet minimum production quotas. With no national dealership network to serve as retail showrooms, this worthy endeavor seemed like a battle that could not be won. After years of struggles designing and engineering the vehicle, sourcing the appropriate materials and production facilities, negotiating the necessary partnerships, and obtaining the required regulatory compliances, the goal of getting this much-needed vehicle onto the streets of Canada seemed to be as far away as it was on day one.

When the Grandes' decided to import, market, and sell the MV-1 in 2006, they could not forsee the impending collapse of the American auto industry. Throughout the next 5 years, as they lobbied for the necessary government compliance and safety certifications to get the MV-1 on the road, the auto industry experienced an unprecedented crisis. The dramatic increase in fuel prices between 2003 and 2008 amplified the crisis when the financial markets crashed in 2008, leading to a bailout of the US auto industry. Fallout from the negative publicity and global financial downturn created an additional PR and branding challenge, which they had to overcome. Undeterred, they turned to their history in auto retailing for inspiration. Their father, Joe Grande, purchased a GM auto dealership in 1977, so they each grew up with auto retailing in their blood. This gave them the necessary insights to tackle the obstacles in front of them. "The old model of auto retailing stopped working because auto manufacturers stopped selling cars that people wanted, they were selling payment plans," said Nick. He argues that manufacturers built relationships with dealers and financial institutions instead of with the end customers.

This experience was the basis for their initial retail strategy to market the MV-1 in Canada: Build a socially responsible company that invests in the customer experience first, thus becoming part of the lives and community of its customers. They understood the need to build a different channel to the same customer. "We knew that a PR and word-of-mouth marketing strategy would be required, but we could not dedicate the required capital to hire a national PR firm," said Peter. "So we chose a grassroots, guerilla marketing tactic that could generate tons of earned media (publicity earned through non-paid advertising)." Peter and his team embarked on a cross-country tour, driving the MV-1 from coast to coast. Along the way they participated in local festivals, trade shows, and community events that were hosted by and for the disabled community. Their "on-the-road" strategy was designed to meet as many people in the community as possible and to support local activities with test drives and product information.

Fueled by their commitment to give back to the community, they became more deeply involved with specific organizations they met on their travels. One such organization was Vita Community Services in Toronto, Ontario, that offers a wide range of services for people living with physical disabilities, including residential adult programs, day services, respite, and crisis and clinical support. MV-1 Canada partnered with this organization in its fundraising efforts, which resulted in the purchase of the very first MV-1 vehicle in Canada. As they toured the country, attracting the attention of community leaders and the media wasn't a problem. "I would call television news stations and newspaper editors in advance of arriving in a city, and they were all too happy to greet me upon my arrival," said Peter. Their efforts resulted in many features on televised news programs across the country, front-page features in the automotive section of national newspapers, and word-of-mouth promotion within targeted communities coast to coast.

Having achieved their goal of earning national media attention, word-of-mouth buzz from community leaders, and deep involvement with their targeted customers, the Grandes were surprised to see sales orders failing to meet expectations. Their guerilla campaigns were successful at generating national attention and awareness but did not convert that attention into the required sales, even though their product was significantly less costly than the available alternatives.

Adding to the challenge was the fact that the public had been trained to purchase vehicles from auto centers with a fleet of cars, salesmen and mechanics working in their service bays. "Auto retailing has been about bundling massive, high-tech showrooms with the retailer's true profit center, the service bay," said Nick. "Building such a network is not about building community but selling services." The Grandes envisioned a different future for auto retailing and servicing but we had to overcome public perceptions. So MV-1 Canada struck an innovative partnership with an independent national auto servicing business that already had physical locations in each province. Each service center and mechanic would be trained and certified to support the vehicle in their service bays.

By unbundling the authorized, post-purchase service from the vehicle's sales and marketing efforts, we could focus all our efforts and budget on developing the sales and marketing strategy. Still, a national sales team without showrooms seemed implausible. Learning from the previous campaign, we knew we could not rely solely on cross-country, face-to-face engagements. Knowing the Grandes' disinterest in building traditional auto showrooms, we choose to create a virtual sales organization by embracing an influencer marketing strategy that identified key individuals and businesses that had the power to drive brand awareness and encourage test drives and sales among their audience. We knew we had our work cut out for us; developing a strategy based on online social activity to keep costs down and take advantage of the growing social media landscape had been hit-and-miss for other businesses.

The 90-9-1 Rule

Initially, we took the traditional approach of identifying communities made up of prospective customers and applied the 90-9-1 rule, which states that in most communities 90% of users are followers who seek information but never or rarely contribute, 9% of users contribute a little, and the final 1% account for almost all the content and engagement. It's this 1%—the holy grail of traditional influence marketing—that public relations and marketing professionals have long courted. This small but active group commands the attention of their larger community, and when successfully co-opted into advocating the business's brand, it gains a cost-effective marketing channel. Of course identifying the 1% is not always straightforward.

Using social monitoring software (see Figure 1.2), we found consumer communities around key content that included people with disabilities, their caregivers, and charities for business-to-consumer (B2C) campaigns. Corporate networks, which would be used for business-to-business (B2B) initiatives, were also identified and included representatives from associations, health-care providers, insurance companies, and governmental agencies.

Within each community, the marketing team cross referenced the names with additional data, including the number of people that read their blogs or printed articles, the popularity of their websites and social influence scores from Kred.com to rank the members as illustrated in the Figure 1.3.

This process allowed us to understand who the 1% and 9% were, as well as their individual abilities to amplify the brand message within their online and offline communities. However, experience taught us this wasn't enough. To successfully engage a community and their influencers, we needed to understand the nature and tone of their dialogue. So we had to apply additional filters and considerations to further segment the identified audience. For example, we searched for "hot button" topics and news to help us understand the obstacles that needed to be overcome through our messaging strategies.

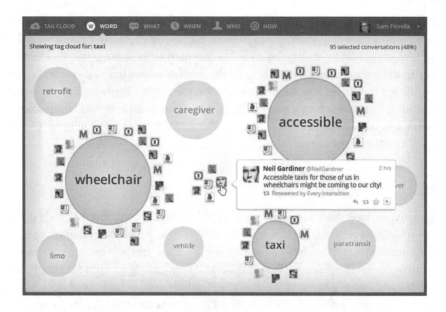

Figure 1.2   *"Social Visualizer" courtesy of Jugnoo.com*

	# of Printed Articles	Print Readership	Freq. of Pub. Articles	Television Reach	Radio Reach	Facebook Friends	Twitter Followers	Site Alexa Score	Reputation Rank	Weekly Blog Views Est	Kred Score	Weighted Score
Tom Allan	12/mo			2MM	95K	1						85
Susan Smith	13	9,550	1/mo	1MM		32K	14,045	76,369	2,049	2,000	650	74
Haydon Telus	400	1.3M	0	0	45K	1,000	10,222	76,265	1,701	1800	643	74
Walter Bobcock	124	89,500	20/mo	0	10K		4001	44,600	1953	1500		70
...	...	...	...	...	...	...	...	...	...	...	...	...
Tim Wallows	0	0	0	0	0	765	1,456	na	na	500	456	49
Alison Jones	0	0	0	0	0	654	1,398	na	na	500	409	49
Depak Cransen	1	na	0	0	0	554	1,167	na	na	500	389	46
Harold Wu	0	0	0	0	0	509	765	na	na	250	375	45
Yennicka Dules	0	0	0	0	0	509	755	na	na	250	364	45
Karen Yeung	3	na	0	0	0	400	604	na	na	250	333	35
Samantha Spade	0	0	0	0	0	567	571	na	na	250	297	34
Guiermo Lopes	0	0	0	0	0	123	0	na	na	0	0	25
Frank Sapone	0	0	0	0	0	102	0	na	na	0	0	23
Wilbur Hanks	0	0	0	0		56	0	na	na	0	0	10

Figure 1.3   *Sample community ranking matrix (Note: Names replaced to protect the individual's privacy.)*

In the case of the B2B audience, using social monitoring software we identified online conversations surrounding the issue of accessibility in municipalities including sentiment analysis (positive and negative-toned commentary). We displayed the results in a tag cloud that illustrated the most used terms and phrases with larger, bolder font. Next, we conducted a supplemental search using online government procurement services to identify which municipalities have public transportation contracts coming up for renewal within two years, which we overlaid on the tag cloud. Figure 1.4 presents a sample of the result. The blue circles represent municipalities where transit contracts were ending in less than two years; red circles represent those with transit contracts coming due in more than two years.

Figure 1.4   *MV-1 Canada B2B target community identification*

By drilling down through the tag cloud, we were able to identify individual communities that formed around relevant issues and by applying the community ranking matrix shown previously in Figure 1.3, we selected those deemed most influential. Based on the research we gathered from directly engaging with this online audience, we developed specific content marketing and sales tactics based on the immediate needs of the local communities as we prepared to respond to the upcoming RFPs.

Further, the exercise allowed us to segment primary and secondary markets to better focus our offline and online efforts. Primary markets had immediate commercial sales opportunities as determined by largely negative sentiment in the online dialogue and transit contracts coming up for renewal within two years. Secondary markets were those with high negative sentiment but where transit contracts were not coming up for renewal within two years; these were deemed longer term opportunities.

For primary markets, a more aggressive, short-term strategy was required. Top influencers, regardless of their role in the group (media, charity, municipal employee, health-care facility, member of the public), were approached as "media

personnel" and invited to be exclusive members of their communities to participate in the launch of a revolutionary product that would impact the freedom of
its members. Appealing to their egos garnered immediate attention and increased
their willingness to be associated with the brand. They were all eager to be seen
as the person or business introducing the MV-1 to their community. Among the
engagement tactics were

- Direct sales calls to municipal and community leaders
- Aggressive distribution of press releases and engagement with the local
  media
- "Live Launch" events within the local city and online through local
  community websites
- A community manager hired to acquire, incentivize, and manage influencers to advocate our product to the community and municipal leaders through op-ed commentary and introductions

In secondary markets, our team took a less aggressive role with influencers by
seeding content in digital and live channels that they were already engaged in. The
content included specific calls to action complete with the option and incentive
to virally share the information. For example, we created sharable videos for local
charities and associations who were in the middle of fundraising or awareness
campaigns. The short co-branded promotional videos featured the charity or association's message and drove awareness to their cause, not the MV-1. We posted
these videos online with "one-click" tools that enabled influencers to share them
with their communities or embed them onto their sites. The viral nature of the
video spread the awareness of the MV-1 as a community advocate, further embed-
ding ourselves into the community. Such tactics allowed us to begin a long-term
relationship building process by supporting the needs of the community instead of
directly pitching our product.

The strategy deployed in these secondary markets included

- Driving awareness and building relationships with associations by supporting their needs, causes, and members.
- Seeding the Internet with research and consumer feedback that supported the economic and political benefits of accessibility vehicles
  designed and built like the MV-1.
- Charting communities, engaging identifiers, ranking opportunities,
  and crafting messages; every part of a social influencer and word-of-
  mouth marketing campaign was planned to the letter.

Our expectations were high, yet as the campaign rolled out, the results again
failed to meet expectations even though we successfully identified influencers and

co-opted them to amplify the message we gave them. Their followers were aware of the MV-1 and many did respond through social shares and website visits, but while greater than the previous grassroots campaign, not enough sales were generated from the influencers' referral.

A lot of effort went into selecting the right communities with the biggest opportunities, the most active and credible influencers within them, and the content that should have resonated with each, yet sales were few. Awareness was high; purchases were still too low. As we monitored the communication paths from chosen influencers to their respective communities and mapped the resulting activity, a new reality began to sink in: There was a disconnect between the audience's willingness to accept a recommendation and their willingness to take action on it. We began experimenting with different message tactics and incentives, but the results were the same. The next obvious consideration was the vehicle's price, but customer research showed that price was not an obstacle, especially since competitive options were equal or more expensive, and in many cases, subsidies were available to offset the cost.

A (Not So) Surprising Discovery

The results proved that our chosen influencers did in fact have the eyes and ears of their communities; however, the lack of adequate return on the marketing costs of generating influencer referrals told us there was still something missing from the equation. We began a campaign postmortem with a detailed investigation into the profiles of the audience who failed to purchase once their identified influencers made the recommendation. The results should not have surprised us; many of the profiles were inactive or fake. Names of members listed in the databases who were reportedly active in offline communications were of people and businesses collected over the years from trade shows, mailing lists, and other promotions but never updated or verified. The online audience was made up of Facebook fans who never engaged online after the initial act of clicking "Like" or Twitter followers who turned out to be fake accounts or real people simply swapping follows to increase their own numbers.

A margin of error is accepted when estimating the reach of an audience in all forms of marketing from direct mail to email marketing to newspaper advertising. We know that not all direct mail is received and if received not always opened and read. We know that not all email addresses in a business's email list are valid or current. We know that not everyone who reads a newspaper reads the ads, and if they do, there's no guarantee that they're a prospective customer or in the market to buy. It's always been a numbers game; cast a net wide and chances are you'll attract enough of the right audience.

We also realized that the percentage of invalid data among prospect and customer databases has grown with the increasing number of interactive options consumers have to engage with a business online. This fact drove home the point that extra time and budget would be needed if we were to continue the general trial-and-error tactics across the entire network. In the end, it was too much time and too much money, and neither was available in abundance. It was a risk we simply could not take at this stage.

So we turned our focus to the other half of the audience, the half that was real and verifiable. Why did they not respond in droves to the seeded introductions, recommendations, and calls to action shared by leaders in their respective communities? They reacted to television publicity by visiting the website; they engaged on social media with shares, "Likes," and comments, yet few were making a direct purchase. A survey of the active followers in the chosen communities we were targeting revealed that while the influencers had their eyes and ears, they did not necessarily have their hearts and wallets. Survey respondents shared factors such as competition, buying cycles, distrust of the influencer, and other personal factors as reasons they chose not to act on the recommendations (see Figure 1.5 for a summary of the top responses).

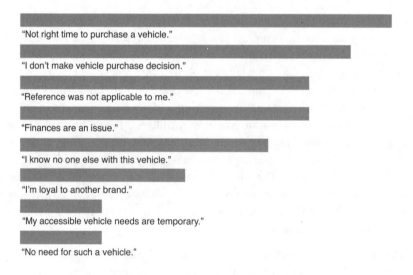

Figure 1.5 *MV-1 Canada influence campaign survey results*

We learned that the influencers indentified were popular among the target audience but, for the most part, did not sway purchase decisions. Their influence was one-dimensional; relationships without depth, amplification without action, and recommendation without comprehension of the audience's need. While the audience willingly read, heard, and even engaged with the seeded messages influencers were broadcasting on our behalf, we didn't really know if they were the right audience. Were they even in the frame of mind to purchase a vehicle? For those who were potential customers and in the market for a new vehicle, what value did they place on the information shared or the source sharing it? We understood that if we wanted to quickly and cost-effectively gain traction within our target audience, we needed to better comprehend what the *audience* considered influential at the moment they received the marketing message.

At the time it seemed counterintuitive, but the influencers and their attributes had to be ignored temporarily to achieve that better understanding of the customer's role in the influence marketing campaign. We embarked on an exercise to identify the decision-making process of our target customers and how internal and external messages impacted those decisions. Simply put, we asked ourselves better questions.

- What is the exact profile of a target customer who is ready to purchase today?
- Who are the "direct-line" influencers in the lives of the decision makers (e. g., family, colleagues, medical professionals, insurance brokers)?
- What are the emotional, social, political, and financial factors that play into the decision-making process?
- Are internal or external factors at play that might interfere with the decision to take action based on an influencer's recommendation?

The responses led to our third and final rethink of the MV-1 Canada influence marketing strategy.

Focusing on the Customer, Not the Influencer

We learned that the value of the amplified message had to resonate more with the target audience than the influencer if we had any hope of it leading to a purchase decision. Further, we began to grasp the reality that the manner in which a message is received and processed by the audience had less to do with the person sharing it (although important) than it did with the myriad of situational factors the customer was dealing with when he received the message.

We redesigned the program to focus on the reasons why each subset of the audience might want to purchase the MV-1. While no other manufacturer was offering a vehicle originally designed and built for people with disabilities, there were other options. This vehicle is clearly a choice, and so the factors that play into the decision-making process had to be merged with the influence paths we were trying to create.

For example, among the audience that required the use of a wheelchair there were subsets from those with long-term to short-term needs. Someone with a disability such as an amputation requires a wheelchair permanently and so transportation is a long-term need. On the other side, someone with Amyotrophic Lateral Sclerosis (ALS), more commonly known as Lou Gehrig's disease in North America, sees rapid muscle atrophy and a life expectancy of 3-5 years. For this person and their caregivers, transportation needs are short-term. For the latter, the decision to purchase an accessible vehicle takes on a different meaning and urgency. Understanding the physical, financial, social, and emotional factors at play when someone decides they need such a vehicle is critical to predicting which they'll ultimately choose and why.

Another group within our target audience was commercial transportation businesses that service those in wheelchairs, such as public transit and private livery services. Within a secondary market identified were hospitals, hospices, and other facilities that care for people requiring wheelchairs. The impact on the organization's ability to make money in a for-profit business or maintain the lowest operating costs in a not-for-profit business were key situational factors impacting how they reacted to messages received from our selected influencers.

When we analyzed who the community influencers were based on their social followers and their ability to amplify a message within target audiences, many of the same names kept surfacing. These were active online broadcasters within the social media space that promoted the needs of the disabled and their caregivers. However, as we discovered, while each was popular and captured the attention of the audience as a whole, subsets of the audience responded to their amplified messages in different ways.

So our team looked at who exactly made the purchase decision within each of the targeted subgroups. In the consumer market, decision makers were clearly those with disabilities and their caregivers. In the commercial space, identifying decision makers was more difficult. Most public transit authorities are managed by municipal governments whose city councils must vote on the procurement department's decision. Private transportation services followed a more typical business model where the COO or CFO conducted the financial assessment and made the decision to purchase certain vehicles.

We began by adding customer profiles to a decision matrix in which we appended factors that might impact a purchase decision (see Figure 1.6 for a sample). This matrix helped to identify and sort the factors that influenced how and when buyers made purchase decisions. For example, due to the effects of Lou Gehrig's disease, those in a wheelchair were impacted by financial factors (the short time period a wheelchair accessible vehicle was required versus the costs of purchasing a dedicated wheelchair accessible vehicle). Public transit purchases requiring a city council vote were impacted by factors including "financial" (cost of vehicles versus available budgets) and "political" (public perception of purchase, first-to-market bragging rights, etc.).

Audience	Situation	Situational Factors	
		Internal Factors	External Factors
1 Wheelchair Users	Permanent Disability Temporary Disability/Short lifespan Need, Finances No Issue Need, Finances An Issue Physical Challenges Caregiver	Dignity/Quality Of Life Living Alone Employment Status Brand Affiliation Owns Retrofitted Vehicle Uses Normal Vehicle Forced To Use Public Transit	Geography Available Financing Employer Associations
2 Public Transit	Request For Quote No Request For Quote Political Financial Environmental	Political Alignment Budgets Population Existing Relationships/Contracts	Public Perception News/Media Coverage
3 Private Transport Companies	Request For Quote No Request For Quote Financial		
4 Medical Care Facilities	Request For Quote No Request For Quote Financial		

Figure 1.6 *Sample MV-1 decision matrix*

In the scenario illustrated in Figure 1.6, one of the profiles identified is that of a wheelchair user with a permanent disability that had the financial means to purchase accessible vehicles. However, for those in some geographic locations (downtown urban core), the steep slope of the retrofitted minivan's add-on ramp becomes an additional "external factor" to the purchase decision. The fact that he or she has an affinity for the minivan manufacturer that is already active in the community adds yet another disruptive factor to the decision-making process.

Looking at the emotional, logical, and social factors that impact the decision-making process of customers in this profile allowed us to better strategize communication paths to their target customers. Yet, even among customers who were similar in our profiling, the impact of various situational factors was given greater or lesser importance. So we began adding positive and negative ratings to each situational factor to further identify the possible impact of these additional influences on a customer's reaction to the messaged received.

For example, "Shirley" is one of the prospective customers identified with this category. She's a single woman and successful wheelchair athlete living in Toronto, Ontario. She requires the use of a chair because of a spine defect at birth. "Daniel," a second prospective customer in this same category, is a father of two in a suburb of Vancouver, British Columbia, and requires the use of a wheelchair because of an amputation later in life. Each prospective customer is permanently disabled, and in each case, finances are not an obstacle to purchasing a vehicle.

Figure 1.7 illustrates the positive and negative ratings we added to the situational factors that impact Shirley's decision making. Her satisfaction with her existing retrofitted van is seen as a large obstacle so it's rated -10. She and her community expressed loyalty to her vehicle's brand, which is active in her sporting community. This clearly has a negative impact on the influence paths so it was given a -5 score. There are potential issues when using a retrofitted vehicle ramp in a city (due to the typically limited roll-out space on sidewalks), which is a positive impact on the decision to purchase our vehicle (allows for various lengths and pitch in ramp deployment), so it was scored +5.

Customer Category		Situational Factors			
Audience	Situation	Internal Factors	#	External Factors	#
1 Wheelchair User	Permanent Disability Need, Finances No Issue	Living Alone Brand Affiliation Owns Retrofitted Vehicle	0 5 10	Geography Associations	5 0

Red numbers represent negative values. Green numbers represent positive values.

Figure 1.7 *Sample MV-I ranked decision matrix—Profile: Shirley*

While Daniel falls into the same category, his decision making is impacted by different levels of the same situational factors. He also owns a retrofitted vehicle but does not have the same challenge with city streets and the limitations of add-on ramps in urban centers. Unlike Shirley, neither he nor his community have any affiliation to the vehicle brand, and so Daniel's decision matrix (see Figure 1.8) has different positive and negative ratings on these situational factors.

Customer Category		Situational Factors			
Audience	Situation	Internal Factors	#	External Factors	#
1 Wheelchair User	Permanent Disability Need, Finances No Issue	Living Alone Brand Affiliation Owns Retrofitted Vehicle	0 0 10	Geography Associations	0 0

Red numbers represent negative values. Green numbers represent positive values.

Figure 1.8 *MV-I ranked decision matrix—Profile: Daniel*

Both customers appeared similar on the surface; however, because each was exposed to different stimuli in processing recommendations, they reacted differently to the same influencer's recommendation. The underlying factors that influence their decision are different; therefore, the way they interpret a recommendation is different.

By overlaying influencer categories and profiles with the situational factors that impact their decision making and the degree each affects those decisions provided us greater insight into influencer-audience relationship. So our next challenge was to attempt to map the combination of factors that impacted those decisions and who was most likely to influence the consumer's consideration or purchase decision in each case.

With mainstream car retailers, the conversations between the customer and a salesperson might uncover these nuances. Within physical showrooms, the salesman can react to the situational factors discovered and respond with the appropriate sales presentation and corresponding call to action. However, general online recommendations rarely accommodate those nuances in their recommendations. To be successful, we had to overcome yet another obstacle.

Winning Strategy: Charting Influence Paths

Once the customer decision-making variables were charted, it was time to recreate the messages and tactics we would push through the newly identified influencers. At first we mistakenly fell back into old habits of creating general content that would resonate with influencers versus customers, and they kept getting derailed by all the external situations that negatively impacted the actions we were trying to influence. Further, we came face to face with the reality that most influencers would not take the time to identify the situations impeding their amplified messages from being received by the right customers.

Word-of-mouth marketing used to be so simple: Identify the audience and the people who influence them, drop a well-crafted and creative message into their communication paths, and advocates would take care of the rest. It was a clear and direct path from the brand to the end customer. The reality of today's socially connected and information overloaded society forced us to reconsider the linear nature of these communication paths.

We had to re-architect content and brand message tactics so that they could self-adapt to the customer's personal situations and where customers were in the purchase life cycle. In fact, we had to plan how to directly exert influence over the target audience even when an influencer was the middleman in that effort. Outside their amplification service, we had to remove the influencer from "active influence" and simply use them as the conduit to the end-customers. We started by creating a baseline for each message within each community.

For example, the base-line communication path would look like this: we broadcast a message to the influencer who shares that message with his audience, who in turn takes the desired action. On top of this we mapped the situational factors previously identified that might derail that message from resulting in the desired action by the end-customer. What if the customer already had an accessible vehicle? What if they worked for a competitive auto manufacturer like Honda? What if they were not the final decision maker? What laws applied in local communities? What if geography made use of the vehicle impossible?

Once these situational factors were mapped over the base-line message path we could identify many of the options consumers would be faced with when receiving the influencer's message. We were then able to determine whether another person or group could exert specific influence over the prospective customer's reaction to the message in each situation.

This required an additional understanding of where the prospect was in the purchase life cycle. For example, a person who becomes disabled as a result of an accident is first influenced by a medical care facility and health-care providers. Alternatively, those undergoing physical therapy are influenced by at-home care providers and physical therapists. Wheelchair athletes are influenced by their sport associations, sponsors, and other athletes. All the above might be influenced by insurance providers. We termed these connections "micro-influencers" because their reach was not a broad amplification across a general community but specific to smaller target groups in specific situations.

The resulting map formed an influence marketing decision tree (see Figure 1.9). It was the foundation of our "influence reverse engineering" process, which is a term we coined to represent our strategy of first identifying the various situations customers might find themselves in when receiving a marketing message, the micro-influencers most likely to confirm or sway that decision, their relationship to the identified influencers, and the adaptive messages required to connect them all.

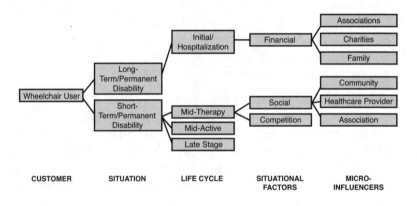

Figure 1.9 *Sample of MV-1 Canada influence/decision tree*

The tools and incentives we placed in the hands of the chosen micro-influencers contained calls to action that could drive consumers to a variety of interactive digital media. We tagged prospects with the influencer and campaign that drove the action, tracked the response, and measured the advocacy and revenue each generated. This allowed us to directly manage the engagement with the prospect regardless of the active or passive nature of the influencer's relationship with them. When the action taken was not the intended goal of our messaging, or if the prospect provided additional information, we would cross reference the response with the decision tree to reevaluate the factors that might be at play in their decisionmaking process. Based on that analysis, we could re-engage the prospect with a follow up message and renewed call to action.

As each communication path was executed, modified, and tracked, the influence matrices and decision trees were updated with the results and lessons learned. This facilitated more targeted and effective communications in future campaigns. In addition, we were able to track, manage, and score individual micro-influencers within specific communities based on the impact their referrals had on warm leads and the speed at which purchase decisions were made among a target group.

Unsuspectingly, we were forging new relationships between the influencers, who were simply broadcasting and sharing information to the larger community with micro-influencers, who were already directly and personally engaged with the target customer.

Finally, because we had direct knowledge of who the influencers were communicating with, we were able to survey prospects and clients to determine the perceived value and authority of the micro-influencers' recommendation. That feedback became another data point in the growing list of profiles we were gathering.

In the end, we created a multidimensional influence strategy that did not rely on casting a wide net but a deeper understanding of the nature of the relationship between our target audience and those who have influence over them. The effort yielded a substantially larger lead funnel with a higher conversion rate, a more detailed and accurate database of prospects and influencers, and an improved relationship with the each community. The result? Before the one-year anniversary of the first MV-1 entering Canada, we were able to secure a 20% ownership of the accessible vehicle market.

Thinking Forward

The lessons learned from this experience inspired us to reconstruct traditional influence marketing strategies that we marketers fall back on—and that are still being taught in colleges—for this and other industries. The impact of traditional amplification-based campaigns that were successful pre-Internet have been disrupted by the hyperconnected communities creating, consuming, and sharing content through an ever-growing list of Internet-enabled devices. In a world where everyone is truly "six-degrees of separation" away from everyone else and digital channels allow us to fabricate a worldwide audience, we're technically all influencers. And when everyone is an influencer, does anyone really have influence?

Current communication and technological trends continue to push for bigger and wider connections with greater and more frequent interactions, more tools to generate content with, and more networks to share that content in. We claim the world is getting smaller when our personal communities' reach and access to information are growing, yet the more people and networks we connect with, the thinner our connections to those people and communities become.

In our rush to engage more people, build bigger databases, and more aggressively compete for our customers' decreasing disposable income, marketers lose the ability to identify the context of the relationships and connections being built. So much focus has been placed on amplification such as number of followers, number of fans and "Likes" on social networks, and number of shares on micro-blogging platforms that software and campaign strategies have become less effective and measurable, especially in the area of influence marketing.

The concepts of word-of-mouth and influence can still be effective and measurable. Our MV-1 Canada case study demonstrates how we must shift our focus from amplification to better segmentation of the target audience, develop a clearer understanding of the relationships between them and their communities, and the factors that disrupt our brand messages.

Now, with this case study in mind let's break down influence marketing. First it's important to quickly review the origins of influence marketing and how social media changed the trajectory of this once effective marketing tactic. With that foundation, we are able to reconstruct influence marketing for the post-digital era and provide a blueprint for how to effectively create, manage, and measure brand influencers for your business.

Endnotes

1. There are many studies that show the decreased impact of search engines for sites on page two or beyond. Most are reported in whitepapers such as this study by Optify: http://www.optify.net/ inbound-marketing-resources/new-study-how-the-new-face-of-serps-has-altered-the-ctr-curve.

2

Influence and the Human Psyche

"What we believe is heavily influenced by what we think others believe."
—Thomas Gilovich

As we discovered in Chapter 1, "Logic and Reason (Or How We Learned to Love Influence Marketing)," with the MV-1 case study, many factors come into play when identifying and marketing to influencers and their audience. Timing, placement, product, and relevance all play a key part in whether a brand message is accepted and shared by the influential targets. The ability to adapt on the fly and shift focus to other influencers based on feedback and metrics are also important. However, as we introduce later in this book, one of the key elements of any decision-making process is the emotional aspect of the brand message and the timing when sharing with the recipient.

As the quote at the beginning of this chapter highlights, people are emotional creatures. We make decisions based on logic yet allow these decisions to be overridden when emotion comes into the equation. We resume a broken relationship because our hearts rule our heads; we make an extravagant purchase we can barely afford because it makes us feel better; we make spur of the moment decisions that make us feel good in the short term but impact us negatively in the long term. This almost domineering-like control that emotion has over logic is a leading factor in why social scoring platforms, like the ones we look at in Chapter 4, "The Current Influence Model and Social Scoring," are good for early identification of influencers but show limitations when adding context, relevance, situation, and emotion into the equation.

In his 2009 blog post on the Neuromarketing website titled "Emotional Ads Work Best," Roger Dooley shared a graph comparing emotional purchases to rational purchases.[1] Using data taken from the U.K.-based Institute of Practitioners in

Advertising, the graph clearly highlights the appeal of using emotional triggers in promotional messages. The graph in Figure 2.1 clearly highlights the campaign effectiveness of emotional messaging was almost twice as successful as rational messaging—31% and 16%, respectively. Brands that used a combination of emotional and rational messaging enjoyed a 26% success rate, still second to a purely emotional approach.

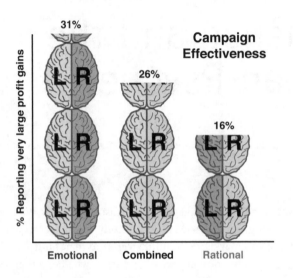

Figure 2.1   *Emotional ads work best*

Emotion, Logic, and Success Above Criticism

The Super Bowl is the perfect example of emotional triggers offering a greater return than a comparable ad that offers more information about a product but less emotional appeal. The cost of a 30 second ad at the 2013 Super Bowl was $4 million, raising the stakes for brand managers and advertising partners. Analysis of the various ads at the 2013 Super Bowl show web host company GoDaddy enjoyed the most successful campaign, with both social engagement[2] and financial return after its ad aired, placing the company ahead of the other ads aired during the game. The combination of earned (online conversations about a brand), owned (unique content produced by the brand), and paid media (ad space on the Super Bowl as well as media channels like YouTube) resulted in a successful ad campaign for GoDaddy.

GoDaddy enjoyed the amount of success it did despite the ad being consistently voted one of the worst Super Bowl ads of the year on numerous online news articles, blog posts, and social network updates. Beginning with GoDaddy celebrity spokesperson Danica Patrick, the ad celebrated "the two sides of GoDaddy"—the sexy side, as portrayed by female models in the company's other TV ads, and the business side. It featured Israeli model Bar Refaeli and actor Jesse Heiman, who played a geek named Walter. As Patrick finishes her introduction, the two begin to kiss passionately, depicting the two sides of GoDaddy complementing each other perfectly.

The success of this ad wasn't accidental—the campaign appealed to both the emotional factor of an admittedly stereotypical geek making out with a beautiful model and logical examples for using GoDaddy's business services. Despite criticism of the ad for being sexist, its message reached its target audience as highlighted by sales figures released by GoDaddy after the ad aired:[3]

- Web host sales rose by 45%.
- Domain sales for dot.com URLs rose by 40%.
- 10,000 new customers signed up for GoDaddy's services.
- Mobile customers rose by 35%.

Emotional triggers like the ones employed by GoDaddy and other brands during Super Bowl 2013 highlight the importance of understanding the audience's mindset. Chrysler's "Whole Again" video for its Jeep product enjoyed positive sentiment and online buzz thanks to its emotional message versus a pure sales one[4] when it aired at the end of the half-time show. Built around the message "America Will Be Whole Again," the ad shows American servicemen and women returning home to their families after active duty abroad, and how the country can only truly be whole again when these families are reunited. By showcasing the partnership between Chrysler and the United Service Organization to bring home these servicemen and women, combined with a stirring soundtrack and voiceover by Oprah Winfrey, the Jeep commercial offered a subtle yet powerful reason to buy Jeep.

The GoDaddy and Chrysler examples are polar opposites in message and execution, but they're tied together by emotional resonance. It's this emotional connection that brand managers are constantly seeking, yet frequently fail to identify when creating a brand campaign. As this chapter shows, however, that failure needn't be so frequent.

The Emotionally Connected Consumer 1: The IKEA Effect

In March 2011, the Social Science Research Network published a paper titled "The IKEA Effect: When Labor Leads to Love."[5] Coauthored by Michael I. Norton of Harvard Business School, Daniel Mochon of the University of California, San Diego – Rady School of Management, and Dan Ariely of Duke University – Fuqua School of Business, the paper studied the emotional sense of accomplishment when consumers completed various challenges. According to Mochon, the reason for the IKEA effect is simple:

> *Imagine that you built a table. Maybe it came out a little bit crooked. Probably your wife or neighbor would see it for what it is, you know? A shoddy piece of workmanship. But to you that table may seem really great, because you're the one who created it. It's the fruit of your labor. And that is really the idea behind the IKEA Effect.*

The interesting premise the paper takes is that we, as emotional beings, don't do something because we love it; instead, love comes from the act of doing something or, in the case of the IKEA Effect, labor. The perception of value increases on projects that people build on their own—even part-fabricated products such as IKEA self-assembly—versus buying prebuilt products and placing them in a household instead. Over the course of a series of studies and experiments, this IKEA Effect became more prominent, and a true feeling of pride and accomplishment was evident. This perception of a higher value continued into the evaluation part of the experiments, where people were asked how much they would pay for the finished products. Those that had been self-assembled scored higher than those that were already fully built.

This study has particular interest for marketers on both traditional marketing spend and influencer outreach. While push (broadcast) marketing pre-social media was the norm, and can still be successful today when part of a larger tactic, the Connected Consumer prefers pull marketing techniques that are simple, make them feel involved, and involve researching their purchase decisions.[6] This is the IKEA Effect of involvement and sense of accomplishment in play from the consumer angle. As we see later in this chapter and further in the book, the goal of an influencer campaign is to build advocacy—how successful this building of an advocate army is is determined by the involvement of both the influencer and his or her audience.

For brands looking to succeed in today's increasingly digital marketplace, the IKEA Effect offers a valuable insight into the way accomplishment and involvement dictate the decision-making process.

The Emotionally Connected Consumer 2: 12for12k and Emotional Guilt

In January 2009, Danny was one month into 12for12k, a 12-month social media-led charity project whose goal was to raise $12,000 each month of 2009 for 12 different charities throughout the year. Founded by Danny and supported by a core team of friends offering various expertise in social media and fundraising, the first charity to be supported was War Child Canada. Despite the campaign receiving airtime on major TV stations and media features across Canada, by the second week the amount raised was less than $600. Danny and the team needed to act to reverse this and made the decision to take a more hard-hitting and emotionally charged approach over the previously "soft sell" tactic of the initial campaign, which was more geared around simply encouraging friends and online connections to help support this new initiative by sharing news of what War Child Canada did.

The 12for12k team collated numerous graphic images from the War Child Canada website, depicting children in war zones with severe injuries, and crafted a "What if this was your child?" message to be shared across social media. The impact was immediate—in the last two weeks of the War Child Canada campaign, the donation needle moved from less than $600 to just over $6,500. While the monthly goal of $12,000 wasn't met, 12for12k support for War Child Canada—as part of a larger promotion by the organization—helped raise awareness of the program and resulted in an increase in both supporters and donors for War Child Canada.[7] It also highlighted the power of tapping into the emotional psyche of human beings for a marketing message, particularly when the message is both relevant and contextual.

In the case of the "What if this was your child?" campaign, the marketing specific was getting the story of War Child Canada in front of as many people as possible, while raising donations at the same time. The emotional angle came from how the message was portrayed and who was targeted. Since the 12for12k demographics showed the majority of supporters were parents, the new promotional approach hit home much harder than the previous one, as is borne out by the exponential increase in donations. Supporters felt compelled to help: Status updates across various social networks shared a common thread of parents horrified by the thought of their child being one of those featured in the images.

The pivot in that first campaign shaped the emotional marketing tactics for the remainder of the 12for12k project throughout 2009, which saw the eventual amount raised for charities totaling just over $100,000 (including January 2010), as highlighted in Figure 2.2. The new direction was simple: Connect emotionally with the supporters and instill a feeling of accomplishment that lives had been changed by working with the various charities 12for12k supported.

Organization:

- 12for12K

Social Media Stats:

- Twitter: 3,600 followers @12for12K
- Blog: 3,000 subscribers
- Facebook group: 700 fans
- Ning network: 200 members
- YouTube.com
- Viddler

Results:

- A 12-hour Tweet-a-Thon raised $15,500 for Share Our Strength.
- Traffic at 12for12K.org increased by 4000% during the Tweet-a-Thon.
- A Twitter avatar "frame" helped bring in 3,600 followers.
- 12for12K.org raised $91,275 for charities in 2009–all with volunteers.

Figure 2.2   *Overview of the key 12for12k components*

The Intelligence Behind Emotional Marketing

The two examples highlighted here are a perfect fit for connecting with human emotions. Charitable causes involving children and pride in self-accomplishment evoke our basic inner need to help others as well as prove to others we're worthy. However, while these responses are instinctive in nature, other emotional triggers can be illuminating when it comes to a marketer's understanding of his or her customer(s).

In a 2007 U.K. case study titled "Using Neuroscience to Understand the Role of Direct Mail,"[8] global research agency Millward Brown shared the results of a project it had worked on for the Royal Mail. The mail service wanted to understand the differences between the same message when it came to online and print media distribution. Millward Brown already knew the importance of emotional connection in marketing; what Millward Brown wanted to do was offer an insight into how brain activity changed when presented with the same message via different methods. Millward Brown partnered with the Centre for Experimental Consumer Psychology at Bangor University in the United Kingdom, and used a brain activity monitoring process known as functional magnetic resonance imaging (fMRI).

For the test, Millward Brown showed two sets of ads to each of the 20 participants in the experiment. Each set of ads was printed on a flyer as well as shown onscreen, to emulate the feeling of seeing them online. Brain activity was then measured each time the ads were presented to the participants. The results were fascinating.

The ads that could be physically touched as well as viewed stimulated the most activity on the brain when it came to both visual and spatial information about the product being viewed. By having something physical in front of it, the brain placed more authority and emotional resonance to that ad versus the one that the participant could see only via a monitor. The takeaway from this experiment was physical involvement versus just visual involvement equated to a deeper connection. This sense of physicality correlates with the findings from the IKEA Effect study earlier in the chapter. It's also an important reminder that effective marketing needs to integrate all facets of the tools available, from print media to email, display ads to social media, and word-of-mouth to influencer marketing campaigns.

The Search for Emotional Loyalty

The ability to connect at this deeper level is, for many, the Holy Grail of marketing. Brands pay thousands of dollars for study groups, and technology companies allocate manpower and resources to develop algorithms, to identify the intent behind a public update on social networks. Emotion in humans can override the most logical argument for not doing something; if we, as marketers, can tap into that emotion, the logic that tells us (as consumers) we don't need to make that purchase today is replaced by the spontaneity of buying it regardless of need. A perfect example is in the smartphone market.

Once You Go Mac...

Since its launch in 2007, the iPhone has become a cultural phenomenon. Its capability to interact with other Apple products through the iCloud solution makes it a must-have accessory for more than 85 million users and plays a large part in the iPhone's success. Users are emotionally attached to their iPhone, much like they are with other Apple products, hence the saying, "Once you go Mac, you never go back."[9] This emotional resonance to iPhones causes users to upgrade their handsets even when there have been minimal changes to the hardware, leading to criticism about lack of innovation from Apple[10]—criticism that has had little impact on the success of the newer models. This emotional resonance has ensured the iPhone's continuing success, despite Google's Android platform challenging the loyalty of the iPhone's user base.

More Than Just a Game

Hard-core video gamers have the same loyalty and emotional connection to their hardware platform of choice. The mid-1980s and early 1990s witnessed a turf war that began in Japan between two highly aggressive competitors and spread to the rest of the world, and was equal to any in the corporate business world. Nintendo and SEGA had both survived the video game crash of the early 1980s that claimed Atari, the other leading player in the market, and now had their sights set on each other. The technology at the time was similar in both companies' platforms, but their approaches were very different.

Nintendo employed a very strategic approach to owning the hearts of gamers in both Japan and America. Courting and winning the support of third-party developers, albeit under strict licensing agreements,[11] ensured gamers who wanted to play their favorite game could only do so on the Nintendo platform, and the cult of Nintendo fandom was born. Despite SEGA's Genesis platform regaining some market share for the company in the 1990s, developers continued to offer exclusives to Nintendo's hardware, enhancing the emotional relationship between gamer and company. Nintendo's continued dominance in the space, along with the emergence of the Sony PlayStation, resulted in SEGA eventually leaving the hardware market altogether in 2001.

The examples of both the iPhone fans and the Nintendo fans illustrate the tangible benefits of connecting to your customer's emotion. However, as SEGA found out, even having hard-core fans isn't always enough to make your product a success. So why did Nintendo and Apple succeed where SEGA failed? The answer could be as simple as the former understood emotional marketing better than the latter.

The Manifestation of Emotional Marketing

As discussed throughout this chapter, the ability for marketers to connect with consumers on an emotional level can result in both longevity for a business and ongoing loyalty and advocacy from customers. The problem for many marketers is how to identify the opportunities and connect meaningfully.

In his 2010 paper titled "A New Concept of Marketing: The Emotional Marketing,"[12] Domenico Consoli of the University of Urbino, Italy, presented his case for emotional marketing. By collating 23 case studies and white papers spanning 35 years, Consoli identified the key proponents of emotional marketing, including measurement of the various stages of identifying emotional resonance in consumers. By drawing from the lessons of philosophers Aristotle and Rene Descartes, as well as naturalist Charles Darwin, Consoli presented a cohesive overview of the various facets of emotion, including physiological emotions such as crying and sweating—all core to a brand looking to connect emotionally with its next marketing campaign.

For example, Consoli found that people would become emotionally attached to their surroundings if there was a certain ambience. Coffee shops that used certain background music and had aromatic candles resulted in customers using that coffee shop versus one that simply sold coffee in generic surroundings. The same would go for shops that sold perfumes and scented products—the right mix of scents would make customers feel more at ease in their surroundings and engage their senses more. This would encourage patronage and sales. The increasing use of a cake baking in the oven or the aroma of freshly brewed coffee by realtors presenting a home is a by-product of emotional marketing and the psychological effect it has on potential buyers. Consoli posits emotional marketing as having a fundamental role in today's marketing landscape.

Emotions in the Purchase Cycle

As we see later in the book, social media and influencer programs—including the platforms built around this new realtime marketing landscape—offer the ability for instant feedback on a campaign or product/brand, as well as the fluidity to make changes to that campaign instantaneously.

This instant ability correlates perfectly with emotional marketing; as humans, we can immediately sense the change in someone's demeanor through the emotional tone in her voice, or a change in facial expression.

This also translates to the online space—people connected to each other for any long period of time can identify the change in someone's content, from a simple Twitter update to a Facebook status or Google+ post, as highlighted in 2012 when Danny's Facebook account was hacked.[13] Friends of Danny's on Facebook soon realized the account had been hacked due to the tone and grammar used by the hacker. This recognition helped counter the negative updates by the hacker until Danny was able to regain control of the account.

By using platforms that identify the current emotional state of the online user, brands can understand and answer both the emotional and psychological needs of the consumer:

- Is the product functional for the target consumer's needs?
- Does it instill an emotional response?
- Will this help build a longer-term relationship?

Measuring Online Emotion

As the Millward Brown study for the Royal Mail showed, measuring brain activity around emotional responses to ads highlighted the preference for physical touch when it came to the decision-making process. However, brands looking to be successful in the social media space, through either digital marketing or influence marketing campaigns, don't have the luxury of being able to physically see that depth of emotional response when monitoring someone's social feeds.

Consoli's solution combines a methodology that delves into the context of the words in the update.

- Break down the distinction between key grammatical areas—verbs, adjectives, nouns, and so on.
- Identify words that make up the verb section, including "admire," "hate," and "rejoice."
- Repeat this with adjectives ("angry," "happy") and other parts of the equation, including nouns ("awe," "disorientation") and adverbs ("sadly").

By breaking down the parts of a public update in this manner, it differentiates each word, enabling technology and algorithms to learn the intent behind someone's statement(s) online. As we see in Chapter 6, "The Consumer Decision-Making Process," and Chapter 7, "Reversing the Social Influence Model," the ability to identify when this intent turns into an action is a crucial component of the new influence methodology this book presents.

Emotional Resonance Versus Controversial Disconnect

When we begin to look deeper into the power of emotional marketing and the way it can overcome even the most logical arguments, it becomes apparent just how powerful emotional resonance can be. When people are emotionally invested in a brand or product because of the positive sentiment invoked within them, this can result in them choosing to continue their relationship with that brand despite controversy around some of the brand's other activities.

American Apparel is one of the largest manufacturers of unisex knitwear materials, as well as children's clothing and special pet knitwear. The company has championed many causes, both for its employees and for its surrounding community, including reforming U.S. Immigration laws. American Apparel's workforce is made up of a large number of legal immigrants, and in 2002 the company shut down its factory to allow its employees to participate in a pro-immigration rally in the company's home city Los Angeles. American Apparel has also been praised for its wage and benefit structure, compared to competitors in the industry, and is lauded for both its environmentally friendly business practices as well as its support of numerous charitable causes. Customers of American Apparel are emotionally attached to it through the combination of its product and the company's business ethics.

However, American Apparel also has many detractors, thanks to the company's use of provocative advertising and marketing campaigns. Many of its campaigns use overtly sexual images and connotations—one ad in particular drew widespread criticism for using a topless woman, dressed only in tights, leaning over a wall. American Apparel countered by claiming its ads were natural and showcased a typical human's approach to sex.

These ad campaigns were considered counter to the community-minded approach of the company's other business face and led to confusion and conflict for many of its customers. Yet despite the criticism around the ads, American Apparel continues to be successful because the emotional connection to the company is so strong.[14]

Once a brand establishes emotional resonance and creates advocates like the customers of Apple, American Apparel, and Nintendo, negative aspects are more likely to be seen as road bumps in the overall success of the business.

Emotion and Its Role in Influence Marketing

For brands looking to use influence marketing as part of their overall marketing strategy, creating an emotional connection can help foster the relationship and turn initial influence into more powerful long-term advocacy. Influence marketing as it stands today is built around short-term buzz for the brand, and gaining awareness of a product or service. While this approach works for instant results, the longer term goals—sales, customers, repeat purchases, loyalty marketing— rarely come from a campaign built on short-term buzz. True success comes from advocacy—when loyal customers refer friends, family and colleagues to your brand, and there's a two-way relationship between brand and customer to continuously improve and solidify the customer life cycle with your brand.

This is the core component to enhancing a customer's experience with a brand and building loyalty and true influence, and we dissect this in more depth in Chapter 11, "The Business of Influence Marketing." It's also key to the relationships between people and the micro- and macro-influencers in their immediate network, as discussed in Chapter 5, "Situational Influence: A New Model for a New Era." Emotional resonance plays a significant contextual role in the decision-making process. It's also one of the reasons current social scoring platforms like the ones discussed in Chapter 4 receive criticism regarding their data, with actual context of relationships making way for how vocal an influencer based on a social score is.

While emotionally connecting with an influencer can be difficult to achieve, particularly if the influencer is being chosen because of his reach (audience size) versus resonance to the brand and its product, it's not essential. What is essential is the reaction to the influencer's message, and what that means to the long-term return for the brand.

The late public relations pioneer Daniel Edelman understood this when he introduced celebrity endorsements into promotional campaigns. Celebrities didn't need to have a connection to the brand Edelman hired them for; they simply needed to encourage people to buy the promoted product. The celebrities Edelman used were global stars with a huge fan base—people like actor Vincent Price and baseball legend Nolan Ryan. The strategy worked, and celebrity endorsements became a normal part of a brand's promotional outreach.

Today, marketers view online influencers as the new celebrities. As we see in the next chapter, the rise of social media has provided anyone who wants to be heard with the tools and platforms to be heard. This has created an ecosystem of various layers of influence, from the solo blogger with a couple of hundred readers to the professional content creator with video shows on YouTube, syndicated content across mass media publications, and thousands of fans and followers across multiple social networks. For brands, the problem is immediate: Which influencers do they connect with, and how do they identify whether they're even the right ones? Additionally, will these influencers offer anything except an initial buzz or is there any kind of emotional connection between them and the brand, and, if so, where can they find that?

For many influencer programs, the last point is the wrong question to be asking. While this chapter has shown the importance of emotional resonance, it can't be forced. Humans don't fall in love because someone tells them they have to fall in love; it simply happens once the right emotional connection has been made. The same goes for brands and products. As marketers, it's our job to instill a desire to purchase, and, for a split second during an ad, the emotion of desire may be felt. Whether the purchase is actually made or not depends on several other factors, including current situation, financial state, and true physical need for the product at that time, as seen in Figure 2.3.

Figure 2.3 *The short-term emotional connection to ads*

This is why ads and marketing campaigns, both traditional and those run across social and mobile networks, are the equivalent of the first level influencer. First level influencers are those who can share a brand's message to a significant volume of people but don't necessarily have a strong connection to the brand or its product. Companies like IZEA (www.izea.com) and Klout (www.klout.com) offer these types of first level influencer services to their clients. The emotional resonance comes in at the next level—the recipient of the influencer message. When a brand can connect with a new customer and turn initial influencer-led awareness into true advocacy through emotional resonance, that's the kind of relationship that push marketing efforts can struggle to achieve. It is something yogurt producer Chobani understands well.

Chobani is a Greek yogurt produced in the United States by Chobani, Inc. The company is extremely active on social media and has built a loyal community around its product. One of Chobani's community members in particular, Howie Goldfarb, is a perfect example of the power of emotion in converting skeptics to brand advocates. Goldfarb is VP of marketing and corporate strategy at Web Choice Consulting and a vocal critic of the way brands use social media for customer experience as well as lead acquisition. Goldfarb didn't begin as a fan of Chobani, instead preferring its competitors Danone and Yoplait. After Chobani dropped its price in 2010, Goldfarb tried and subsequently loved its yogurt. This started the process of Goldfarb moving from a "just another customer" level to the brand advocacy he supports the company with today.[15]

Goldfarb's relationship with Chobani moved beyond appreciation for the product into true loyalty because of the way the Chobani social media team interacted with him. He reached out to Emily Schildt, who at the time was the digital communication manager for Chobani (today she's director of consumer engagement), and offered to conduct an online and digital audit for Chobani. She agreed, and Goldfarb found they were already carrying out many of the recommendations he would make to brands using social media. Schildt thanked Goldfarb for his time with a case of yogurt and he's received four or five cases since then, just for his support of the brand.

Because of this interaction, Goldfarb recommends Chobani to as many people as he can, and even takes pictures of Chobani products in-store and uploads the pictures to Twitter. The relationship and advocacy are returned by Chobani; in 2012, Chobani representatives knew Goldfarb was moving to a new home and asked him for his new address so they could send some fresh yogurt to him.

The longer-term advocacy built up since that initial contact highlights where emotional resonance sits in relation to influencers. Goldfarb originally tried Chobani through the company's action of a price drop (the first level influencer), but it was the micro-influencer (Chobani's social team) that connected with Goldfarb emotionally and built on positive sentiment (emotion) around the ongoing dialogue. This continued advocacy today is built solely on this two-way relationship between brand and consumer – Goldfarb is not employed by Chobani, yet he promotes them as effectively as any member of their in-house marketing team.

As we discover in Chapter 5, this level of emotional connection between consumers and the micro-influencers who truly influence their decision making is the area brands need to understand and use effectively. As we see in the next chapter, the rise of social media in the last few years has made this identification and understanding process more strategic and driven by actual knowledge of people versus assumption of their persona.

Endnotes

1. Dooley, R. July 27, 2009. "Emotional Ads Work Best." Neuromarketing website. www.neurosciencemarketing.com/blog/articles/emotional-ads-work-best.htm.

2. Kotlyar, B. February 8, 2013. "How GoDaddy Won the Social Media Super Bowl." Dachis Group blog. www.dachisgroup.com/2013/02/how-godaddy-won-the-social-media-super-bowl/.

3. Wasserman, T. February 5, 2013. "GoDaddy Posts Biggest Sales Day in History After Super Bowl Ads Run." Mashable website. www.mashable.com/2013/02/05/go-daddy-biggest-sales-day-super-bowl/.

4. Zeidler S., and L. Baker. February 4, 2013. "Oprah's Jeep Super Bowl Commercial Gets High Marks." Huffington Post Media. www.huffingtonpost.com/2013/02/04/oprah-jeep-super-bowl-commercial_n_2613286.html.

5. Norton, M. Mochon, D., and D. Ariely. "The IKEA Effect: When Labor Leads to Love." www.hbswk.hbs.edu/item/6671.html.

6. Spenner, P., and K. Freeman. May 2012. "To Keep Your Customers, Keep It Simple. Harvard Business Review. www.hbr.org/2012/05/to-keep-your-customers-keep-it-simple/ar/1.

7. Topham, J., and D. Jones. April 29, 2009. "Raising a Social Media Army tor Fight for Child Soldiers." Slideshare presentation. www.slideshare.net/PRworks/war-child-ali2-for-slideshare.

8. "Using Neuroscience to Understand the Role of Direct Mail." 2007. Millward Brown Case Study. www.millwardbrown.com/Insights/CaseStudies/NeuroscienceDirectMail.aspx.

9. "Once You Go Mac, You Never Go Back." July 9, 2012. The New Tech discussion forum. www.thenewtech.tv/forum/threads/once-you-go-mac-you-never-go-back.164/.

10. www.reviews.cnet.com/8301-19512_7-20114949-233/iphone-4-vs-iphone-4s-comparison-chart/

11. "Nintendo Entertainment System: "Third-Party Licensing." Wikipedia. www.en.wikipedia.org/wiki/Nintendo_Entertainment_System#Third-party_licensing.

12. Consoli, D. 2010. "A New Concept of Marketing: The Emotional Marketing." EconPapers website. www.econpapers.repec.org/article/brajournl/v_3a1_3ay _3a2010_3ai_3a1_3ap_3a52-59.htm.

13. Brown, D. July 15, 2012. "Facebook Hacking and the Value of Social Currency." Danny Brown website. www.dannybrown.me/2012/07/15/facebook-hacking-social-currency/.

14. Bigger, M. April 18, 2012. "Why Do Customers Go Bananas for American Apparel?" Bigger Capital website. www.biggercapital.squarespace.com/biggercapital-investment/2012/4/18/why-do-customers-go-bananas-for-american-apparel.html.

15. Goldfarb, H. February 14, 2013. "Dear Chobani: I Love You." Spinsucks web-site. www.spinsucks.com/social-media/dear-chobani-i-love-you/.

3

The Rise of Social Media

In 1998, Francis A. Buttle of the Manchester Business School in England, posted a white paper titled "Word-of-Mouth: Understanding and Managing Referral Marketing." The paper looked at the slow uptake of word-of-mouth (WOM) marketing, and why so few businesses were taking advantage of this powerful form of marketing, despite championing personal referrals. Buttle's argument for increased use of WOM was particularly evident in this excerpt from his paper:

> In the 1980s, the concept of "the marketing maven" was developed. This was a person who enjoys advising friends of new products/services and places to shop.... It is the social integration of the maven rather than any product-related expertise that gives them their power. Market mavens are largely women but indistinguishable in other ways. Gelb and Johnson...noted that "not only does the market maven prompt word of mouth, but those with links to such individuals are disproportionately likely to act on what they are told."

Sound familiar? It should; it's the very essence of today's influencer description and the core foundations upon which success in social media is built. While platforms and tools may bring something new to the marketing table, the discipline of word-of-mouth marketing is still the cornerstone of the medium. The correlation between word-of-mouth and social media has seen many businesses implement social media into their overall marketing strategy, albeit with mixed results, as we show throughout the book.

It's natural for social media, influence, and word of mouth to gel together as business solutions. While social media's strength in marketing is relatively new to the business mix, its core has always been from word-of-mouth marketing and the interpersonal relationships and buzz that discipline creates.

Logic, Branding, and Influence

An example of the return from interpersonal relationships and word-of-mouth conversations and recommendations is author and business strategist Olivier Blanchard, who has carved a very strong niche for himself as an expert at building brands. His blog—www.brandbuilder.wordpress.com—has a strong following among corporate marketers. Whenever Blanchard publishes a blog post, the comments following the post usually number more than 100. His public updates to social networks such as Twitter and Facebook elicit just as much conversation, as professionals from all levels of expertise offer their agreement or discourse. Blanchard has worked with some of the biggest brands in the business world, including The Federal Reserve, Smartbrief, and Word of Mouth Marketing Association (WOMMA). He also is the author of *Social Media ROI*, a blueprint that brands use when setting up their own campaign metrics. The reason for Blanchard's success in the business world can be tied directly to his expertise across more than 15 years of consultancy and brand education. The reason—or one of the key reasons—for Blanchard's success in social media, where anyone can claim to be a brand expert, is simple: He knows his stuff and he presents it in a logical and emotional manner. When Blanchard presents an argument or case study, he complements it with well-researched facts and logical reasons for his point of view.

Another great example is Amber MacArthur—www.ambermac.com—a Canadian entrepreneur, television host, professional speaker, and best-selling author. MacArthur's rise from a small-town television host to the first New Media Specialist on one of Toronto's leading news channels, CityTV, came about primarily from her use of social media channels to build her brand and highlight her expertise in the space. Her book on using social media to grow your business, *Power Friending*, was a national bestseller, and she has keynoted more than 200 events worldwide, where her knowledge of rising trends in the technical and social media space attracts clients such as Tony Robbins, the Discovery Channel, Microsoft, and the American Dental Association. MacArthur also used this knowledge to create and cohost the popular television show AppCentral, which looks at the latest apps for tablets and smartphones and is syndicated in Canada, Australia, and South Korea. She also writes a regular column for Fast Company and has been interviewed on CNN. In short, MacArthur has shown how successful you can be by using social media effectively, and she's widely recognized as a new media influencer in North America and beyond, with the power to sell out events whenever she speaks.

Blanchard's and MacArthur's success, and the power this affords them, showcases the very thing that brands are looking to connect with and benefit from when it comes to both influence and social media/word-of-mouth marketing.

It's why social scoring—the method of taking someone's reach, relevance, and activity on social networks and ranking them based on perceived importance—has become such big business. And it's why software companies are looking to build the golden ticket platform that can truly tie all these pieces together and offer measurement and return on investment.

Yet for all that social media has to offer and the speed at which it has risen to play such a key role in the business plans of forward-thinking organizations, its success has been in the planning and building process for the last 15 years.

Project 1998—The Content Creators

If you were to ask social media experts what the core part of any involvement in social media should be, the majority of the answers would probably center on content.

While content can fall under multiple umbrellas—Twitter posts, Facebook status updates, YouTube videos, Pinterest pins, and more—the overriding definition of content is the type found on blogs, whether this be the written word, videos, or podcasts. The reason for this is simple: Blogging offers the medium where a brand can be truly itself and offer the exact kind of messaging for which it wants to be recognized and respected. While Twitter restricts messaging to short staccato bursts of information, a blog post can be as long or as short as the publisher feels necessary. Even more importantly, blogs are—for the most part—the property of the brand itself. Although you can share whatever you want on social networks as long as it doesn't go against their Terms of Service or Privacy Policy, a blog—particularly a self-hosted blog—allows anything within reason to be published. This allows a blogger the benefit of a far stronger editorial point of view, which in turn helps attract the exact kind of audience—or customers—a brand is looking to connect with. A blog is viewed as the cornerstone of any social media marketing or influence campaign. In this respect, social media looks to its history and origins to help shape where the medium is today.

Although the first personal blog is recognized as having been published by college student Justin Hall in 1994, it wasn't until four years later that blogging truly came into its own. Prior to 1998, if you were interested in blogging, either for personal reasons or business/educational ones, you needed to know how to code in HTML, the web language that dictates how a site looks when viewed online. Coding in HTML can be a long and laborious practice, and the skills and patience needed for it deterred many people from becoming involved online 15 years ago.

That all changed when Open Diary introduced a platform that noncoders and the public at large could publish to, without the need to code in HTML. Additionally, readers of these blogs could interact even further and leave comments after a post.

This level of two-way communication effectively nixed focus groups as the leading feedback platform in the years to follow. This simple change to how an audience connects with a publisher also acted as a forerunner to how brands use content as a marketing channel and tailor promotions geared to a specific audience's needs and purchase cycle—the very essence of a business that knows how to use social media as both a promotional and educational channel.

A Question of Two Cultures

In 2012, one of the fastest growing markets in Europe was e-commerce. The Centre for Retail Research in the United Kingdom showed that online sales totaled just over $255 billion across the main European countries in 2011, an increase of more than $32 billion since 2008.[1] In 2012, that was expected to exceed $294 billion. In the United States, online sales totaled $198.8 billion, with projections for 2012 just short of $225 billion. According to U.S. market research firm Forrester Research, within the next two years of this book being published, online sales in the United States are expected to total $279 billion, as shown in Figure 3.1.

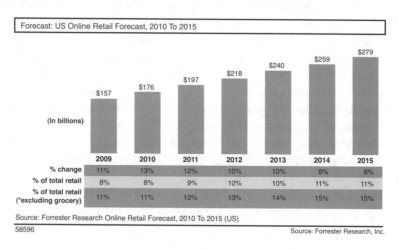

Figure 3.1   *Forrester prediction of U.S. online sales in 2015*

These figures just take into account retail sales online—they don't include social networks, such as Facebook, and their e-commerce solutions for brands, nor do they include the increasing growth in digital downloads from specialist sites and hobby stores. If one thing has changed significantly in recent times, it's the way we shop as consumers—and brands are recognizing this and increasingly looking for solutions to help them better connect with you, the consumer.

Compare this to the consumer experience a few short years ago. In 1994, the introduction of SSL encryption services, enabling purchases online to be made through secure payment gateways, marked the beginning of e-commerce as a key retail solution. The primary outlet for consumers was still brick and mortar retail outlets, with physical transactions remaining the method of choice for consumers. Today, while online sales are still the minority of total retail purchases, they comprise a growing percentage.

This increasing use of digital sales channels has seen businesses of all sizes struggle to understand the new connected consumer and their relationship with a brand. Companies that once flourished with one-sided broadcast relationships now find themselves struggling as they're forced to change the way they interact with customers. However, even as little as 15 years ago, this wasn't something for businesses to worry about.

Because of this, advertising and marketing were very different and, more often than not, defined a business's success. Brands could force-feed wave after wave of direct mail, radio and television ads, billboard advertisements, and more to a public that had no easy way to verify the authenticity of the claim. There were, and continue to be, regulatory bodies to ensure brands were adhering to advertising compliances, but these could only truly be put into action if the regulators were aware of any infractions.

Today, with the instant reference points of Google, crowdsourcing, and online legislation—the Federal Trade Commission introduced regulatory guidelines regarding social media and advertising in 2009[2]—companies can quickly be found out if they're falsely promoting their products and services. Blogs and websites dedicated to calling out bad business practices, customer service, and user experience continue to grow, with many of the more popular ones enjoying an audience in the hundreds of thousands and giving their authors mini celebrity status. This kind of consumer power was brought to the fore in September 2011, with the case of C.C. Chapman and the pasta sauce company Ragu.

Social Media Dads Can Cook, Too

Chapman is a marketing consultant and author who founded Digital Dads—www. digitaldads.com—and Cast of Dads—www.castofdads.com—to showcase content from a father's point of view on what it was like to be a dad. He coauthored the book *Content Rules* to help organizations of all sizes understand the power of content on the likes of Facebook, Twitter, blogging, and more when it comes to promoting your company's story and the people behind its success.

On September 27, 2011, Chapman published a blog post that attacked Ragu for a campaign it was carrying out via Twitter and YouTube. To try and engage the type of audience it was after—dad's who blogged—Ragu created a mock video interview of moms complaining about the lack of culinary skills in their husbands or partners. The campaign's goal was to advise dads that Ragu had them covered in the kitchen when it came to simpler meals.

With the video created and uploaded to YouTube, Ragu then took to Twitter to ask what dad bloggers thought of the campaign, with the question, "Do your kids like it when you make dinner?" During this promotion, Chapman was the recipient of one of these tweets, and his anger at the approach and the suggestion dads couldn't cook anything but quick pasta meals became the fodder for his subsequent blog post "Ragu Hates Dads."[3]

Because of his social media presence, the blog post garnered an immediate and impressive reaction from Chapman's followers and their own connections. As we write this, the post had more than 1,900 shares on Twitter and 1,000 shares on Facebook, as well as more than 250 comments. The majority of these comments and social shares supported Chapman's views—that Ragu was stereotyping dads and that its social media campaign and outreach on Twitter were poorly executed. So incensed was Chapman that he suggested the agency behind Ragu's campaign should be fired. In the immediate aftermath of the post, Ragu stayed silent, and this led to Chapman writing a follow-up post, offering his advice on how the company should have handled its outreach. This post led to a brand manager contacting Chapman to discuss his concerns and the overall perception of the campaign. Ragu admitted mistakes had been made, that the intent had not been to upset dads, and asked how it could better engage dads in the future.

Two key lessons stand out from the Chapman/Ragu case: Had Chapman not been able to blog about his experience to a loyal and engaged community, Ragu probably would never have known just how badly the campaign was perceived by its chosen audience. Second, Ragu could have ignored the online activity and hoped the noise would die down organically, yet it chose the communicative path instead and showed recognition for the consumer's voice and its importance. This ties back to the message we discussed in Chapter 1, "Logic and Reason (or How We Learned to Love Influence Marketing)," about truly understanding the consumer you're targeting.

The Shift to Social Media and the Rise of Citizen Influencers

Many purists of the medium will tell you social media has killed everything traditional media and marketing stood for. While there is some justification for this notion, it's simply not true. According to the 2012 CMO Survey, marketers expect to spend just under 20% of their marketing budget on social media.[4] While this shows companies willing to invest in social media, year-on-year growth was lower than expected. Additionally, B2B-service companies are actually decreasing their spending.

There's no question social media has introduced some key factors into today's business world—open dialogue, increased consumer awareness, and accountability, for example—but the truth is, social media is still just an added component to the bigger business picture. That's not to diminish the importance of social media and its role in today's marketplace—both authors of this book are huge proponents of the space and tools it provides businesses. We're just realistic about what exactly social media is, and what it will never replace.

Undisputedly, social media has completely changed the ballgame when it comes to marketing to your customers. As the Ragu example showed, brands can no longer afford to ignore criticism and customer apathy (if they ever could). Nor can they simply buy mass advertising and hope to drive negative sentiment and awareness around their product into the ground. Today's social channels and ease in sharing and consuming news killed that option stone dead.

Additionally, while many brands and account managers worry about what's being said in public about their products and clients, much of the real conversation happens behind closed doors on forums, community websites, and private Facebook groups. Into this battlefield brands are being thrust, sometimes reluctantly.

While many businesses understand they need to be somewhat active on social media—even if it's just gathering competitive intelligence via social listening versus being actively engaged—they're still afraid of the resources involved as well as how they would manage situations like the one Ragu experienced.

However, the danger for these brands is that social media is no longer a shiny new object—it hasn't been for a while. Businesses have moved beyond questions like "why should we be on social media?" into true actionable integration across different departments and teams.

Businesses now actually measure campaigns effectively and determine where their social media expenditure is successful and where they can cut budgets for weaker results. This integrated approach yields impressive results for the brands that approach social media marketing holistically.

Lebanon Ford, Lebanon, Ohio

Automotive giant Ford has long been recognized as a leader in the social media space when it comes to innovative and successful campaigns. Ford's blogger outreach campaigns, including one that invited bloggers to drive Ford vehicles across America and journal the experience, have been frequently copied by competitors. Ford's corporate website is heavily optimized for social media accounts, with a dedicated Ford Social hub aggregating multiple social accounts and news (www.social.ford.com). However, the Ford corporate approach to social media is just part of the bigger story. Many of its local dealers are not only using social media effectively but also benefiting from impressive financial results.

A good example is the Lebanon Ford dealership in Lebanon, Ohio (www.lebanon-ford.com). In 2010, all Lebanon Ford had was the simplest of websites. This changed when general manager Lisa Cryder saw the potential of social media and hired her son, Jeff Cryder, Jr., as Lebanon's Digital Communications Director. The results were impressive as are shown in Lebanon Ford's Year-Over-Year results in Figure 3.2.

Key Performance Indicator (KPI)	YOY Increase*
Total visits to www.lebanon-ford.com	181%
Unique visitors	125%
Total page views	623%
Average visitors per day	121%
Submitted Internet leads	407%
Appointments made from submitted Internet leads	480%
Total Internet sales	260%
Traffic from Google (organic search)	154%

* Compares May-Dec. 2009 to May-Dec. 2010

Figure 3.2 *Lebanon Ford's Year-Over-Year results (Source: Lebanon Ford)*

As you can see, there's a marked increase in every single category when compared to the previous year, from website traffic and page views to increased traffic from organic search queries. The most impressive statistics, though, are the ones that show the financial return from Cryder's strategies: leads, appointments, and sales from the dealership's increased online presence.

So successful was Cryder's approach to social media for Lebanon Ford that it caught the eye of Scott Monty, Ford's Head of Social Media. The dealership—and by default Cryder—is now held up as a case study of how businesses can truly use social media to their advantage.[5]

The first thing Cryder did was implement a full-on social media makeover. He created two dedicated blogs—For[d] Life and The Ford Project (since merged into one main blog)—and also set up Lebanon accounts on Facebook, Flickr, Foursquare, LinkedIn, Tumblr, Twitter, and YouTube. He overhauled the main website into one with more focus on social media integration. In addition to this, Cryder optimized the search engine visibility of the website so that anyone searching for a specific vehicle would find multiple examples of Lebanon Ford—page one listings on Google for organic results, as well as images of the vehicles for sale and where you could interact with the dealership online.

With videos previewing new models, as well as answering technology questions about pairing your phone to Ford Sync, on YouTube also ranking highly in search engine results (Google owns the video content channel), Lebanon Ford quickly came to own many of the search terms it wanted to be found for. Cryder formed a dedicated team to create, distribute, and promote content, as well as engage fans and new customers alike. This engagement includes inviting active social media users in the local area to test drive a new vehicle and, much like the parent organization's blogger outreach program, share their experience on their own channels.

In addition to the outreach program, special offers via geolocation platform Foursquare, a mobile solution that allows smartphone users to "check in" at a location they're visiting, proved extremely successful.

- Cryder used Foursquare to offer maintenance coupons.
- These coupons encouraged Foursquare users to visit the dealership and have their current vehicle serviced; that, in turn, allowed the sales team to promote Ford's new lineup with the customer while his or her vehicle was in the service bay.
- The dealership replicated the coupon promotion on Facebook to great success.

Lebanon Ford's social media success can be attributed to many factors: Jeff Cryder, Jr., and his understanding of the space; a business and upper management that was willing to take the risk and enter the space wholeheartedly; and the patience to see the strategy through its early days before traction.

For us, though, the core reason for success was that Lebanon Ford focused on limited platforms and excelling there, as opposed to being everywhere and seeing what sticks.

This is where many businesses stumble when trying to use social media. They're unsure of which platforms to be on so they try them all. The problem is, the success of the larger social media networks like Facebook and Twitter have seen scores of similar platforms come into the equation. With Twitter it's Identi.ca; with Facebook it's Google+; with LinkedIn it's BranchOut.

Confusion around the platforms on which to connect continues to hold brands back from fully embracing social media. This is no different from the dilemma brands face when choosing where to place a media buy—the local paper, an ad in the industry journals, TV, radio, or online.

Brands are willing to test the social media waters, however, via individuals already entrenched in the space, and this willingness to use the voice of others paved the way for the social media influencer model, although this can have mixed results.

The CNN iReport Fail

On October 3, 2008, a report that Apple CEO Steve Jobs had died of a heart attack was posted on the website of news giant CNN under its iReport banner. iReport allows anyone to create an account with CNN and become a "citizen journalist." CNN created iReport to offer local people the opportunity to share stories and news articles that would otherwise be ignored or unheard, and it was through one of these citizen journalists the Jobs story broke.

The citizen journalist involved reported the scoop had come from a reliable source inside Apple, but didn't have any further information, so was publishing the story on iReport to see whether anyone could provide further details. The impact was immediate.

Because the breaking story was published on a CNN property, most people took it as authentic. Apple's shares fell 10% in 10 minutes and closed the day 3% down overall. The U.S. Securities and Exchange Commission (SEC) requested the details of the citizen journalist responsible for posting the news, and CNN's reputation was questioned for allowing the story to be published without verification. (iReport has a disclaimer that all stories are published unedited unless they're "compelling, important, and urgent.")

Critics accused CNN of running the piece to drive traffic to its site, a claim CNN refuted. Citizen journalism, which had been growing in popularity for its ability to offer raw opinion unfiltered by editorial restrictions, lost much of its authority and raised questions on how much influence these journalists should be afforded.

This was an early example of both the power and fear of social media. The speed at which the breaking story spread, and the effect it had on shares in an organizational behemoth such as Apple, showed just how viral the nascent social media could be. It's this virality, and the potential for false and damaging statements to be accepted as fact, that brands continue to fear when it comes to adoption of social media.

The Nate Silver Phenomenon

When American statistician Nate Silver correctly predicted the winner in all 50 states of the 2012 U.S. presidential election, it was the crowning moment of a career that has seen Silver recognized as a true influencer across two of America's most popular pastimes—baseball and politics. In 2002, Silver built a predictive algorithm called PECOTA (Player Empirical Comparison and Optimization Test Algorithm), which Silver used to forecast the player performance of major league baseball players. PECOTA's analysis and results impressed Baseball Prospectus, an organization dedicated to specialized analysis of baseball known as sabermetrics. Baseball Prospectus bought the program from Silver, who continued to manage it until 2009, when he left to concentrate on politics, which he had been writing about since 2007.

Silver's logic-based analysis for the 2008 elections saw him predict 49 out of the 50 states correctly and put him on the radar of mainstream media and political pundits alike (in 2009, *Time* Magazine named him one of the world's top 100 most influential people). While critics of Silver question his methods, there's no doubt that his algorithms and affirmation of his method from the 2012 election have changed the landscape of political punditry and made Nate Silver the man the media will go to when election season comes round again in 2016.

The fact that Silver used his blog to publish his predictions, and bypassed the traditional media of newspapers and television, was a turning point in political punditry and how it's reported. Traditionalists may not be fans of Silver but the users of the social web are.

The New Personal Relationship Dynamic

So far this chapter has illustrated the evolution of word-of-mouth marketing from a one-directional communication path to a multidirectional groupthink or digital "bandwagonism." The result of effective traditional word-of-mouth marketing, the bandwagon effect, is a long-standing marketing principle in the offline world that describes a person's willingness to adopt a belief, opinion, or attitude when the majority of that person's community expresses acceptance of it.

Marketers influenced key individuals within a community to state their belief in something expecting others to quickly "jump on the bandwagon" too. The phenomenon was sometimes referred to as the snowball effect because once it got rolling, the sheer speed and size of the movement was next to impossible to stop.

However, consumers have become more interconnected with each other through social channels, which create myriad opportunities to disrupt the path, size, speed, and impact of that snowball. What was once single-direction communication from brand to influencer to community that inspired a specific action is now a multidirectional free-for-all in which any person, comment, or action can instantly change the direction of brand communications and public perceptions alike. In Figure 3.3, you can see exactly how these paths are connected and disseminated.

By facilitating a greater exchange of information, social media has created a disruptive force that marketers must deal with. They can no longer rely on the bandwagon effect to keep consumers loyal because this new access to information dramatically changed not just how consumers engage with products and brand messages but how they make purchase decisions.

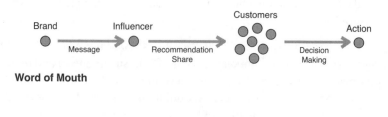

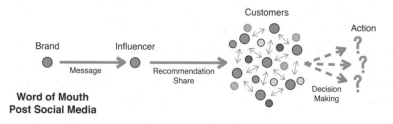

Figure 3.3 *Word-of-mouth communication path, pre- and post- social media*

The evolution of Internet-based technologies, social networking, and the public's growing acceptance of online public communications has altered the dynamic of word-of-mouth marketing forever.

We have identified three major shifts in communications: degree of separation, degree of relationship, and degree of publicity. These shifts have dramatically impacted how people engage with each other and played a disruptive role in not just word-of-mouth but general marketing effectiveness.

Degree of Separation

Think about it: How much more popular is the average high school student today than a student 25 years ago? Before the Internet was common and certainly before social media networks, the most popular high school student might have claimed to know approximately 100 people made up of family, neighbors, classmates, and colleagues at a part-time job. In reality, the student probably only connected on a regular basis with no more than 25 or 30 people.

Today, thanks to technology and social networking, teens could claim to know thousands of people, and the number of people they converse with regularly can easily reach hundreds if not more. Social technologies, including the Internet, social media, and wireless mobile networks have unraveled the definition of friendship. At a minimum, friendships are now a much looser connection of contacts than ever before. Where friends were once people we had some personal, face-to-face connection with, today friends are often people we've never met in person.

Social media did not create this paradigm; technology did. Popularized by John Guare's play *Six Degrees of Separation*, mathematicians and psychologists tested the accuracy of the model during the 1960s and 1970s.

The result was that in reality, the U.S. population is more likely all connected by only three degrees of separation as reported in *Contact and Influences*, a study conducted by Manfred Kochen building on the work of MIT's Michael Gurevich.

Social media has amplified this concept by providing more immediate connections between people. Since 2000, data and social scientists have been applying the Six Degrees of Separation theory to social networks and connections. In 2008, Microsoft conducted research analyzing MSN electronic messages and found that most people in that digital universe were connected by exactly 6.6 degrees. However, that was a limited sampling because it studied MSN users only.

Let's consider our "friendships" on Facebook, the world's largest social network. In 2011, Johan Ugander, a Ph.D. student in math at Cornell University and a former research intern at Facebook, conducted a study that proved Facebook users were only 4.74 intermediaries apart. While there's been debate around the number (some say it's actually 3 degrees since you don't count people on either end of the chain), the fact remains that our social graphs have become bigger and more complex and our ability to connect with more people has increased dramatically.

As of August 2012, there were approximately 143 million users on Facebook in the United States and 1 billion Facebook users worldwide (Source: Statista, 2012). According to the PEW Research Center's American Life Project, the average number of Facebook friends reached 318.5 among Millennials (adults between the ages of 18-34) in February 2012; for GenX users (ages 35-46), that average is 197.6 friends, and Baby Boomers (age 47-65) averaged 124.2 friends, as shown in Figure 3.4.

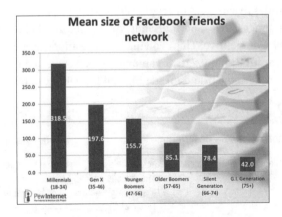

Figure 3.4   *Pew Research Center's American Life Project*

The more people we connect with, the more social networks we engage in, and the more devices we have to access those communities, the more convoluted our personal connections become. The sheer volume of people within an individual's personal network today impacts the nature of modern relationships and how we communicate.

These growing connections, more commonly known as a person's social graph today, define our personal, family, or business communities across social networking sites.[6] This social graph allows us to better connect with those most relevant to us at any given time, as well as make much more effective use of the social web and the various networks we belong to and our connections on them.

This concept is taking hold as social media is starting to map the connections and relationships between people that used to be invisible.

The Five Degrees of Social Relationships

The option—and ability—to connect to a greater number of people via social channels has decreased our degrees of separation from each other but fabricated new degrees of relationships among us. Having different levels of relationships is not a new phenomenon; however, the dynamics of those relationships have changed thanks to social technologies.

Forgotten high school mates are now Facebook friends; old and neglected business card exchanges are now LinkedIn contacts; followers are now social friends. At a minimum, this redefines the characteristics of relationships we once had.

According to Pew Research, as of February 2012, 66% of online adults use social networking sites. In fact, on a typical day, 48% of online adults use social networking, up from 43% in August 2011 and just 27% in April of 2009.

Table 3.1 identifies five degrees of relationships within a person's new list of personal contacts: Inner Circle, Social Friends, Acquaintances, Followers - Colleagues, and Followers - Competitive. This evolving list of relationship types, and the differing communication characteristics among them, has created new pathways through which traditional brand messaging and influence can be disrupted.

Table 3.1   Social Graph Relationship Matrix

Tier	Categorization	Description	Relationship Activity
First	Inner Circle	Personal contacts such as family, neighbors, friends and coworkers with whom you share frequent and personal communications both online and face-to-face.	In-person and digital gathering such as meals, social engagements, telephone and video calls, text messaging, etc.

Tier	Categorization	Description	Relationship Activity
Second	Social Friends	Contacts with frequent personal communications but where the relationship began and, for the most part, remains online.	Digital gathering such as social networking, video chats, etc.
Third	Acquaintances	Contacts formed or solidified through a one-time or infrequent meeting such as at a trade show or past friendships such as old high school contacts reconnected solely through social channels.	Infrequent contact via social networks, mainly focused on business relationships.
Fourth	Followers - Colleagues	Impersonal relationships where no face-to-face connections were made; where communication is limited to the consumption of digital content.	Two-way, impersonal activity including reading each other's blogs, following each other on Twitter, etc.
Fifth	Followers - Competitive	Impersonal relationships where no face-to-face connections were made; where communication is limited to the consumption of digital content.	One-way, impersonal activity where one monitors the actions of another such as competitive analysis.

Prior to the popularization of social networking, this graph might have been a two-dimensional map for marketers seeking to engage an audience of prospective customers; the first degree being the prospect's personal network and the second tier being the larger, general community.

Where the Internet facilitated greater access to information, social networking facilitated greater access to relationships and so marketers must take notice of the nature and context of those relationships when considering how to craft messages and tactics that might assert influence within those communities.

The Degree of Publicity—Online Networks

However many degrees apart we are or to what extent we develop a relationship, the one certainty is that most have become public or, if trends continue, soon will be. People have grown accustomed to sharing every aspect of their personal beliefs, daily activities, and personal or business discussions with the world. Further, they enjoy and expect that those they connect with will also share those engagements publicly.

Photo sharing networks like Instagram are populated with pictures and comments about the food we eat and with whom we eat it. Geonetworking sites like Foursquare or Facebook Places allow us to report to the world the stores we shop at, the cities we visit, or the airports we connect through. Presentation sharing networks like SlideShare announce what presentations we download to our Facebook connections.

Websites like Yelp.com encourage us to publicly document and share personal experiences about the hotels we stay at and the restaurants we frequent. Travel site TripIt.com posts your travel plans and history to your LinkedIn profile page. Friends tag us in the pictures they post on their social sites or online groups that we don't even belong to. Blog commenting tools such as Livefyre turn basic blog commentary into public displays by displaying our personal profiles and aggregate our comments across everyone's blog posts on those profiles.

The once friend-only, private Facebook now provides public pages and defaults our posts to share across those public connections. We can now subscribe to personal Facebook pages without having to be friends. Others, like professional networking site LinkedIn, are quickly enhancing our public page profiles and features so we can provide a richer and more robust interface to share our information and activity with the world.

And when we consider the number of smartphones, cameras, digital music players, and tablets that can record audio, images, and video and instantly distribute them across the Web, we quickly realize there's little we do not share publicly anymore. We're moving toward a society where all offline relationships will eventually be, even if only in part, online.

When Everyone Is an Influencer

What is the result of this shift in how we communicate? The growing volume and degree of connections we have have increased the data we consume and the influences we're subjected to every day. The increasing trend to share those connections and relationships publicly further amplifies personalities, opinions, and messages. With more people joining social networks every day, more of the world's population gaining access to the Internet, and more devices being equipped with wireless technologies, there's no end in sight.

By connecting with friends on social networks, rating a meal at our favorite restaurant, or checking in to your local coffee shop, we all become prolific content producers. When combined with our ever-expanding social graph, our amplification makes each and every one of us a potential influencer. And when everyone is an influencer, is anyone really an influencer? The reality is that by connecting through our growing social graphs, all we've really done is muddy the waters.

Complicating matters further, businesses, identifying the threat and opportunity that lie in newly connected communities and their groupthink, are expanding the noise by hijacking those networks and conversations with their own messages. Not only do they add to the noise, they distort it with attempts to manipulate the conversation in their favor.

So who—if anyone—is really an influencer anymore? When everyone is free to produce whatever content they want and publish it without fact checking or compliance, how can online recommendations be trusted? Our increased access to each other, as well as each other's relationships, experiences, and opinions, has increased the likelihood that disruptive factors will creep into the communication mix and impact the natural course of someone's influence over another.

So even if you could identify a true influencer, would it do you any good? However, with so much to gain by businesses that can successfully identify and leverage these influencers in our highly complex and connected society, this challenge will not be left unanswered. In the next chapter we introduce the first wave of businesses and platforms that have accepted this challenge and discuss their implications on influence marketing.

Endnotes

1. http://www.retailresearch.org/onlineretailing.php

2. http://www.ftc.gov/opa/2009/10/endortest.shtm

3. www.cc-chapman.com/2011/ragu-hates-dads/

4. http://www.cmosurvey.org/blog/social-media-spend-continues-to-soar/

5. http://www.closingbigger.net/2012/04/ford-dealer-social-media-success-story-lebanon-ford-podcast/

6. http://www.web-strategist.com/blog/2007/11/10/what-is-social-graph-executives/

4

The Current Influence Model and Social Scoring

In the spring of 2011, Sam was going through the recruitment process for the position of vice president at a large Toronto marketing agency. Sam felt extremely confident regarding his chances, given his background of more than 15 years of major brand consultancy expertise.

This confidence continued into the early part of the main interview, where Sam and the interviewer spoke of the successes Sam had achieved with the types of clientele that the new vice president would be working with at the marketing agency.

Halfway through the one-on-one, the interviewer asked Sam what his Klout score was. Sam drew a blank stare; he had never heard of Klout. Was this recruitment talk for senior level executives?

The interviewer shared his computer screen with Sam, showing him the website for social influence platform Klout. On the screen, Sam could see a profile of himself, with a large number 37 next to his details—his Klout score.

The interview ended shortly after that revelation, and Sam wasn't invited back. Instead, the position he'd been so confident in winning was given to another applicant who had a Klout score of 67.

Welcome to the world of social scoring for influence.

Sam's experience has been well documented across several blog posts, news stories, and case studies on the phenomenon of social scoring. It was one of the first examples of the rising power of social scoring, and how influence measurement platforms such as Klout, Kred, PeerIndex, and others are now taken seriously.

That was two years ago, and the marketplace has shifted dramatically since then, with even more platforms to gauge how influential you are online, both as an individual and as a brand or brand advocate.

If the rise of social media as discussed in Chapter 3, "The Rise of Social Media," impacted the way businesses interact with their customers, the growth of social scoring has forever changed the way these businesses approach their marketing campaigns with these very customers in mind—and it's only going to continue to grow, as we see in the next section of the book.

To understand where these platforms are going, first we need to understand where they came from and—more importantly—why they arrived in the first place.

The Carnegie Principle

When Dale Carnegie released his seminal book *How to Win Friends and Influence People* in 1936, he probably didn't realize just how much he would shape business mindsets for the next 70 years.

While primarily one of the first self-help books to be published for the general public, Carnegie's book also set the tone for how businesses could appeal more to their customers, existing and potential. This was based on six of the key tenets throughout his book, which we recognize as The Carnegie Principles:

1. Become genuinely interested in other people.

2. Smile.

3. Remember that a person's name is, to that person, the sweetest and most important sound in any language.

4. Be a good listener. Encourage others to talk about themselves.

5. Talk in terms of the other person's interest.

6. Make the other person feel important—and do it sincerely.

While at first these principles might not all appear to be ideas that sit comfortably with the average business, you only need to look at how these beliefs have entrenched themselves in today's social media-led business for validation of how far each one has been recognized as a business mantra.

The success of Carnegie's book—15 million copies sold worldwide and counting—introduced a somewhat foreign concept to many businesses: that people truly are the lifeblood of any successful business. This includes employees as well as customers.

As the book found its way into the hands of more than just people looking for self-improvement, business ethos began to change. It was far from an overnight swing, though; even today, there are still hundreds of thousands of businesses where it's clear the culture of the company isn't aligned to its people, whether internal (employees) or external (customers).

The Marketing Shift from Brand to Consumer

Three years after Carnegie's book came out, Europe was at war. When Hitler invaded Poland on September 1, 1939, Great Britain and France declared war on Germany. The United States entered the fray in 1941 when Japan bombed Pearl Harbor, and the Second Great War became truly global. Surprisingly, during this period of turmoil the present business landscape—at least as far as research is concerned—was shaped.

As discussed in Chapter 3, prior to social media businesses had to follow a certain path to access the thoughts of their customers:

- Questionnaires on a website
- In-store promotion
- Outbound telephone calls
- Emails

If the budget allowed, focus groups could be used. These first came into general use in the United States during World War II, when scientists worked with the Ministry of Defense to gauge public perception of the war. These focus groups led to propaganda campaigns, both at home and abroad.

The potential of taking these focus groups into the marketing world was evident. By working directly with customers, existing and new, brands could pivot if a product didn't live up to pre-public promise, instead of continuing to spend money on a project that seemed doomed to failure. Where Research and Development previously cost millions of dollars before feedback could be given, now businesses could spend a fraction of that cost throughout the development cycle and adjust accordingly.

It wasn't just the marketing world that benefited from focus groups, although they were the natural fit. Usability engineering focus groups, for example, enabled feedback on websites and software, with companies relying on these specific types of focus groups to shape what would hopefully be the next big thing in technical design or website user interface.

It's clear that the advent of focus groups introduced a major shift in how businesses and their customers interact with each other. Like any result-driven parameter, though, the power and usefulness of focus groups also became their Achilles' heel.

Brands shared their prototypes of early visions of a product and group participants offered feedback on what worked, what didn't, and whether the market was ready for this new addition.

As consumers began to understand the value of these types of discussions to the brands running them, the more savvy among them realized future participation could be gamed. With sites like Focusgroup.com offering over a hundred dollars for a couple of hours of a person's time, some focus group participants ensured the answers they provided were positive, thereby encouraging brands to invite them back for future sessions.

This led to the perception of focus groups as brand cheerleading rather than informative feedback opportunities, a view reinforced by Jonathan Ive, Apple's senior vice president of industrial design, who blamed focus groups for producing "bland, inoffensive products."

While focus groups continue to be used today, their appeal has diminished because of the questions surrounding the transparency and authenticity of the answers. Focus groups show how the power of a few can shape the outcome of many.

However, focus groups also highlighted the limitations of this approach—gaming the feedback to encourage repeat attendee participation, as well as retaining that feedback behind a closed door ensured that true innovation in the marketplace wasn't being fully encouraged or acted upon. The business landscape was changing—print media, as well as television and radio ads, were still the core part of a business's go-to-market strategy—but now there was a new component, the Internet.

A new model was needed—one that benefited brands and consumers, and offered true feedback as well as the ability to connect with more than just the participants in a focus group.

Enter influencer marketing and outreach.

The People Paradigm

In 1906, a West Jersey and Seashore Railroad electric train derailed on a bridge in Atlantic City, New Jersey. The two lead cars derailed as the train made the crossing, with the third car eventually toppling into the river below. As the tragedy unfolded, former journalist turned PR pioneer Ivy Lee worked closely with the company to openly share the details of the tragedy with journalists and reporters. This partnership ensured the factual version of the tragedy was released, as opposed to supposition and guesswork on the part of the media. Widely recognized as the first news release, this was a pivotal moment in the history of modern media where the voice of one could be used to convey a message to the many.

This event could be viewed as the birth of word-of-mouth marketing via mass media consumption—one of the core disciplines in today's influencer marketing approach. By using a single point of contact (Lee) that the audience (journalists) respected due to his background in their industry, West Jersey and Seashore railroad used the same techniques that brands today pay thousands of dollars for, whether via a social scoring platform or a marketing agency running your targeted outreach campaign(s).

The story of Ivy Lee is just one of several early examples of the power of one to drive the attention of many. In his book *The Tipping Point*, published in 2000, Malcolm Gladwell shares the story of Paul Revere and William Dawes, two revolutionaries who rode through the night to warn of the advancing British forces prior to the battles of Lexington and Concord in the American Revolution.

While both men shared the same warning, only Revere's resulted in raising the kind of defenses needed to push the British back. The reason? Revere was a Connector, the kind of person who knew everyone and who would be listened to—just the kind of person to ensure an important message reaches the right audience and—crucially—is acted upon.

Ivy Lee. Paul Revere. Dale Carnegie. Whether you call them Connectors or pioneers, they all showed the potential of the right person at the right time spreading the right message. As we saw in Chapter 3, this is the core tenet of word-of-mouth marketing, which in itself is the core tenet of influencer marketing. Everything we know about influence, and spreading a message organically as well as virally, points to the start of the last century and even earlier to Revere's celebrated ride through the night that changed the course of a war. That's why the primary strategy behind any word-of-mouth campaign centers around the Four As, as shown in Figure 4.1.

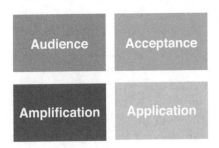

Figure 4.1   *The Four As approach to word-of-mouth marketing*

Audience

It doesn't matter what type of campaign you're running—social media, traditional ad spend, pay per click—you need an audience ready to receive your message. Paid media offers the benefit of having others identify your audience—Google's Pay Per Click (PPC) solution allows you to target by demographic, location, whether your audience uses tablets or smartphones to browse the Web, and so on—while Facebook Ads uses its Insights algorithm to identify how many people your ad will reach based on the information you feed into its filters.

With organic media, though, which is where word-of-mouth marketing and blogger outreach campaigns come into play, the audience needs to be found and cultivated. This is where social scoring platforms such as Klout, Kred, Peerindex, Ecairn Conversation™, and others offer specific services to help you identify your audience. We look at these platforms in more depth at the end of this chapter. Whatever campaign tactic your business uses, having a receptive audience is key to any success you're hoping to achieve.

Acceptance

Unless your audience is ready to accept your message, then no amount of budget or clever marketing copy is going to change their minds—at least not initially. To have your audience accept your message, it needs to trust the medium you're using. A generic ad isn't necessarily going to build that trust. It may spark desire, but desire doesn't always lead to a purchase. This is why brands look to influencers to increase the likelihood of a message being accepted.

Think about your own decisions, particularly larger purchases. Do you buy a car because of the way it looks and sounds, or do you also take into consideration viewpoints of friends who are mechanics, family members who have owned that particular brand before, as well as journalists or reviewers in publications or television shows who you respect? When you respect the broadcaster of a message, your decisions are influenced by their advice. Brands realize this and are increasingly moving away from celebrity endorsements to social influencer endorsements because of the greater probability of the message being accepted.[1]

Application

In theory, the application of your brand's message should be the simplest part. Unfortunately, social media can be fickle—one brand's successful application can be another brand's failure, as Oracle found in 2012.

Primarily known as an enterprise-level software solution, the company took a large step into the social space in 2012 when it bought Involver, a developer of

Facebook applications; social media and social relationship management company Vitrue; and monitoring and sentiment analysis specialists Collective Intellect. In November of that year, Oracle decided to work with Facebook and merge all the business pages of these three new acquisitions under one main umbrella page, Oracle Social.

In the early hours of Saturday, November 10, a mini crisis erupted as the Oracle Social page was besieged by people asking why they were suddenly fans of this new page. Even worse, users recommended that other fans report the page as spam, primarily due to the sudden and inexplicable growth of the page—in the space of three days, Oracle Social had grown to more than one million fans. Many people complaining about Liking the page saw this as proof that Oracle had bought all these new fans. As this outbreak of complaints took place, there was complete silence from the Oracle account.

It wasn't until later that day, after several blog posts about the incident as well as hundreds of Facebook complaints, that Oracle published its first update to the page—an apology and clarification that the Likes were a result of the three previous company's pages being merged into one. However, this still didn't appease the majority of the complainants, who felt they had been automatically added to a page without prior discussion or warning. Nor were they totally buying the explanation Oracle gave that Facebook had instigated the merger four days earlier than expected. They also felt Oracle had been lax in addressing the problem, especially given the fact that the company page was promoting how effective Oracle was at social media solutions. Social media marketers and consultants highlighted the incident as the perfect case study of how not to approach a social media campaign.

The Oracle example shows that even companies that have the resources and manpower to execute social media well can get it wrong. Had this been a marketing campaign versus a simple Facebook page issue, the consequences for Oracle could have been much worse. It's a strong reminder of why the application—or execution—of your message needs to be seamless and planned down to the minutest of details.

Amplification

When you consider that almost a thousand tweets per second are shared on Twitter, and that more than three million blogs are reported to be started every month, the amplification your brand creates for your message is key to its success and subsequent campaigns. If your marketing team doesn't identify a way to ensure your message cuts through the online clutter and finds its way to the ears and eyes of your target audience, then you may find yourself struggling to succeed in social media.

This enigma has encouraged brands to use the services of social scoring platforms versus identifying how their message can be spread organically and by internal teams. True word-of-mouth marketing is an artform that takes experience and deep strategy to successfully navigate. It's why nonprofit organizations like WOMMA—the Word of Mouth Marketing Association—exist, to advise on best practices and educate its members on marketing through brand advocates and viral buzz. The problem for many businesses, however, is they simply don't have the time or resources to implement WOMMA's solutions. This can be due to financial restrictions, or manpower, or even time constraints. A strategic word-of-mouth campaign can take months to come to fruition, and in this always-on, instant-result business world we live in today, many brands can't afford to wait that long.

This realization opened up the doors for social scoring businesses to enter the marketplace.

The Power of One

The concept of influence is not new. On October 30, 1938, CBS aired the radio drama *The War of the Worlds*, based on the book by English author H. G. Wells. It was narrated by Orson Welles and presented in the same manner as news bulletins of the time. Because of the gravitas of Welles's delivery, many listeners of the show believed they were hearing the account of a real alien invasion of Earth. When it became clear that the show was fictional, newspapers and public figures decried the approach, and several members of the public sued, although only one person received compensation. Welles became famous for his part in the drama.

The power of one—the ability of one person to shape the thoughts and/or desires of many—is highlighted perfectly with the CBS radio drama. It also shows how the Four As were used to increase the success of Welles and CBS in convincing the public of its authenticity.

- **Audience**—As World War II loomed, the listeners of the show were already on edge and wary of invading armies. They listened to their radios for news from Europe as well as where the United States stood on the growing threat of war.

- **Acceptance**—There was little to no reason to doubt the validity of the broadcast. CBS was a national station and Welles a respected actor. It also helped that an announcement prior to the broadcast, stating the show was a fictional theater production, was missed by the vast majority of listeners due to the show running at the same time as NBC's hugely popular *Chase and Sanborn Hour*. When listeners of the NBC show tuned into the CBS broadcast, it was already well into its depiction of an alien invasion and the disclaimer long gone.

- **Application**—By keeping the tone authoritative and presenting the first two-thirds of the broadcast in the style of a news bulletin, the presentation of the story became so real that listeners called police stations for advice on how to prepare for aliens.

- **Amplification**—Although televisions were around in 1938, radio was in its heyday. Welles and CBS chose the perfect platform to ensure as many people could hear the broadcast as possible, and in doing so their message spread virally within a short time.

Imagine if this same broadcast happened today but instead of a radio show, the updates were news snippets shared in short and panicky bursts on Twitter. The microblogging platform has repeatedly shown its value as a news service and disseminator of information. It was the first service to break the news of the Mumbai terrorist attacks in 2008, as users in the Indian city immediately started sharing eyewitness accounts of the carnage around them. When US Airways flight 1549 had to make an emergency landing in the Hudson River in New York in 2009, Twitter beat the mass media news networks again when residents near the river shared pictures and updates about the plane crash.

Had Welles's narration been via tweets to a global public audience instead of just the listeners of the CBS radio show and had been accepted as fact, then the virality of his message would have been enormous. Social media has taken the ability to impact the lives of others to a height previously unheard of, unless you were a celebrity or public figure.

This potential for anyone to assert influence over others has changed the way brands look at marketing their products and services. Advertisers have to adapt to smarter approaches that include digital channels, and media and news organizations no longer have the monopoly of their audience's attention that they used to enjoy.

The problem for brands in this new democracy is many don't know how to attract these influencers, particularly in the B2C market where social media adoption is currently more widespread. The company may have superstar salespeople, and the CEO may have good connections at the C-suite executive level, but none of that can help when it comes to the nuances of building an outreach campaign to target influencers and brand advocates. This is a skill that requires not only knowledge of the various social platforms, but also the language and user behavior for each one.

Twitter characteristics are different from Facebook, and Facebook user behavior is equally as different from LinkedIn. The strategy behind a word-of-mouth campaign requires a specific person to be driving it—and many companies are unwilling to take a chance on employing that person in the event the strategy doesn't pay off and they're left with an employee with no role. This conundrum opened up the opportunity for today's social scoring platforms. While numerous social scoring and influence measurement solutions are in the marketplace today, some have risen to the head of the queue.

Klout

Although not the first social scoring platform, Klout (www.klout.com) is, arguably, the most well-known. Released in 2007, its name is synonymous with social influence, and it's the platform that divides opinion the most—a true sign that a company is doing something that people are interested in and watching closely. Klout's methodology is shrouded in secrecy, although its front-facing approach is simple. The company scrapes publicly available information and creates a profile of you on its site, and then assigns a score to you between 1 and 100 based on an algorithm. This score is made up of several metrics, although there are three key analytics that Klout bases its score on: How active you are online; how much amplification you have when it comes to having your message shared by others; and the perceived influence of those with whom you're connected. The more you have of each of these metrics, the higher your influence will be, as shown in Figure 4.2.

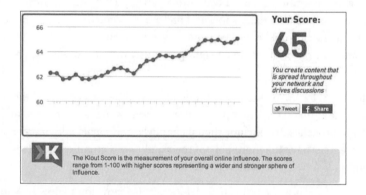

Figure 4.2 *The Klout influencer scorecard*

Klout initiates this process via your Twitter account. If your profile is set to public, Klout accesses Twitter's API and uses the information its engineers find to set up your profile and allocate your score. The platform then encourages users to sign up and connect their other social networks to increase their Klout score. This opt-out process has garnered Klout its biggest critics. Many people are unaware they even have a Klout profile as Sam found out to his detriment at the beginning of this chapter, and are unhappy at having to sign in to a service they didn't opt-in to in the first place to delete their information. Klout has also come under fire for the way its algorithm created profiles for minors, which the company countered by improving its database and resolving to be more stringent in policing how profiles are created.

While Klout has its critics, it also has a strong and loyal user base. Additionally, brands and partners have embraced the platform to offer Klout Perks to connect with that user base. Introduced in 2010, Perks are rewards that only users with a certain Klout score or higher can apply for and range from something as simple as a Sharpie pen to a weekend with a new car to test drive. The hope from the brands is that, by accessing people with influence in the market they're competing in, they'll enjoy the extra exposure an influential blogger or social media user can give them. Recipients of Klout Perks are encouraged to share their experience with their audience, and brands hope this organic promotion and sharing will deliver their desired results, whether that be awareness of the brand, increased social followers or mentions, or—ideally—sales.

Since Klout's inception, the company has received more than $40 million in funding, a clear sign that social scoring, while still considered to be in its infancy, is something that brands and organizations are looking to better understand. Compounding this validation was the integration of Klout into Microsoft's search engine Bing in late 2012. When web surfers use the Klout sidebar with Bing, not only do they see the score of any individuals being searched for but also the topics where they're influential. This partnership and others like it—Klout also partners with industry heavyweights like Hootsuite, Radian6, and Salesforce—have strengthened Klout's position in the social scoring industry, as well as the growing maturity of the industry.

Kred

Launched in September 2011 by social analytics leader PeopleBrowsr, Kred (www.kred.com) is seen by many to be the natural competitor to Klout. Both companies took existing words and altered them to offer a relevant yet cooler description of their service—with Klout it was clout, and with Kred it was cred, or credibility. Both companies also highlight the capital K as a core part of their imagery and logos, and they both allocate social scores along with rewards for users that meet a certain criteria (in Kred's case, these are Kred Rewards). However, a few key differences set the two platforms apart, as shown in Figure 4.3.

Whereas Klout is protective of its approach and how its algorithm computes the raw data that makes up your score, Kred is open and public about its methods. This openness to discuss its results and dissect its data is a direct result of Kred's roots in its parent company PeopleBrowsr, but it also endears the company to marketers and brand partners since they can actually see how the data is being collected, segregated, and actioned.

Figure 4.3 *The Kred story for individuals*

Kred is also proactive when it comes to ensuring its platform isn't being abused. When Klout introduced a new feature called +K in the middle of 2011, it was seen as a way to help identify influencers beyond Klout's own algorithm. Users could give a recommendation of someone's influence, by awarding them a +K for a certain topic. Unfortunately, savvy users of the service soon found a loophole where you could allocate +K's in topics the recipient knew nothing about.

In one particular instance, Danny became known as an expert in sheep as his friends and connections across social networks kept giving him +K's in sheep as a joke! This flaw resulted in Klout having to adapt the feature so that only approved topics would be counted. To avoid the same thing happening to its influence metrics, Kred actively monitors its platform for any suspicious behavior or questionable metrics and scores. If it finds people gaming the system, Kred removes them from the lists it sends its clients for their influencer campaigns.

These lists are another key differentiator that separates Kred from its competitors. Whereas Klout identifies influencers based on its algorithm and then acts as the conduit between the brand and Klout's database, Kred acts more as a consultancy. It collects the names of its members and sells them to advertisers and brands directly, and then works with the brand on how best to approach these influencers. By taking this approach, Kred can isolate specific influencers and their communities effectively, which helps target a Reward or similar incentive for a Kred member to interact with an advertiser or channel partner. It's an old approach (list-building) given a modern twist (social media influence).

Kred's connection to PeopleBrowsr's social analytics, and the multitiered approach it takes to identifying influencers and helping brands work with them, has helped the platform separate itself from its early mover peers. Kred's implementation of campaigns for multiple audiences across different verticals has resulted in the ability to measure results in a more actionable manner for their partners.

PeerIndex

Founded in July 2007, PeerIndex (www.peerindex.com) measures a person's influence by three core metrics: Activity, Audience, and Authority. Much like Kred, PeerIndex is keen to avoid the kind of spam and gamed aspects of social scoring that Klout fell victim to with its +K system. By choosing these three metrics, PeerIndex looks to concentrate more on relevance and insights, which proponents of social influence, as well as marketers, place more value on (see Figure 4.4).

The Activity metric measures your personal activity across the Web compared to other social media users; the Audience metric measures your overall reach, and how that can be dissected across different social networks; and the Authority metric measures your overall relevance to the community to which you're connected.

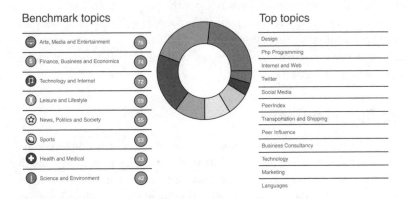

Figure 4.4   *PeerIndex ranks benchmark topics to identify relevance*

PeerIndex also offers users of its service special brand promotions, called PeerPerks. For smaller businesses that can't afford full promotions like PeerPerks, the company introduced Perklets, targeting local businesses, startups and up-and-coming entrepreneurs, and small business owners. With social influence programs and perks often being prohibitive in cost for smaller business owners, PeerIndex's initiative allows lesser-known brands to reach a wider audience at a fraction of the cost of traditional marketing and advertising.

Empire Avenue

While not a social scoring platform in the same sense as Klout, Kred, and PeerIndex, Empire Avenue (www.empireavenue.com) helps brands connect with relevant influencers by mimicking the stock market, only virtually. Users—or players—of the platform are given a stock price when they sign up, based on the connections they have across Twitter, Facebook, Flickr, YouTube, LinkedIn, Foursquare, Instagram, and their own blogs. This stock price is then publicly displayed, and other players can buy shares in you based on their perception of your future value. Your activity on the Web, as well as your interaction with other members of Empire Avenue, help to increase your value, which attracts further investors. The more investors you have, the more likely you are to be seen as someone of influence.

While Empire Avenue defines social equity by the value of a player's stock and connects brands with these people to spread a promotional message across their networks, the platform has been criticized for the apparent ease in which it can be gamed. Since Empire Avenue rewards you by dividends paid out by other players you invest in, as well as your own activity across the Web, several players have simply interacted more with those they've invested in.

By sharing that person's content and promoting him or her to their own networks, it raises the share price of that person. Once the price goes up your own value increases, much like in the stock market. By following this practice, the player whose share value is raised doesn't even need to be influential in any way, nor does the person have to be very active on other networks, if she plays the social stock market in Empire Avenue effectively.

eCairn Conversation™

Specializing in community and influencer marketing, eCairn Conversation™ (www.ecairn.com)—from parent company eCairn, Inc.—stays away from the gamification approach of other social scoring platforms and concentrates more on raw data and context to identify almost half a billion influencers across hundreds of industries and topics.

Founded in 2006, eCairn takes its cue from the ideas presented in Malcolm Gladwell's *The Tipping Point* and Seth Godin's *Tribes* and scans the social web to identify like-minded individuals that are both connected to each other and talking about similar topics. They then identify how these people are connected—from a simple link on a blog to more in-depth connections and reference points. Once eCairn finds that connection, it uses it to build personas of the influencer in question to provide their clients.

This information can then be broken down into three core competencies:

- **Research and insight capture**—eCairn Conversation™ takes the relevance and authority of an influencer's content and delivers it in a more granular fashion, ensuring only the most relevant and authority-driven data is captured.

- **Influencer profiling and outreach**—As influencer programs mature, and the audience of these influencers become influential themselves, the ability to connect brands to the right audience becomes increasingly important. eCairn identifies targets through a mix of relevance to a topic (both negative and positive), their social graph (their activity online, who they're interacting with and how influential that person is), and geography and demographic match.

- **Content engineering**—With social media's and social influence's growing importance in the overall strategy of businesses and marketers, the role of content in that strategy has also grown. Blog posts, social updates and statuses, online presentations, web copy—all are key parts of a successful presence on social media. To meet the demand of this new paradigm, content engineers have come to the fore. One part strategist, one part analyst, one part creator, and one part product marketer and manager, the content engineer is a gatekeeper of your business's success on the social web. eCairn recognizes this new role and helps identify the influencers and community leaders that can help your business share its message more effectively and strategically.

eCairn uses several other metrics for identifying influence, including

- **Cluster Neighbor Identification**—Highlights close-knit communities and who's leading them as shown in Figure 4.5.

Figure 4.5 *The eCairn Cluster Neighbor Identification*

- **Conversations Explorer**—An aggregated feed of real-time conversations across multiple platforms.

- **Trend Analytics**—Allows brands to identify trends within a specific topic, the peak time for these conversations, and the ability to identify the people driving these peaks and spikes.

- **Expressions Explorer**—Takes the expressions and phrases within a community and highlights those that are the most relevant to your outreach campaign.

Because of this approach, eCairn has established itself as one of the leading influence platforms when it comes to actionable data.

The Domino Effect of Social Influence

As discussed in Chapter 3, the rise of social media and its acceptance by the mainstream saw a glut of similar platforms in a short timeframe. Some of these thrived and flourished, while others became a shadow of their former popularity or disappeared altogether. It's a position social influence finds itself in now, as new platforms come onto the scene hoping to replicate the success of the early movers like Klout and create an influence platform in their own niche industry. Whereas Klout, Kred, eCairn, and others are geared solely toward the marketing needs of social influence, new platforms are looking outside that box and offering more specialist solutions.

- **Tawkify** (www.tawkify.com)—Although Tawkify is primarily an online dating site that uses real people to match members with each other versus an algorithm, it also uses Klout scores to advise who is a better match for your potential future partner.

- **Reppify** (www.reppify.com)—Taking the hiring process away from the standard resume and into the social space, Reppify uses a combination of features to match employer requirements to potential employees. Employers can set up screening filters for their vacancy, and Reppify will only allow those that pass that filter to the next stage. Here, they analyze candidate profiles and connections across LinkedIn, Twitter, Facebook, and GitHub. Candidates are then compared with each other and allocated a rank based on reputation, influence, social footprint, and overall candidacy appeal. Reppify claims to improve the selection process by performing up to 10x faster than manual screening.

- **Pinpuff** (www.pinpuff.com)—Building on the popularity of online image curation site Pinterest, Pinpuff analyzes your Pinterest account and assigns you an influence score based on your interests, your followers as well as those you follow, your uploads (pins), and repins (people who have shared your content), comments, and likes. Depending on the activity around you and your pins, you are allocated a monetary value for each individual pin. The goal with Pinpuff is to help marketers and brands that are struggling to integrate into the Pinterest ecosystem and work with influencers to promote their goods and products via Pinterest boards that are heavily trafficked and engaged.

These are just a few of the newer platforms taking advantage of early mover opportunities in social scoring across other niches and verticals—and they're just the tip of the iceberg. As social scoring matures even further, and algorithms improve to include more context around communities and relationships within them, the industry will only grow and expand into other areas not yet considered. Brands will be able to filter out the people they have no interest in working with, and end users will, in return, be able to be much more fluid in how they're targeted and approached by these brands.

The Looming Storm Clouds of Social Scoring's Effect on the Conversation

This in itself raises a new problem, though. As the Power of One example earlier in the chapter shows, with the abundance of platforms coming to the market and the gamification angle of these platforms, how does this affect the natural conversations that made social media the mass market medium it's become? While it may not be a major problem at the minute, the very fabric of how we communicate with each other is shifting.

Instead of brands and social scoring platforms leading the charge to the new marketing landscape that word-of-mouth marketing promised, there's the real danger that these programs can be rendered ineffective by consumers gaming the way they're perceived. Now that perks and rewards are part of the equation, everyday users of social media are trying to make themselves seem more influential by adapting their language and public profiles to be more attractive to the brands that are looking to use social media outreach for their next promotion.

We're already seeing blog posts and tweets geared toward attracting brands through meticulously crafted wording and copy optimized for search engines. We're also seeing hashtags on Twitter—the method of isolating topic-specific updates—hijacked and abused by nonrelevant users, some who are using them intelligently enough to look a normal part of the conversation and present themselves to any brands monitoring that stream.

Social groups are forming where bloggers and social media users share each other's content above others to be seen as influencers and thought leaders, again with the hope of attracting advertisers and sponsors to their blogs, or capture lucrative book deals and speaking gigs. While the likes of Kred are active at finding and punishing rogue accounts and users, it's a job that will only become more difficult as more users flock to each of the platforms to see which offers the most return for activity and membership.

If the abuse of Klout's +K system was a blip on the radar of social scoring's growth, the potential for the complete social media ecosystem to change based on language and gaming the platform presents a real problem for the brands and businesses looking to allocate a large amount of their marketing budget to this nascent industry. If social influence is to grow into the medium that truly delivers the golden egg of social media and business success, it needs to rely less on the social scoring solutions and more on the true relevance and context behind a person and his or her community.

Just as true measurement and return on investment (ROI) have always been key performance indicators for marketers and businesses, so will true influence and contextual relevance be the solution to take us forward into the next generation of influencer marketing. The rest of this book is your guide on doing exactly that for your business.

Endnotes

1. http://www.mediapost.com/publications/article/100350/brands-more-wary-of-celebrity-endorsements.html#axzz2LyZl3tgM

5

Situational Influence: A New Model for a New Era

The end result of any good marketing effort is to identify, engage, and nurture the most qualified prospects, ensuring the leads generated drive the highest customer acquisition rate—or at least it should be. There's been a backlash against the marketing industry, marketing professionals, and even some marketing software platforms because of what many see as their inability to measure the direct result of their efforts vis-à-vis the business's bottom line.

The study of marketing—and social media in particular—is often criticized for being a soft science. Critics point to exercises such as branding, community building, and social engagement as examples of efforts that may raise awareness of the brand name but are rarely able to link directly to the specific sales or profits generated by those activities. The need to measure the return on investment (ROI) of social media activities—and by extension marketing—has become a rallying cry of business executives and pundits alike.

Others claim that many modern social engagement programs are ineffectual due to their focus on short-term strategies instead of long-term value. Here critics point to the trend in acquisition of simple measures of success such as followers, "Likes," and shares. Others cite the use of social influence scoring platforms to identify brand advocates as short-cuts driving poor and inaccurate results because they avoid the real work required to drive long-term business value and bottom-line results.

Criticisms aside, the practice of influence marketing must be restrategized if it's going to become an effective marketing tactic for businesses and gain the favor of executives who control marketing budgets. The advent and use of today's popular social influence platforms and scores is not influence marketing. These platforms are a good exercise in product and brand amplification, whereas true influence marketing is about measurable customer acquisition and lead conversion. This chapter lays the foundation for an influence marketing blueprint that demonstrates how the practice of influence marketing may return to driving measurable sales instead of just broad brand awareness.

Trend Currents

Business models and methodologies are constantly evolving to adapt to consumer trends, technological advances, and socio-economic changes. It's a common occurrence; in fact, evolving business thinking, strategy, and process is essential for corporate growth. The key, of course, is to stay ahead of consumer needs and preferences so that your product, operations, and marketing are ready when consumers make the shift. Better yet, influence them to shift toward your product. Today we have the advantage of Big Data, a term used to describe the increasing amount of unstructured business and consumer data being collected and stored by organizations. However, the term is also associated with the fact that real insights from this collection of data are difficult to ascertain due to the current limitations of commonly used software tools that capture, manage, and process that data. Ironically, technology has created an environment where we produce and collect data faster than technology permits us to effectively store and intelligently analyze it. This fact hasn't stop marketers from basing decisions on such data, however.

Steve Woodruff, president and founder of Impactiviti, a professional pharmaceutical and health-care industry referral network, states that too few marketers pay attention to the *trend currents*, which he defines as unstoppable forces (social, technological, economic, etc.) inexorably shaping the cultural landscape. He warns that the *current trends* most businesses focus on are merely metrics that contribute to much larger *trend currents*. He argues that a business's quest to mine data and manage current trends blinds them to the long-term shifts in communication; they do not see the proverbial forest for the trees. His views are an astute observation, as we're seeing more and more businesses crippled under the weight of Big Data and more and more marketers—faced with so much online data—jumping on the bandwagon of quick-fix social media solutions instead of doing the requisite work for success.

For many years now, Apple Computers has been the go-to case study of a business that stays ahead of the curve, with some arguing that its real success comes from creating the curve that people subsequently follow. Whichever you believe, the late Steve Jobs, founder of Apple, was the epitome of someone who saw only trend currents. For example, in 2000 when the music industry was focused on fighting individuals sharing copyrighted music for free across peer-to-peer networks like Napster, Apple was monitoring the trend currents. What others saw as a copyright or financial issue, they saw as a fundamental change in how people purchase and consume music. The music community was trying to manage the current trend while Apple focused on the trend current. Jobs set out to create a solution that leveraged the Napster revolution to create an entirely new business model. Less than a year later, he introduced iTunes to the world, and within a few months was boasting a million downloads. Later that year, it launched the next iPod featuring a brand-new version of iTunes that seamlessly integrated with the songs and playlists stored on Mac computers. Within a year, Apple reinvented the industry, identifying and adapting to the trend current, not the current trend.

Arguably, at least in modern times, technology has had the biggest impact on consumer habits, business operations, and the economy in general. Social scientist Everett Rogers outlined an adoption life cycle of technology in his book *Diffusion of Innovations*, shown in Figure 5.1, which explains how technology is first embraced by a few innovators and early adopters before the majority of the public embraces it. These innovators who tend to jump on a trend quickly to gain the first-to-market advantage often fail to understand the trend current. The crossroad is typically traversed by the "early adopters" who are equally quick to jump on new technologies, but whether the path chosen leads to "early majority" adoption is based on how well the innovators understood the trend currents.

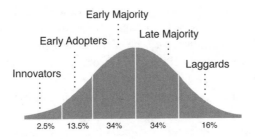

Figure 5.1   *Innovation adoption life cycle*

We're at just such a crossroads today with influence marketing; what is the current trend and what are the trend currents? Innovators, such as PeerIndex, Klout, and Kred, witnessing the change caused by social technologies, pervasive communication, and the disruptive impact they had on word-of-mouth and influence marketing practices, developed first-to-market technologies to leverage the Big Data available across social networks to identify influencers through their level of social activity, the size of their network, and how much other social media users engage with them. They sought to provide marketers a new tool that could once again effectively identify influencers within their communities. Marketers, or the innovators and early adopters using social scoring platforms as the basis for influence marketing campaigns, are embracing current trends. However, if we suspend our focus on the current trend, we might see where we're missing the opportunity to truly create, manage, and measure brand influencers in the future. We're not suggesting that social scoring platforms are useless, only that basing influence marketing campaigns on them is shortsighted. To measurably and effectively generate business value from influence marketing, we must first understand and navigate the disruptive forces created by social media and the pervasive technologies previously outlined in Chapter 4, "The Current Influence Model and Social Scoring." In addition, consideration for how consumers make decisions at different stages of the purchase life cycle adds a new dynamic to influence marketing strategy.

Gravity

In 1610, Galileo Galilei, an Italian scientist and philosopher, helped start the Scientific Revolution, in part, by expressing his belief that the sun, not the earth, was the center of our universe. He was branded a heretic by the church and his peers for challenging widely believed—and church-sanctioned—doctrine. Through fear, ignorance, or public pressure, his peers were comfortable with the status quo, and challenging it was unthinkable. Rebel Brown, author of *Defying Gravity*, updates this theory: "We are humans in business and humans don't like change, yet our markets, buyers and competitors are changing as we speak." Business leaders and marketers tend to seek the path of least resistance and when given the choice, opt to do what's always been done or take advantage of services offering shortcuts for jobs that require more consideration and manual work. Why do the work when others offer the tools to do that work for us? It's easy to become complacent. Throughout history, those who have benefited most from the status quo have proven to be the most resistant to different points of view, no matter how logical or how many countering views are offered. "It's this gravity that prevents business leaders and marketers from innovating," argues Brown.

Today, the media, businesses, and software vendors seem stuck on the notion that social network amplification is an effective baseline for influence marketing strategies. The conversations around influence marketing have typically been debates over the accuracy of the numerical scores assigned to individuals based on their social reach and engagement or the merits of one platform over the other. Elsewhere, heated arguments erupt over whether social media engagements can, in fact, measure any form of influence at all; they're stuck in their own gravitational pull, propelling the status quo. If we were to break free of this gravity, we'd gain the required altitude to view the trend currents and strategize how influence will eventually be used in social media marketing.

If social influence scoring platforms are the gravity preventing us from seeing the trend currents in influence marketing strategies, how do we break free?

Repositioning the Customer at the Center

The current paradigm of influence marketing places the influencer at the center of the marketing universe. The popularity of social influence scoring platforms listed in Chapter 4 has helped propagate this belief. The scientific truth that the status quo is hiding is that the customer, not the influencer, is at the center of the marketing universe; ultimately, it's the customer who makes the purchasing decision, not the influencer. Our strategies must be dictated by that truth, not the fanfare over current technologies. Influencers, along with business brands and their marketing messages, are simply planets circling the customer, vying for his attention.

Let's break down both theories. With influencers at the center of the influence marketing strategy, as shown in Figure 5.2, marketers must identify people who have a wide reach and/or a deep reach within communities focused on specific interests or keywords. To be effective, they must then attempt to understand the nature of each community and the role that the influencer has within that community. Brand messages and campaign tactics are then crafted in such a way as to piggy-back on that relationship. Influencers amplify the brand's message or offer recommendations to a wide cast of characters in hopes that some will embrace the message and, in turn, share it with their audience.

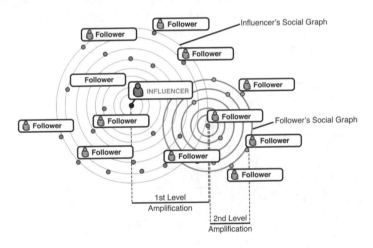

Figure 5.2   *Fisherman's Influence Marketing Model*

Even with a great deal of research and preparation, such campaigns are always a gamble because the basic tenet of the campaign is amplification with little knowledge or design toward converting a prospect to a customer. It's what we call the Fisherman's Influence Marketing Model: Identify the fish you're trying to catch; choose the right body of water; and then cast the widest net possible and hope for the best.

Fisherman's Influence Model

Applying the concept of "casting a wide net to catch the most fish" to Influence Marketing strategies, which suggests that leveraging those with the largest following and reach among large social communities will drive the greatest brand awareness and, eventually, a purchase.

Good marketers may choose to use the Fisherman's Influence Marketing Model as a first step only. The model can help identify potential influencers and their communities, which in turn may be used as the basis for further research and analysis into those relationships and their context. That additional insight and data may help create a more targeted customer acquisition campaign to fill the sales funnel with better leads. This is certainly a better strategy than sending product samples to a mass of loosely qualified followers; however, the campaign life cycle is long and still based on a faulty foundation: the influencer.

Now let's consider what happens when we shift this universe, as illustrated in Figure 5.3, to position the customer at its center. The first thing we notice from our *Customer-Centric Influence Model* is that it's not a direct reversal of the former. When influencers are at the center, the orbiting planets are their various followers. When the customer is placed at the center, an entirely new universe opens up. In this universe, the people, institutions, technologies, and communities that impact purchase decisions orbit the customer.

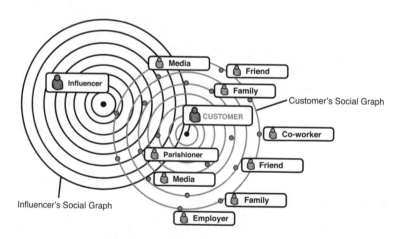

Figure 5.3   *Customer-Centric Influence Marketing Model*

Customer-Centric Influence Model

Identifying product or service decision makers, the micro-influencers in their social graphs, and aligning influence marketing campaigns around their interactions throughout the decision-making process.

When marketers orient their campaigns and technologies around the influencer, the focus becomes their attempt to drive awareness or possibly even sway purchase decisions, instead of addressing the decision-making process. Placing the customer at the center forces us to look at the decisions he or she makes and what impacts those decisions. Referencing the pervasive communication theory discussed earlier in this book, we can visualize the many interconnected factors that impact those purchase decisions. This model enables us to drill down to the people that directly interact with decision makers when they are making decisions. In this model, influencers can be seen as contextual relationships, not just broadcasters. In fact, the very flow of communication is different. In the Fisherman's Model above, the focus of the strategy is outbound or push-communication to the influencer's social graph. In the Customer-Centric Model, the focus is on identifying the context and impact of the influence flowing in from the various players in the customer's social graph.

To better illustrate this concept, consider a mobile phone provider that wants to introduce a new phone model to the market. The manufacturer could choose the Fisherman's Model, in which case it would seek the favor of individuals and com-munities perceived as influential across their target market.

The first step involves the identification of the target audience's demographics and the communities they engage in most often both online and offline. Typically, experienced brand marketers will invest in analyzing the subject matter and tone of the conversations occurring in those communities to identify the opportunities and challenges in promoting the new product. Individuals with the greatest reach and perceived authority are identified in hopes of converting them to brand ambas-sadors or, if they're current customers, to advocates. These are *macro-influencers*, people with a large, general audience made up of communities with whom they have varying levels of relationship. Today's trend has marketers turning to social influence scoring tools discussed in Chapter 4 to help quickly identify these macro-influencers or to help further segment them into specialized groups.

Once the communities and their influencers are identified, the manufacturer's marketing team attempts to educate, encourage, and incentivize the chosen influencers to broadcast encouraging brand messages through the influencer's media channels (radio shows, magazine columns, etc.) and social channels (blogs, Twitter, Facebook, etc.). Leveraging gamification strategies, they further engage the audience with awards and status gimmicks to encourage them to rebroadcast and share those same interactions with their own social graphs.

Gamification, the use of addictive game mechanics in nongaming scenarios, has proven effective in many marketing campaigns.[1] Marketers create tactics and leverage technologies to motivate specific behaviors in selected influencers by appealing to various human needs and senses. Some of the common tactics are the use of badges awarded in exchange for a required action, an achievement status bar demonstrating progression along a desired path, or virtual currency earned and exchanged for other products, services, or future considerations.

Gamification

The use of addictive game mechanics in nongaming scenarios to encourage greater participation and use.

When completed, the Fisherman's Influence Marketing campaign is typically measured by the earned media it acquired for the product. Earned media is the free, favorable publicity gained through promotional efforts as opposed to paid media, which is publicity gained through paid promotion and advertising.[2] Success is also gauged by the increased website traffic, volume of online discussions, and positive sentiment in those discussions. More sophisticated marketers and software may track sales volumes to the amplification created by their chosen influencers; however, in most cases these measures are unreliable.

If the manufacturer chooses the Customer-Centric Influence Model, the first step is the same: Identify the target audience's demographics and the communities they engage in most often; however, that's where the similarities end. The subsequent study of the subject and tone of conversations within those communities take on a different meaning. This analysis isn't undertaken to identify keywords and sentiment to fuel influencers' amplification but to identify the individuals and categories of individuals who are engaged with the target customer on specific subjects.

By using social monitoring technologies, the marketing team first looks at trending topics and sentiment of conversations within the target communities. Once grouped, they can drill down to the individuals engaged within those conversations. By applying user profile filters or by appending third-party data, they can tag customer profile types to the individuals engaged in those discussions. As shown in Figure 5.4, this provides the phone manufacturer in this case study a unique insight into who is talking to whom.

Our experiences support this scenario and point to the fact that true influence—that which impacts a purchase decision—is based on dyadic relationships. A dyad is a group of two people, the smallest possible social group. A dyadic relationship refers to discussions or communication between two people involving their mutual ideas, thoughts, behaviors, or ideals. A chance meeting between two persons at a trade show or between the host and participant within an online webinar, for example, that does not continue after the initial event does not have a lasting effect on each other. The theory suggests that the impact of personal interactions between two people with shared culture, ideals, or circumstances is greater than the looser interactions such as someone reading another's blog. Because of the dyadic relationship between coworkers, for example, a product recommendation is more likely to be acted upon than a recommendation by a well-respected journalist in a trade publication. The power in these relationships is based on the time the individuals spend together and the emotional intensity of their connection.

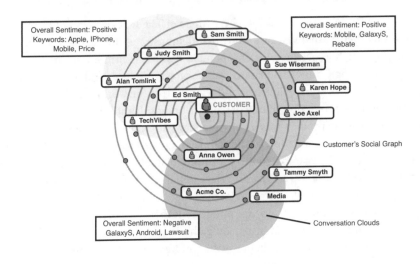

Figure 5.4 *Conversation/influencer profile segmentation*

Identifying dyadic relationships among a brand's audience is not easy, especially for larger organizations with many prospective customers and followers. However, the goal is not to identify each individual and all those they speak with most. Instead, we identify user profiles and formulate models that can be extrapolated across the entire audience, as illustrated previously in Figure 5.4.

This study allows us to plot connections around specific individuals' profiles. For example, instead of knowing that John is talking to Karen, Sue, Joe, Acme Co., and TechVibes, this model allows us see that a prospect is having conversations with peers, a coworker, parishioners, and a blogger. Overlaying the roles of the people engaged in this conversation begins to apply context to the conversation, which, in turn, allows us to establish the context of the relationships.

Extending this exercise across other discussions and communities creates a powerful, contextually oriented database of users. The lesson learned by applying this filter in the Customer-Centric Model is the identification of user profiles and relationships that most influence other decision makers in specific conversation types (subject matter, tone, and sentiment of conversation). In contrast to the Fisherman's Influence Model, we can narrow the prospect's social graphs and apply a new, more accurate metric for the identification of influencers. Much research has been done on the greater impact of one's close social circle over celebrity dating back as early as 1944. That year, Paul Lazarsfeld published his book *The People's Choice* in which he outlined his study of women in Decatur, Illinois. Lazarsfeld's study proved the women's decision-making processes were more influenced by interaction with personal contacts over prominent media personalities.[3]

Marketers Kevin Casey and Ed Roche, owners of The Idea Factory, a full-service marketing agency, shared a case study that demonstrates this fact is still true today, even in our highly social world. This popular marketing firm boasts many national clients including Corby Distilleries Limited, which produces and distributes many popular brands of spirits, liqueurs, and wines across the world. The agency was tasked with the promotion of one of Corby's brands: Lamb's Rum. Market research identified that the product was mostly popular within the Canadian Province of Newfoundland and Labrador, so the campaign created sought to capitalize on its local popularity. The campaign titled, "Lamb's Nation," featured endorsements by celebrities and well-known citizens. When initial results fell short of expectations, the agency surveyed customers and learned that its sales growth was attributed to the brand's die-hard fans not speaking about their love of the product publicly but among their "buddies" at in-person gatherings. Lamb's Nation, the sentiment behind the campaign's theme, was accurate and on-target, but the product's growth was based on a one-on-one personal experience between friends—who wanted to keep it that way. The resulting shift in tactics from online influence strategies to traditional, offline word-of-mouth ground-swell campaigns proved successful at driving up sales.

Understanding that prospects are engaged in direct conversations with specific types of social contacts such as peers, coworkers, family members, journalists, or bloggers is more meaningful to the purchase decision-making process than identifying individuals who have a large online following. Today's influence marketing strategies are typically based on identification of influencers, including social celebrities, popular bloggers, or any individual with high scores on social influence scoring platforms. While this model might be quicker and require less effort, it's also less effective. The value of broad amplification and recommendations is lessened by the unidentified quality of relationship, context of conversations, or accuracy of the target audience, all leading to a lower conversion and purchase rate. Forrester analyst Michael Speyer confirms this analysis in a published report[4] where he states that to be successful, "vendors need to identify and characterize the influencers in their specific market...which requires a comprehensive influencer identification program." Determining the characteristics of influencers within a community becomes critical to success.

Robert Axelrod, professor of political science and public policy at the University of Michigan, produced another study on social influence, which claimed that people are more likely to interact with others who share many of their cultural attributes and that these interactions tend to increase the number of cultural attributes they share (thus making them more likely to interact again).[5] In our model, these people are called *micro-influencers*, meaning they're individuals with whom prospective customers are more closely engaged at the time a purchase decision is being made. Because of the dyadic nature of their relationships, these people are the key to a successful influence marketing effort in our hyperconnected digital world. But before we discuss micro-influencers, we need to better understand the situations that impact those relationships and our decision making.

Micro-Influencers

Individuals within a consumer's social graph, whose commentary, based on the personal nature of their relationship and communications, has a direct impact on the behavior of that consumer.

Situational Influence

Understanding the profiles of consumers and those they engage with more personally in their social graphs is only step one in the Customer-Centric Influence Model. Be they online or in person, personal interactions are affected by external factors that impact—positively or negatively—the reception of a recommendation from any influence. Known as "situational influence," they're factors that exist independent of the communication between influencer and prospective customer but also impact the customer's decision-making process. The theory is deep rooted in the study of psychology and sometimes referred to as *situationism*, which has proven that people are as influenced by external, situational factors as they are by their internal traits or motivations, if not more.[6] These situations act as a disruptive force in the brand and influencer communications, which further derail current amplification-based influence models.

Situational Influence

> The external or societal factors that surround a community and consciously or subconsciously influence the nature of their interpersonal interactions such as geography, religion, or economics.

Four types of external situations may impact the influence that macro- or micro-influencers exert over their social connections, discussed in the following sections.

Communities

The nature of the relationship or conversation between people morphs when they are experienced in different communities, even when it's the same two people engaging in different communities. A conversation about mobile phones, for example, between a person and a coworker will take on a different meaning, and potentially result in a different outcome, than if that same conversation occurred between the person's spouse or friends on social networks. The community situation coworkers find themselves in skews the conversation toward the mobile phone's use in a professional environment, such as its capability to easily sync to the corporate email exchange server or how it meets security requirements. The same conversation with a spouse might focus on the monthly costs, availability of family call-free plans, or connectivity with home computers. When discussing the choice with friends on social networks, branding and status enter the discussion with specific groups advocating for the brand they believe is "coolest." The coworker, the spouse, and the social networking friend are all micro-influencers that directly impact the decision-making process, but in different ways based on the micro-community they belong to.

Economic

Economic forces, defined as personal, business, or national financial consider-ations—real or perceived—that affect purchase decisions made by consumers, also interfere with the normal communication path between influencers and consumers. This is a broad category that can be impacted by something as specific as the individual's credit card debt to something more generic such as the international debt crisis that most countries are struggling with currently. In either case, consumers weigh the impact of their needs and desires, regardless of the recommendations and social pressures, against their comfort level at spending money in the face of financial pressures. Economic uncertainty is a powerful force in the decision-making process and in most cases effectively halts influence marketing messages from converting to purchases.

What should be of further concern to marketers is that economic situations don't need to be as overt as the U.S. "debt-cliff" crisis of 2012. They can be more subtle and personal. For example, in the spring of 2011 Apple, Inc., and Samsung Electronics, two of the world's biggest mobile device manufacturers, went to war. Apple struck the first blow with a multinational lawsuit against Samsung, claiming it infringed on many of Apple's technology patents. Devices listed in the lawsuit included some of Samsung's most popular and high-profile devices, such as the Galaxy S2, Galaxy S, and Nexus S, as well as the Galaxy Tab 10.1 tablet.

In July 2012, a U.S. judge awarded Apple a preliminary injunction pending the outcome of the trial that could have forced Samsung to remove its Galaxy Tab 10.1 tablet from stores. News of the injunction spread like wildfire through blogs, social networks, and news channels. Influencers speculated that by being served an injunction, Samsung devices would start disappearing off store shelves and/or technical support would not be provided to those who managed to scoop up one of the extremely popular Android-based tablets. Fear and uncertainty was echoed by the journalists, bloggers, and analysts who publicly predicted that a successful suit could lead to higher costs and diminished user experiences on Android-based phones from all makers. "Consumers may pay more for these devices. Consumers may have a device that solves the same issues in a less elegant feature set," predicted Jefferson Wang of IBB Consulting Group. According to Anthony Scarsella of Gazelle, a popular phone trade-in company, "consumers seem to be jumping ship [and] we expect this trend to continue." Regardless of the initially fast-paced sales of the Samsung mobile products, fueled by the positive advocacy of influencers across social channels and the fact that no final court verdicts were in, consumers were fearful and making decisions based on that fear.

On April 24, 2012, a federal jury in San Jose ruled that Samsung infringed on multiple Apple patents, awarding the Cupertino, California, maker of the iPhone and iPad more than $1 billion in damages. However, during the same time period other jurisdictions such as South Korea, Japan, and the United Kingdom ruled in favor of Samsung. Regardless of the rulings in favor of Samsung, the market was still concerned; the uncertainty was deep rooted, especially since the one jurisdiction that favored Apple's suit was in the large U.S. market. Gazelle reported that the company had seen a 50% increase in the number of customers looking to unload Samsung devices during this period, regardless of the continuing positive product reviews shared by Samsung advocates.

Social and Cultural Groupthink

Another disruptor in the influencer's amplification path is social or cultural groupthink that consciously or subconsciously contradicts technical influencers. Groupthink is a psychological phenomenon that describes how the need for harmony within a social group forces its members to assume a belief, opinion, or attitude, even when some leaders provide a genuine evaluation of the virtues of the alternative. Originally explored by Irving Janis, a research psychologist from Yale University[7] in the early 1970s, the concept has been given renewed importance due to the mass adoption of social media communication by the global community. A modern application of Janis' groupthink is the "wisdom of crowds," which represent the sentiment: If enough people post something online—regardless of whether or not you know them—what they say must be true. Crowdsourced opinion has become fact. Consumers are almost blindly accepting commonly shared opinion (via online posts) without seeking alternative viewpoints or assessments.

Keeping with the theme of mobile device manufacturers, let's consider the case of Research in Motion (RIM), maker of the landmark BlackBerry smartphone. RIM, credited for inventing the smartphone industry, was once the most valuable company in Canada and essentially owned the world's smartphone market share. In 2011, reported profits were more than $1 billion, but RIM's fortunes reversed almost overnight; it recorded a net loss of $753 million in the first half of 2012. While technology analysts continued to advocate for the vastly superior phone, email, security, and instant messaging (BBM) service available on the BlackBerry, the once dominant mobile phone manufacturer lost its market share to rivals Apple and Samsung in meteoric fashion. Pundits argued that the decline in market share was a result of the company's fixation on the phone's business function, resulting in a small ecosystem of personal and gaming apps and the lack of innovation in the device's graphical user interface, two areas where the company's rivals excelled. Eventually, even security-concerned IT managers bowed to the pressure of their employees demanding they adopt Apple's iPhone or the plethora of Android-based mobile devices by Samsung, Motorola, and others.

The one certainty is that the public perception of the Blackberry's brand declined even faster—and with more verve—than its stock price. BlackBerry owner Rachel Crosby, in an interview with the *New York Times*[8] in October 2012, referenced her BlackBerry phone the way someone might speak of an embarrassing relative. "I'm ashamed of it," claims Crosby, a Los Angeles sales representative who acknowledges she no longer publicly uses her BlackBerry at cocktail parties or at conferences. In business meetings, she admits to hiding it behind an iPad so that clients won't judge her. This was not a case isolated to individuals but businesses as well. To upgrade Yahoo's failing public image, the newly appointed CEO, Marissa Mayer, offered employees the option to trade in their BlackBerrys for iPhone and Android devices.[9] Owning a BlackBerry or publicly praising the device's functions branded you a social outcast and the butt of everyone's jokes.

In some cases, the need for harmony isn't about the group publicly sharing the group's belief but not talking about it. During her 2005 tour of Japan, worldwide music superstar Madonna publicly praised Japan's "Washlet," an "intelligent" toilet that provides—among other features—posterior-cleaning water jets, hot air dry function, ambient background music, and odor-masking technology. "I've missed the heated toilet seats," the pop-diva promoted upon leaving the country. She was not alone in her praise, many famous and well-connected people have gone on record promoting the virtues of the ultra-modern toilet.

It's the earned media and public advocacy that brand marketers would die for, the type of public promotion many try to emulate when accessing social celebrities and socially active people with high Klout scores. Find people who are perceived to have a popular voice and get them to talk about your product, and their audience will beat a path to your door, open wallets in hand.

Yet, while the ingenuous toilets are found in 70% of Japanese homes, hotels, and businesses, they're one of world's best kept secrets. Hiromichi Tabata, head of the international division at Washlet-maker TOTO does not hide the company's desire to become a major player in international markets. The company has attempted to crack foreign markets, including the lucrative U.S. market, for more than 10 years with little success despite the volunteer endorsements by many internationally known celebrities (such as Madonna) and business executives. "It's because of the cultural taboo over talking about toilets," reports Tabata. "Americans avoid talking about those kinds of things so we can't expect success from word-of-mouth, even if they recognize our products are excellent."

Psychologists and social scientists continue to explore this phenomenon by demonstrating how groupthink impacts collective avoidance as well as collective advocacy.[10] Interestingly, there is growing evidence that groupthink's impact is moving beyond publicly shared beliefs and impacting the decisions people make.[11] Clearly, this is a critical consideration in planning influence marketing strategies.

Personal Ideology

Ideology, such as political and religious affiliation, is becoming an increasingly disruptive role in influence marketing. This is not a new concept: Politics and religion have always been divisive forces in society; however, as with social and cultural groupthink, social media and pervasive communications have increased our ability to both amplify and share personal views. In fact, it has emboldened people to share those views more than ever before across social channels and, more to the point, reject and rebel against the views others share.

Consider the comments made by Dan Cathy, the chief operating officer of fast-food chain Chick-fil-A, opposing same-sex marriage in the middle of 2012. Cathy publicly opposed gay marriage rights in an attempt to influence his followers in the months leading up to the November 2012 U.S. presidential election. The buzz around his comments escalated when it was reported that his company's family-run charitable foundation donated millions of dollars to political parties that opposed same-sex marriage. His attempt to influence voters was seen as a "line in the sand," and people gathered on both sides based on religious and political affiliations. Protesters called for a permanent boycott of the restaurants. In reaction, counterprotesters organized mass "eat-ins," encouraging supporters to purchase more of Chick-fil-A's food and more frequently.

The effects of ideological disruption can be calculated and planned as part of an influence marketing strategy designed to earn much desired viral marketing effect and earned media. In the case of Chick-fil-A, the public reaction was definitely a disruption in consumers' purchase decisions as evidenced by the company's statement in July 2012, which stated "Going forward, our intent is to leave the policy debate over same-sex marriage to the government and political arena." However, ideological disruption can work in a brand's favor, as exemplified by the Kraft Oreo campaign in June 2012, which saw a picture of the iconic Oreo cookie posted on Facebook with the typical white cream center replaced with rainbow colored cream layers as a show of support for the lesbian, gay, bisexual, and transgender events being held later that week. The post received 150,000 likes and 20,000 comments on the company's Facebook page; most were positive comments with a few negative ones calling for boycotts of the popular cookie. Analysts called the threats by would-be boycotters "empty threats" and reported no negative impact on sales.[12]

Situational Factors

Just as influencer communications are impacted by community, economic, sociocultural groupthink, and ideological situations, these universal situations are further impacted by local "situational factors;" they represent the personal factors in the consumer's life that interact with the universal situations outlined previously to further impact the purchase decision-making process.

Situational Factors

Personal circumstances such as household finances, lifestyle, and relationships that influence the decision-making process of individuals within communities.

Situational factors are discussed in the following sections.

Personal Situational Factors

The consumer's familial situation is a key disrupter to a marketer's brand messaging and call to action. Personal situational factors are typically dictated by proximity, intimacy, and nature of the consumers' personal relationships. For example, a woman who is the mother of three young children makes purchase decisions differently than a woman without children. If the three children, for example, are grown and off to college instead of young and at home, purchase decisions take a different form yet again.

Thousands of women may actively follow a popular Mommy-blogger, reading and even commenting on her every post. Yet, for example, when the blogger recommends a particular game system, the age and sex of the reader's children will dramatically impact her decision to purchase that product or not. If a business' audience is mothers, simply broadcasting recommendations to all of them through popular bloggers without an understanding of their personal situational factors will miss the mark with most of them.

Environmental Situational Factors

The environments, both physical (geography) and digital (devices), where brand messages and recommendations are received are yet another disrupter of the brand's messaging path. Brand messages received on mobile devices while in a store versus a desktop computer when at work are interpreted in vastly different ways. For example, a positive rating on a restaurant by a friend is more impactful on the consumer's purchase decision if received on Yelp or Zagat's mobile app while walking down the street searching for a place to eat, than if they viewed a positive brand mentioned by that same person when reviewing their random positive comments or pictures on social sites such as Facebook or Instagram.

Consider the decision-making process of this same consumer looking for a restaurant when travelling in a new city while using the geolocation social networks such as FourSquare or Facebook's Places. They see who of their friends or colleagues have "checked in" in that city or at a specific restaurant in the city and choose a location based on their need to connect with a friendly face.

Emotional Situational Factors

Emotions or the emotional state of a consumer might have the most effect on a consumer's final decision-making process. For example, consider the state of mind of auto workers in December 2008, when the three major U.S. auto industry companies—GM, Chrysler, and Ford—asked the federal government for a $34 billion bailout to avoid bankruptcy. The emotional state of the millions of workers associated with the industry was decisively negative in the months after this presentation. Or, on a more micro level, consider the emotional state of the possible consumer of a wheelchair or other accessibility device in the weeks after an accident that gave them a permanent disability? The emotional state of prospective customers have a significant impact on their motivation to embrace or ignore an advocate's recommendation.

Life Cycle Situational Factors

The final localized factor to consider is where the customer is in the purchase life cycle of a product. A consumer who is in the *needs identification* or *awareness* stage of the purchase life cycle will react differently to an influencer's message than someone at the decision stage. Similarly, if the audience receiving the message is already a customer, are they at the loyalty stage where they're willing to buy more from you or are they at the advocacy stage where they're willing to voluntarily advocate your brand to their audience?

This is the blueprint that we use when servicing our clients, moving people along the customer life cycle to build business value and profit by improving the customer experience. As part of that methodology, we recognize that not all customers are—or will be—advocates. Once they become a customer, there's a period of "satisfaction" where customers look to have their purchase decision justified by good customer service, product utility, and so on. Once proven, they move toward "loyalty," which is represented by their willingness to buy more from the business based on its continuing good service, utility, and possibly recognition or rewards for continued patronage. Some, but not all of those within the loyalty stage of the life cycle, become so happy that they choose to voluntarily advocate the product and service to their business.

Micro-Influencers

When we apply the situational influences and situational factors that interfere with our brand message, we can visualize how these influence disruptors impact the communication path. It becomes evident that a host of factors can conspire to derail an influencer's intended conversion. Or are they opportunities?

Adequately identifying prospective customers, and further segmenting them based on situations and situational factors, enables us to identify the people and businesses—or technologies and channels—that are closest to them in each scenario. We call these *micro-influencers* and see them as the business's opportunity to exert true influence over the customer's decision-making process as opposed to macroinfluencers who simply broadcast to a wider, more general audience. In short, it's the difference between a branding exercise among a loosely defined audience and a formal lead capture and conversion strategy.

Geofencing

When collected, these contextually based dyadic relationships form what we call *geofenced communities*. Geofencing is the influence marketing tactic of identifying where the prospective customer is in the purchase life cycle, and the profiles and roles of micro-influencers who impact their decision-making process as filtered in various situations and situational factors. Charting customers in this manner allows us to identify true influencers and create influence marketing campaigns that are less likely to be disrupted by situational influences and factors. Further, it helps define the content marketing strategies and highly targeted calls-to-action that are more likely to convert prospects into customers in each scenario.

Geofencing

Segmenting decision makers and their personal social graphs, including micro-influencers, based on specific situations and situational factors as applied to a specific stage in the decision-making process.

To illustrate this concept, let's explore the case study of a computer manufacturer that sought to increase its sales of laptops to college students. Having identified a growth opportunity in this category, the marketing and R&D departments developed a product at the right price point with the features and software most applicable to this audience. The following sections explain the steps taken in the Customer-Centric Influence Marketing Model.

Step One: Community Identification

Social media monitoring and analytics software was used to identify communities engaged in discussions around the keywords: "laptops," "college applications," "college tuition," and "student loans." User profiles were displayed around the keywords in a tag cloud along with other keywords that the software identified as related to the main terms. A social graph was drawn using the connected people around the chosen terms and both community and user profiles were saved. A thorough vetting process that scrubbed each audience group included clearing out the fake or little used profiles and the identification and categorization of user profiles within each group.

For example, in the discussion community that formed around "college tuition," the marketing team identified profiles that included college applicants/high school seniors, college applications/adults, parents of high school seniors, the business's employees, competitors' social media accounts, competitors' employees, official brand accounts for colleges, college alumni, media and blogger profiles, and so on.

Step Two: Situational Analysis and Factors

Next, contextual analysis was performed to identify the nature of the conversations occurring among each community to identify the situational influence that might be at play. For example, within the "college tuition" discussion community, two situational influences were identified: economic (associated to cost of tuition in a tightening economy) and cultural-socio groupthink ("cool-factor" associated with certain brands). Next, marketing analysts applied the localized situational factors (or combinations of factors) that might impact a purchase decision. These included, among others, personal factors, such as the household income and availability of funding; emotional factors, such as the distance college was from parents' home; environmental factors, such as the location where discussions were occurring (e. g., on school forums or on social networks); physical location (geography) of those identified; and so on.

Step Three: Identification of Customer and Micro-Influencer

This analysis allowed the marketing team to understand, among those in the online community, who the decision makers were, such as parents of teens applying for college or adult students returning to college. With each group profiled, the community social graph was reoriented around the decision maker to help identify who their micro-influencers were, as illustrated in Figure 5.5. Profile data pulled from data suppliers such as Kred and PeopleBrowsr, collected data such as degrees of separation, relationship status, sentiment of discussions, and traditional analysis including past knowledge, experience, and market research were used to further segment the profiles of the micro-influencers.

However, to develop the correct influence marketing strategy and corresponding communication and promotional tactics, they went one step further. As highlighted by the situation formulas denoted in each quadrant of Figure 5.5, the marketing team matched the situation(s) with the situational factor(s) that might impact the purchase decision.

As an example, in Figure 5.5 the formula for the top-left quadrant breaks down like this:

Situation A: Economic Situational Analysis: Cost of tuition was unaffordable by those in the community identified.

+ Factor 3: Personal: Household income of parents below national average.

+ Factor 4: Environmental: The availability of funding for students, geography of students and available colleges.

+ Factor 7: Timeline: More than 12 months from college application due date.

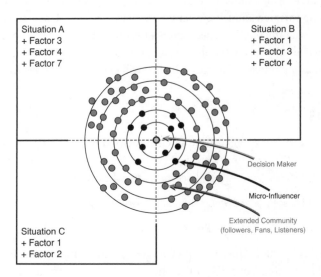

Figure 5.5 *Geofenced communities*

With decision makers identified and each social graph filtered by the possible situations that impact their decision making, the marketing team was able to craft the appropriate influence marketing campaigns that targeted the micro-influencers at key moments in the online conversation. Situational forces determined the urgency of influencers' recommendations and impacted the conversion ratio from those same recommendations. In the end, the geofencing exercise increased the number of warm leads and the overall sales of the product within the target audience.

Applying Situational Factors

It's important to note that the situations and factors outlined within this chapter don't necessarily apply to every business. Different industries and geographies are each impacted by different combinations of factors. Further, as our society, technologies, and the manner in which people communicate change, so too will the situations and situational factors that impact influence marketing change. However, all businesses can use the customer-centric influence model and geofencing to identify, chart, and track the situations their customers find themselves in when making purchase decisions.

Pervasive communications combined with these situations and situational factors impact the business-influencer-customer communication flow and have changed the nature of influence marketing forever. The key consideration is no longer an influencer's reach and amplification but who and what influences their followers to make purchase decisions. One more area of study is required before we can look at leveraging this new model: the actual purchase decision. Understanding the factors that impact the purchase decision is important, but we cannot predict what path influence will take, without a strong understanding of the consumer's actual decision-making process. The next chapter will explore this process.

Endnotes

1. Woods, D. 2012. "Gamification Grows Up to Become a CEO's Best Friend." *Forbes*. http://www.forbes.com/sites/danwoods/2012/05/14/gamification-grows-up-to-become-a-ceos-best-friend/.

2. McFedries, P. *Word Spy*. 2008. New York: Broadway Books.

3. Lazarsfeld, P. 1944. *The People's Choice*. McFadden Publications.

4. Speyer, M. 2007. "Identifying IT Buyers' Hidden Influencers: Finding and Nurturing Your Brand Presence Beyond Your Formal Channels." Forrester Research.

5. Axelrod, R. 1997. *The Complexity of Cooperation*. Princeton, New Jersey: Princeton University Press.

6. Krahe, B. 1993. *Personality and Social Psychology: Towards a Synthesis*. London: Sage.

7. Janis, I. L. November 1971. "Groupthink." *Psychology Today*.

8. Perloroth, N. (2012). The BlackBerry as Black Sheep, *New York Times*, Business Today/Technology.

9. Ibid.

10. Hart, P. 1998. "Preventing Groupthink Revisited: Evaluating and Reforming Groups in Government." *Organizational Behavior and Human Decision Processes*.

11. McCauley, C. 1989. "The Nature of Social Influence in Groupthink: Compliance and Internalization." *Journal of Personality and Social Psychology*.

12. Ford, Z. 2012. "ABC News Invents Anti-Gay Oreo Boycott." thinkprogress.org. http://thinkprogress.org/lgbt/2012/06/27/507005/abc-news-invents-fictional-anti-gay-oreo-boycott/?mobile=nc.

6

The Consumer Decision-Making Process

In Chapter 5, "Situational Influence: A New Model for a New Era," we outlined how a business's marketing messages are disrupted by global and local situations, which increases the risk that the message will be received at the wrong time, by the wrong people, or simply ignored. As a result, for influence marketing campaigns to work, they have to be more focused and targeted to the customer's decision-making process. But how do consumers make a decision to purchase a product when presented with a recommendation? Current influence campaigns typically ignore the fact that consumers have a choice to accept or ignore the amplified recommendation. If the practice of influence marketing is to improve, its strategy and tactics must progress beyond simple broadcasting by third-party anointed influencers to become campaigns that inform, sway, and create purchase decisions.

What is the tipping point that pushes a customer from initial product awareness to serious consideration to purchase? We know that customers are turning to the Internet and social channels to seek information and opinions that might better inform their choices, but does access to a bevy of online data and recommendations impact the consumer's decision-making process? We submit that broadcast recommendations are only half the battle; prospects have to decide whether to believe the recommendation and then decide whether they're going to make a purchase decision based on it. In this chapter, we break down consumer behaviors and their decision-making processes along with the factors that disrupt them. Understanding the dynamics of decision making within specific communities is a critical skill that must be mastered before we can apply the "reverse engineering influence" and "predicting influence paths" methodologies outlined in the next few chapters.

Situational Factors Disrupting Purchase Decisions

In the upcoming chapters, we identify how to plan for and possibly predict the situational factors on influence messages and purchase decisions, but before we can identify which forms of influence marketing campaigns or content strategies are most suitable, we have to consider what factors impact those decisions. This is not a new concept; marketers have typically turned to the study of behavioral science to understand consumer motivations that lead to when, why, and how they choose to purchase a product. Within behavioral sciences is a section dedicated to consumer behavior, which deals with the buying behavior of individuals, including how they make purchase decisions. For example, the decision to purchase a specific product can be motivated by different factors for different customers. In one case, the consumer has a utilitarian need that the product fulfills, whereas another consumer may purchase it for the social status gained through ownership. The reverse is also true; the decision to not purchase a product might be due to the lack of utilitarian need for one, while others may choose not buy that same product because they can't afford it or simply because it doesn't suit their personal tastes and preferences. In fact, several factors can influence the purchase decision of any consumer including psychological, social, and economic factors.

As there are situational factors that disrupt an influencer's amplified brand message (see Chapter 5), so too are there situational factors that disrupt the consumer's decision-making process. Factors such as selective exposure to various advertisements and promotions or the consumer's selective attention to those that appeal to their emotions or physical circumstances impact the choices they make. Other factors such as the consumer's interpretation of the messages they're exposed to or the recollection of messages and advertisements seen in the past are also disruptors in the decision-making process.

The people in proximity to the customer when they're making a purchase decision as well as their physical surroundings, such as music and decor, have all been proven to impact the choices made, effectively disrupting any influencer's recommendation. Temporal effects, such as lack of time or the time of day a consumer is making a purchase, also play into the decision. Finally, antecedent states of the customer, such as their mood, the day's previous events, or even the amount of cash on hand, create significant disruptions in the choices made.

Complicating matters further, behavioral science has identified that some consumers may skip phases within the decision-making process based on their involvement with a product or business brand, their personal circumstances, social environment, or the cost of the product. All these disruptive factors highlight the need for marketers to better identify the unique decision-making processes of their customers and map communication strategies for each to maximize the effectiveness of influence marketing campaigns.

Missing Data Inputs

How do consumer behaviors impact their buying decisions in the markets businesses are attempting to influence? To answer this, marketers collect psychographic data, such as the personality, values, attitudes, interests, and lifestyles of their consumers, as well as demographic information including the age, gender, geographic location, and household income of prospective audiences. Developing full customer profiles using this data has served to better understand the customer's activities, interests, and opinions, which have traditionally informed branding, advertising campaigns, media buys, and market research. As outlined in Chapter 4, "The Current Influence Model and Social Scoring," social conversations between peers—and between the brand and its customers—have added new data points that we must now factor into the customer's decision-making process. Additional decision-making references are required if we're to shift campaigns from amplification mode to the decision-making mode.

Initially, we considered how the Elaboration Likelihood Model (ELM) might drive influence decision-making through influence marketing. ELM informs marketers whether a direct or peripheral communication strategy is best for influencing consumer behavior. When a consumer is highly engaged with a product, a more direct path of communication is warranted to influence her behavior, which might include an in-person or online demonstration, a salesperson visit, or a direct email. Alternatively, when consumers are less involved, meaning they're not currently using the product, not sure whether they need it, or just becoming aware of it, a combination of less-direct tactics is useful, such as banner ads, webinars, and trade shows. The theory states that the more involved customers are with a product or brand, the more likely they are to accept direct attempts to influence their behavior, whereas less-involved customers see it as obtrusive.

There is a challenge with this approach to decision making as it relates to influence marketing, however; it does not take into account the situational influences that impact the recommendation shared, nor the relationship and dynamics of the micro-influencers within the decision maker's social graph. Be it direct or peripheral recommendations, the results are still just amplification and not measurable attempts to change the customer's behavior or decisions.

Conflicted Decisions

A decision is the choice one makes when faced with several alternative options; it can be a physical action, forming of an opinion, or acceptance of a belief. The decision to buy a product, for example, is the result of a complex cognitive and social decision-making process. Customers choose to purchase one of your products instead of your competitor's offerings; they choose affinity to your company's brand instead of pledging it to another. The key is choice, and consumers have many choices.

Judi Samuels, a brand and communication strategist with a focus on emotional marketing, argues that consumers "make purchase decisions based on emotional connections but immediately seek rational or logical inputs to justify those decisions....It's about risk and reward," she continues. "The greater the risk, the more logical inputs the brain requires to justify the emotional attachment initially created." For example, a low-cost product with a shorter purchase life cycle such as soap or fruit requires fewer and less logical justifications than larger, longer-term investments such as a home or a vehicle. When faced with these decisions, consumers turn to a variety of conscious and subconscious inputs such as past experiences, personal feelings and attitudes, peer recommendations, lifestyle, and social pressures to accept or reject the desire or need to make the purchase. The more choice and the more data available to consumers, the more conflicted decision making can be. As outlined in Table 6.1, from the time a consumer identifies the need for a new product—or is exposed to a new product through an advertisement or recommendation—to the time the consumer uses that product, he is making decisions. Consciously or subconsciously, consumers are asking questions that need to be answered satisfactorily if they're going to take the action.

Table 6.1   Decision-Making Conflict in the Purchase Life Cycle

Stages in Consumer Decision Making	Decision-Making Conflict
Perceiving a Need	Do I really need this? Can I afford it?
Seeking Value	What else is available to me? Do I have any history with this product? Who else is using this product? What do others think of this product?
Assessing Value	Will I be alone in using this product? What will people think of me for using this? Is considering another option too costly or time consuming? Are there other options worth considering, which are the few I will consider?
Buying Value	Is this the right business to buy from? What is the risk of using this product? Can I wait or is this urgent now? What immediate pleasure will I get from purchasing this now?

When planning influence marketing campaigns, marketers must identify the behavior consumers are engaged in when their advocate's recommendations are received. More importantly, they must learn to connect the advocate and the decision maker with a message that answers the consumer's decision-making conflict instead of offering generic statements or symbols of product support. Later in this chapter, we break down the disruptive factors in consumer purchase decisions but for now, let's explore these stages in consumer behavior.

The purchase decision-making process typically starts when a consumer perceives a need. The need could be the result of a problem that needs an immediate solution, such as a hole in the bottom of a pair of shoes on a rainy day. Alternatively, the need may be fabricated by marketers or peers who convince the individual that a specific pair of shoes is trendy and although he already has three other pairs of shoes, not having this one particular pair is somehow a problem that has to be resolved. In the latter case, the need really isn't a need but a want, which involves an entirely different decision-making process. Identifying the catalyst of the decision-making process can have a dramatic impact on the success of an influence marketing campaign; there is a time sensitivity with the prospect who identifies he has a need because of the hole in his shoe versus the one who doesn't know he has a need. In the first case, the recommendation must be crafted to sway or resolve an existing decision-making process, but in the other it must initiate a new decision-making process.

When a problem has been identified—based on a need or a want—consumers instinctually move into the three stages of the consideration value process: Seeking value, assessing value, and buying value. The first stage is *seeking value*, which begins an active search for solutions to the problem. The search for solutions take on different meanings based on the scenario that started the decision-making process. For example, the consumer with the hole in his shoe has a different set of criteria than the one considering another pair to satisfy a fashion need or social acceptance. Consumers with urgent needs use location and convenience as possible criteria, utilizing mobile devices to access information, whereas those with perceived or real problems that aren't considered urgent may access crowdsourcing applications and use social acceptance or peer recommendations within their communities as their criteria.

When consumers gather all the data required, they move into the second stage called assessing value. Here they attempt to *assess value* by identifying and comparing the available options and input received from various sources. How many choices were identified? Were any recommended by peers or experts? As outlined in previous chapters, the availability of product information and on-demand peer reviews has propelled our need to seek and process even more information before making any purchase decision. Marketing managers and search engine optimization (SEO) teams are responding by ensuring their products and positive reviews are available across as many websites and social networks as possible, and that each is search-engine friendly and ranking highly. This data collection is critical to the decision-making process we're outlining; however, the sheer volume of data and the situational factors exerting pressure on the brand message and the consumer's situation are disrupting an otherwise predictable choice. This is the most critical stage for influence marketing; understanding the unique disruptive factors that affect the recommendation offered, and the consumer's decision-making process, enables marketers to craft campaigns that are more likely to result in a purchase decision.

The final stage is *buying value*, where consumers make the final decision to purchase a product (or not) based on all the available information gathered and vetted against personal circumstances and decision-making criteria. If a product has passed the second value stage, the consumer—often with input from peers—has determined it's the best option. However, that's not enough. There's still a question of value in purchasing this product; what is the risk in buying it? This is where the logical justification of the initial emotional or social attachment is most evident. This is where the final decision is made, yet this is also where numerous factors may interfere and disrupt the justification.

Psychological Factors Disrupting Decision-Making Processes

Regarding the situational factors impacting decisions, marketers must delve into psychological concepts such as motivation, personality, perception, and lifestyle to properly map how consumers make decisions and thus how they might be influenced. The situational factors that impact decision making discussed in a previous section were predominantly external, where psychological factors are typically internal. Influence marketing that impacts the decision-making process understands these psychological factors and appends them to communities or subcommunities being targeted for influence. These factors help resolve conflicted decisions and add the missing data points outlined previously; the most common are summarized below.

Motivations Disrupt Decision-Making Processes

Motivation, as defined in the Oxford English Dictionary, is "a reason or reasons for acting or behaving in a particular way." The motivation to purchase a product is often linked to our basic human needs. Subconsciously—and depending on the product in question—purchase decisions are driven by basic survival instincts, including

1. **Self-preservation**—This is the base physiological requirement for human survival, which motivates people to avoid pain and protect themselves. Note that the avoidance of pain here isn't physical but social, financial or emotional. For marketers, it's important to note the past

negative experiences (cause of pain) that their target audience has had with their product or that of their competitor's product because of the learned response to avoid that pain.

2. **Love and belonging**—This is our need to belong and be associated with a group or a community. For consumers, this is the motivation that drives the need for peer acceptance of the purchase we make and share.

3. **Achievement, status, or prestige**—This is the individual's need to meet realistic goals, receive feedback, and experience a sense of accomplishment; to win and not lose. For consumers, this translates to how well a product or service moves them—physically, socially, or emotionally—toward a self-defined victory.

These different motivations are present at different times during the customer life cycle and are further affected by the sex of the target being influenced. A simple example can be illustrated when considering the personal motivations of an 18-year-old male purchasing his first vehicle versus the personal motivation of a 45-year-old woman purchasing a vehicle. The 18-year-old male is commonly fueled by love, status, and self-respect, whereas the 45-year-old woman's purchase decisions might be motivated by physical well-being, achievement, and personal fulfillment. Now overlay the situational factors described previously, and the motivational factors on decisions can change. For example, if the 45-year-old woman is a single mother of four children, her circumstances will affect how she makes decisions.

Personality Disrupts Decision-Making Processes

Behavioral science has shown that relationships exist between an individual's repeated response to specific situations and their affinity or preference for specific brands. Extending the concept to larger groups, such as the population of a country who have embraced a common national identity, their affiliation to a common ideology or set of characteristics becomes a decisive factor in the purchase choices they make. When people see themselves in a particular way, their behavior and their choices tend to be skewed by that belief. Marketers seeking to influence these consumers must understand the depth of conviction with which most hold these personality-based biases. The stronger the personality trait associated with the individual, community, or nationality of the audience, the more difficult it can be to influence their purchase decisions.

The people solicited to act as influencers, the channels selected, or even the content of the influence messages become an even bigger challenge in this case. In fact, this disruptive psychological factor might result in an influence marketing campaign achieving the opposite result of that which was intended. For example, a gun manufacturer in the United States choosing people to recommend their products based on a high influence score on the keywords "guns" or "ammunition," as rated by one of the social influence scoring platforms outlined in Chapter 4 runs the risk of a public backlash by the more liberal citizens of the country. Public outcry and boycott threats can positively impact the purchase decision of those who support gun ownership or might negatively impact the decision of those who don't have a strong affiliation to either side of the debate. Understanding the personality of the target and larger audience allows influence marketing campaigns to avoid such public debates by carefully crafting the context of the message that is being shared based on the context and relationships of the geofenced community selected.

Learned Reactions Disrupt Decision-Making Processes

Behavioral and cognitive learning are other psychological concepts that marketers must factor into the influence marketing model. The behaviors most commonly associated with customers and their purchase decisions are the result of repeated experience and thinking. Essentially, we've been trained to think and react in certain ways to specific stimuli. Marketers seeking to exert influence over purchase decisions who don't embrace this learned reaction might find their messages landing on deaf ears.

Learning to leverage consumers' learned reactions requires an understanding of how consumers learn from repeated experiences. Behavioral learning is based on the physical actions taken by an individual over time when seeking—and purchasing—products. As illustrated in Figure 6.1, there are four stages of purchase engagement most consumers repeat that form common reactions. The first stage is Desire, which is the activity driver, the desire that starts a decision-making process. Next, we have the Search or the input and call-to-action that the consumer recognizes when seeking solutions and that forces him to react or make a decision. The third stage, Reaction, is the response or specific action taken by the consumer to satisfy his original desire. The last stage is Justification, specifically, the logical or social justification sought to confirm that the decision made was the right one. Over time, the positive justifications train us to react in a specific way to the advertisements, recommendations, and messages presented to us at the Search stage, the point when influence marketing intersects with the intended audience.

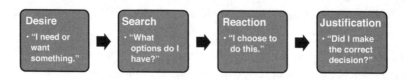

Figure 6.1 *Four stages of learned purchase engagements*

Influence marketing campaigns can adopt two strategies learned from this behavioral learning theory. The first is to leverage a general stimulus to the target audience at the Search stage. This is based on learning that a specific brand name, person, advertisement, or image produces a favorable reaction for the brand and positive justification to the consumer across multiple products. A simple example is a study of repeated decision-making processes among consumers that were presented with the Nike logo at the Search stage based on the need for shoes, clothing, athletics, professional, or amateur sports information. Assuming that in each experience, the decision-making process generated a consistently positive justification in those who chose to purchase one of its products, the Nike logo and brand become a general stimulus that can be used to influence decision making to multiple or broader influence marketing efforts.

Alternatively, if the results of repeated purchase engagements demonstrate a consistent negative justification result to a purchase decision based on the presentation of specific logos, advertisements, images, or people during the Search stage, we know that that target audience identifies the stimuli differently.

Another form of learning in consumer behavior is cognitive learning. Unlike behavioral learning, which is based on justifications to the repeated decisions by the consumer, this type is based on the connections consumers make between multiple stimuli, concepts, or group activity. For example, consumers who consistently see a major news source and a popular local blogger, each promoting a similar view on a topic, begin to form connections that influence their purchase decisions. The opposite scenario is also true; when specific and familiar media and blog sources are always diametrically opposed in the views and recommendations they share, our brains connect this situation to our repeated affiliation with one or the other and automatically make decisions based on that cognitive learning. By observing others' behaviors, we often adjust our own behaviors in common patterns.

Attitudes Disrupt Decision-Making Processes

Consumer attitudes are learned predispositions to react favorably or unfavorably to a specific brand or product. Often, attitudes are formed by the values and beliefs we learned from childhood or shaped through interaction with our peers. Yet another psychological factor impacting decision making is the established attitudes of the product brand's target audience. Attitudes are difficult to form and more difficult to alter when formed because most consumers are not aware of their predispositions. The common values we share with our families and communities establish commonly accepted behavior patterns and form a biased perception of the standard, quality, or function of a brand, sometimes despite proof to the contrary.

This is experienced often by marketing teams attempting to influence voters in election campaigns. Each attempts to leverage influential people to sway public opinion favorably toward their political party and candidate's platforms. Yet, the voter's learned attitudes create a predilection toward the performance of that party or candidate regardless of the genuineness or validity of the influencer's recommendation. The desire or need for factual data is often suspended during heated political campaigns in favor of social proof. Because we live our lives so publicly, being seen as part of the crowd becomes more important than challenging the status quo.

Understanding the attitudes of individual prospects and the communities they belong to provides an insight into what influences their decision-making processes. This enables marketers to add a layer to influence marketing content and strategies that allow the campaign to ride the collective groupthink or counter it while driving customers toward the purchase decision. In some cases, a less-direct approach is required. For example, when influence may have to be exerted toward changing the perceived importance of the attributes consumers hold dear, or by showcasing new characteristics or features that forces the consumer to overcome their biases. In others, influence marketing might be used to change the association between a brand and the attributes that the public has an attitude toward; in either case, this is an important filter that must be applied.

Social Proof Disrupts Decision-Making Processes

In practice, the concept that decision-making is based on emotional connections and justified by logical connections has morphed due to the change in how we access and exchange information. The high use and penetration of the Internet and social channels across multiple desktop and handheld devices, including tablets, smartphones, and more, have added another dimension to the concept of decision justification. While decisions may still be made emotionally, justification is now being negotiated between social and logical connections. Turning to social media for references, recommendations, and peer reviews has become an automatic step for most people when making a purchase decision; some conduct their research on their desktop computers, while others use their Internet-connected mobile devices to seek decision-supporting data at point of purchase.

In many cases, social proof has replaced logic in the decision-making cycle. Social proof is a psychological factor in that it reveals how people emulate the actions of others to demonstrate appropriate behavior in a specific situation. Consumer purchase decisions are often chosen in an attempt to reflect the attitude of their community. Consumer attitudes shift based on that community groupthink, which requires influence marketing efforts to be shaped to either support or counter the impact on the individual's decision-making process. Consider the public's changing attitudes toward trusted news sources as an example. In the 1960s and 1970s, CBC News anchorman Walter Cronkite was widely recognized as the most trusted man in America. However, during the 2008 U.S. presidential election, *Time* magazine conducted a nationwide poll to identify the most trusted anchorman, and the public's choice was satirist Jon Stewart, host of the televised *The Daily Show*, beating out the traditional networks' top news anchors by earning 44% of the national vote.

Jon Stewart, Stephen Colbert, and other satirists became very influential over a large demographic of the U.S. population because they understood that social attitudes were changing. The public had grown cynical of big business, government, politics, and religion. A litany of events, including the conviction of trusted international professional services firm Arthur Anderson in 2002, the multiple arrests of priests charged with child molestation, and the impeachment of former U.S. President Bill Clinton, combined with a high unemployment rate among Millennials, all collided to create a generation of cynics. The loss of trust with institutions previously considered trustworthy changed how the public viewed information sources, so it's not surprising that the satirists became so influential. Instead of packaging news in the same format popular with cable news networks such as CNN, they craft and present news in a tone and format that is where their audience is, not what they want them to be.

Lifestyle Disrupts Decision-Making Processes

The consumer's lifestyle, or the activities and interests that he engages in—and associates with publicly—contributes to the factors that impact decision making. The lifestyle disruptor, unlike the previous factors, is more easily recognized and managed through influence marketing; nonetheless, it's an important consideration when planning how your brand influencers engage with the audience.

As part of a new influence marketing methodology, we must include information about the decision maker's lifestyle in the target audience's profiling to better predict how consumers will react to various decision-making stimuli. For example, consider an influence marketing campaign for a health supplement product targeting those with active, outdoor lifestyles. Based on social influence scoring platforms or other tools, a community might be geofenced to include consumers with an affinity toward snowboarding, surfing, or skateboarding. These might be existing customers or advocates of clothing and leisure brands such Billabong, Vans, and Toms. However, within that same geofenced community might be another group whose active, outdoor lifestyle is more closely aligned with international travel and cruises or eco-tourism. The endorsement of an influencer such as a professional athlete will have a different impact on each of these sub-lifestyle groups within this same geofence.

Closely related to how lifestyle impacts purchase decisions is the social class of the target audience. Social classes don't tend to change frequently during the lifecycle of the consumer, so it is also a relatively simple profile to attach and manage within the geofenced community you're targeting. Since social class is often directly associated with—and usually created by—occupation, source of income, and education, such classification is an important criterion. Each group places different emphasis on what it considers important based on the lifestyle and social class the group is—or wishes to be—associated with. When this information is appended to consumer profiles within a targeted community, new insights are gained that can help formulate the choice of influencer, channel, or content strategy.

Perception Disrupts Decision-Making Processes

Consumer perception is a view of a product or brand generated by the brain after it collects, sorts, and interprets data from multiple sources. This view of a product, industry, or even a person's place in the community can be swayed in different directions based on the combination of data sources available or how they're organized by the consumer. Factors such as the amount of exposure consumers have with a product or their ability to adequately connect the product function to a human need impact their perception. Predicting how your target audience perceives your product or services is critical because it impacts their view of the risks associated with sampling or purchasing it.

Consumers tend to experience anxiety about purchase decisions when they cannot adequately predict whether the choice they're making will result in a positive justification; any chance that their choice might not be justified after the purchase and the perception of the product becomes negative. Let's take the example of Green Mountain Coffee Roasters, Inc., which introduced the Keurig coffee machine that brews single cups of coffee in its branded brewers using unique and patented K-Cups. When first introduced, consumers weren't quick to embrace the innovation; based on available information, the perceived risk was too high. "Will I be forced to buy coffee only from them?" "Will I end up paying more for coffee using K-Cups?" "With no competition, will there be enough variety or quality control?" "What if I don't like the flavor of the coffee?" "Will the use of single-brew cups create an environmental impact?" There wasn't enough data initially to offset the perceived risk in purchasing the product and so initial sales to consumers were not brisk.

The company embraced an influence marketing strategy that eliminated the perceived risk associated with the expense, use, limited selection, and eco-friendliness of the K-Cups. Among other strategies, the company aggressively pursued corporate office coffee services and office managers to use the machine and the variety of flavors, since the workplace is where most people consume coffee and where, in most cases, the coffee is offered free. This allowed consumers to gather the decision-making data that might reverse the perceived risk associated with not knowing the flavor, complexity of use, and so on. Then, free trial machines were provided to selected consumer influencers who were asked to join a Twitter Party to share their experiences with the larger community. While some objections (such as eco-friendliness or price per cup) remained in some, the program was successful at overcoming the biggest obstacle: the fear of the unknown (flavor, complexity, availability, etc.). That, coupled with the recommendations from peers, was enough to help turn the single-cup coffee segment into a multibillion dollar industry. Other competitors are now entering the market, including the Starbuck's Verismo premium single-cup brewing system, launched in the Fall of 2012.

The challenge for marketers is that consumers selectively choose what they pay attention to and the information they're willing to accept. They often choose to pay attention only to brand messages that are in line with the current perceptions and ignore those that are not. In other cases, their perceptions interpret the message in a manner that makes it consistent with the current views. Selective retention is another challenge; consumers tend to remember only the brand recommendations that align with their own perceptions. Clearly, understanding brand perceptions among a target audience is necessary if influence marketing strategies are to translate into purchase decisions.

Family Influence Disrupts Decision-Making Processes

The changing structure and nature of families has an increasing impact on how people make purchase decisions. Internal family dynamics, for example, have an impact on how consumers behave for a number of reasons. The family unit is where most people acquire the attitude and perception that guides their purchase decisions when alone; thus, it's critical for influence marketing to profile the family units of the business's prospective customers. Attempting to exert influence over the purchase decisions of geofenced communities, where the profiles include familial profiles, requires a communication strategy based on the identification of the family member and the role she plays in the family's purchase-making process. For example, is the family member the information gatherer, micro-influencer, decision maker, or end user of the product?

Where the family unit exists within its natural life cycle, for example, newlyweds, young family with newborn, mature family with adolescents, or empty nesters, impacts the products they buy and the purchase decisions they make. A young family with one infant child makes decisions differently than an older family unit with a few adolescents. Similarly, the latter's purchase decisions will be skewed differently than a family unit with kids off to college or married and out on their own.

Interpersonal dynamics within the family unit add even more complexity to this process. Some families have a spouse-dominant decision-making dynamic where one of the two has final say on all or some of the family's purchases. Other couples make joint decisions on all major purchases, but their circumstances may alter the definition of "major." Depending on the product a business is promoting, marketing teams must understand and map these profiles to the influence path. In fact, with the growing number of single-parent families, teens are starting to take the lead on some purchase decisions.

The various psychological factors outlined in this section are provided as a checklist for some of the missing profile data in current influence marketing programs. These data points and considerations provide additional context to the brand-influencer-consumer relationship. It aids in better segmenting target audiences and crafting influence marketing campaigns that more closely align to what best influences the unique situations that impact their decision-making process.

Cognitive Dissonance

An often overlooked element of consumer behavior by marketers is that which occurs after the purchase is made. Behavioral scientists refer to the psychological concept of cognitive dissonance, which describes a feeling of personal discomfort that results from holding two conflicting beliefs. For example, when a consumer purchases a product, particularly if it is a high-value or socially prominent purchase, it's common for the buyer to question his decision. Was it the best option? What are the consequences of that purchase? Alternatively, the experience of using the product may not match the original expectation. Further, the discrepancy does not have to truly exist, just the perception that the product experience and pre-purchase impression don't align is enough. In many cases today, such dissonance is created by comments, recommendations, and feedback offered by the consumer's peers after the purchase was made. Now consider the impact of influence marketing efforts to this group. Whenever such a discrepancy between the consumer's satisfaction and the logical or social justification used to make the purchase decision exists, the consumer has to change something to eliminate or reduce the dissonance experienced.

Influence marketing is often relegated to customer acquisition efforts, yet the need to create advocates and social proof around a brand necessitates better engagement with existing customers. Identifying cognitive dissonance in existing customers allows marketers to pinpoint the micro-influencers that may help alleviate the tension and sway their belief toward a feeling of satisfaction with the purchase and possibly even advocacy. Left alone, consumers with these feelings may return the product, or worse, turn to social channels to complain about it. The returns and online negativity can be curbed when influence marketing is applied to this customer segment. It's important to monitor such dissonance in the conversations and behaviors of customers and prospects alike, once this criterion is added to the audience monitoring filter previously outlined.

Purchase Life Cycles

So far in this chapter, we have discussed human behavior, how people make decisions, and the psychological and social factors that can disrupt what might otherwise be predictable behavior and choices. However, as we attempt to shift influence marketing campaigns from broad amplification to decision making, we must also understand where the consumers we're hoping to influence are in the purchase life cycle when a recommendation is received. Influence is a variable concept; what may influence a consumer when comparing two different options is different from what is required for someone who has a need but isn't yet aware of the options. A typical model for the customer life cycle, as illustrated in Figure 6.2, demonstrates the stages of engagement consumers may pass through when purchasing a company's product.

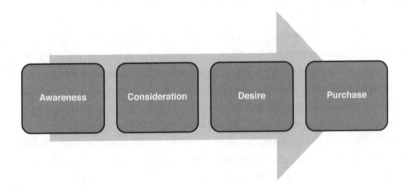

Figure 6.2   *Customer life cycle*

The challenge that social influence score-based campaigns have is that they engage a broad target audience based on keywords and the size of the influencer's reach instead of attempting to identify where groups of prospects are within the purchase life cycle and move them to the next stage toward purchase. Let's consider a scenario in which an appliance company introduces a new, high-end coffee machine into the market. Today, as illustrated in Figure 6.3, a marketer may choose to look at a social influence scoring platform to determine who has the highest score on the keyword "coffee" and related topics and create a campaign to solicit their advocacy. One of the more common tactics is to send those with the highest score one of their coffee machines to test for a period of time with the hope that they'll share the product's name and images with their social graphs, and, if they really enjoy the product, recommend it to those same people. This satisfies both branding/ awareness and advocacy/lead generation marketing goals. Or does it?

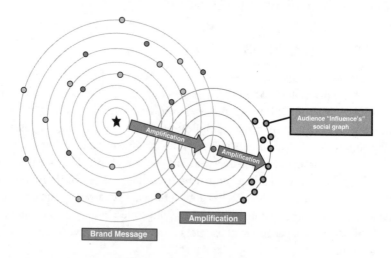

Figure 6.3 *Amplification of recommendation through influencers*

The reality is that when product managers choose an influencer-centric approach, they rarely take into account consumer behaviors. Further, they don't consider where in the purchase life cycle those in the influencer's social graph are. As illustrated in Figure 6.3, a brand may be successful at identifying an influencer(s) to whom they can send samples and also be successful at having them share positive sentiments to their social graph, but are those in their social graph at the "purchase" stage or at the "awareness" stage? Are they even potential customers? Do they already have your or a competitor's product? If marketers are going to use technology to identify influencers online, they should continue to evolve that practice to identify and segment the end prospects they'll be reaching. If we break down those groups, you might have a different opinion of who is—and isn't—influential by the possible purchase transactions they can generate. As highlighted in Figure 6.4, when the end audience is segmented, only a small percentage may be in the buying cycle for the product. With this knowledge, would marketers still choose this same influencer with a high social influence score? If they do, they might better strategize the campaign to more directly target those they're trying to reach.

In Figure 6.4, only 10% of the influencer's social graph are prospects for an immediate purchase, 20% may be potential customers, and the balance are not interested in this company's offering at all. If the product manager chooses to engage this prospect, she may want to focus the influencer on promoting a time-sensitive offer to increase the chances of pushing that 10% from strong consideration to purchase. Alternatively, calculating a bigger payoff from the 20% interested but not currently in the buying cycle, they may choose to use a longer-term strategy that directly engages this group with sampling programs or other tactics that move them closer to product consideration.

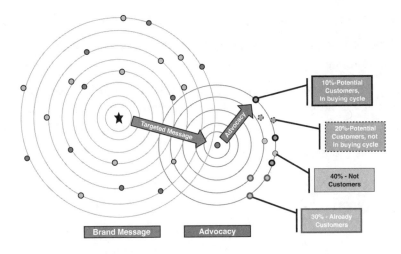

Figure 6.4 *Segmentation of prospects by purchase life cycle*

In this one case, 40% of the influencer's audience, for various reasons, would never purchase the recommended product. Another 30% are already customers and might require a different strategy to increase their purchases, if even possible. Marketers who choose to focus on the influencer's reach and amplification risk lower conversion and success because their tactics end up being more generic. In the next chapters, we explore how to monitor, segment, and market to these sub-group targets with target communities.

Of course, businesses cannot possibly map the situational factors that impact influence and the factors that impact the decision-making process for every single client in their target audience. However, when you understand all the possible factors that can disrupt the influence your chosen influencers are attempting to exert, research and analysis of current transactions allow you to create common consumer profiles and apply what you learn to those general profiles. Once completed, you can more quickly identify the profiles of the geofenced communities you're targeting and create adaptive messages that are more likely to generate a positive purchase decision. But more on this in the next few chapters.

References

Kerin, R., S. Hartley, and W. Rudelius. 2009. *Marketing, 9/e, 7th Edition*. New York: McGraw Hill.

Maslow, A. 1954. *Motivation and Personality*. Harper Collins.

McClelland, D. C., R. Koestner, and J. Weinberger. 1989. "How Do Self-Attributed and Implicit Motives Differ?" *Psychological Review*.

Senise, J. 2007. "Who Is Your Next Customer?" Strategy+Business, Booz Allen Hamilton, Inc. http://www.strategy-business.com/article/07313?gko=1428c.

7

Reversing the Social Influence Model

So far, we've discussed what influence is and how marketers attempt to use influence marketing as a tactic across social channels. We illustrated the cultural, social, political, and economic factors that impact the effectiveness of those campaigns by explaining how current social media-based influence marketing models are missing the target (the customer decision-making process) in favor of influencer identification and gamification schemes. All this brings us to our own business decision: Is influence marketing really effective and should we be investing in it?

The purchase habits of consumers have changed; impulse decisions are fewer, making way for more considered, researched purchases, even if that research is done at point of purchase by scanning a QR code. The availability, volume, and polarity of public commentary, coupled with the situational factors outlined in previous chapters, have swayed the typical decision-making process common 15 years ago. Therefore, to be effective, influence marketing can no longer be based on influencers broadcasting brand messages but must be based on swaying the decision-making process of the individual. Understanding the situations and situational factors that disrupt the influence marketers are trying to exert allows us to effectively reengineer the influence path.

Influence Paths

The pathways that a brand message or recommendation takes after it is issued by a marketing campaign or influencer. Such paths can be direct (from the business to the influencer to the decision maker) or indirect (from the business to the influencer but disrupted and altered based on other peer reviews or situational factors) resulting in an unpredictable outcome in the desired effect on the purchase of products or services.

Reverse engineering social influence paths turns the traditional model on its ear by focusing the strategic planning on the customer instead of the influencer. Influence marketing can be effective at driving sales if we first determine where the customer is in the purchase life cycle, what situations and factors impact their decisions at each stage, and what the nature of the conversations are that they're having with their social graph in each case. By charting these data points and sentiment, we can identify the micro-influencers that have real impact on the prospect's purchase decisions and finally, which macro-influencers influence that community of micro-influencers.

As we discover in Chapter 8, "Managing Social Influence Paths," with this information, marketers can look at creating customized and adaptive messages that have a greater impact on the sales funnel and conversion ratios. However, before we get there we must better understand text analytics, sentiment analysis, and how they're used to collect, sort and map this information.

Macro-Influencers

Individuals, businesses, or media, with a large, active social following comprised of people with whom they have a loosely defined or unknown relationship.

Micro-Influencers

Individuals within a consumer's social graph, whose commentary, based on the personal nature of their relationship and communications, has a direct impact on the behavior of that consumer.

The vastness and complexity of the data analysis required, not to mention the nuances within the conversations and decisions-making factors for each group, are challenges that must be addressed. The larger the business and the more products it offers, the greater this data set will be and the greater the challenge in achieving the influence marketing methodology outlined in this book. However, as social monitoring software and text analytic technologies become more advanced and available, this process will become easier. There are already a number of excellent products that can help automate this new methodology, which we discuss in this and upcoming chapters.

To be clear, the need to identify, segment, and monitor the purchase life cycle, situational factors, and decision-making processes does not require capturing and analyzing each individual customer and everyone they engage with. Our goal here is to create group profiles, as illustrated in Figure 7.1, that represent common prospect profiles at specific purchase stages by gathering data from those we can identify and analyze. These group profiles are used as a baseline from which marketers can continue to add and modify based on the ongoing campaign results. Figure 7.1 demonstrates just one possible sample of a profile framework. This sample has three purchase life cycle stages defined and within each of those are two types of prospects, those that are already customers but might purchase again and those that are competitors' customers but might be convertible. Within each of those categories, six sample customer profiles, based on demographic, psychographic, and social data, have been identified as common among the entire prospect data base.

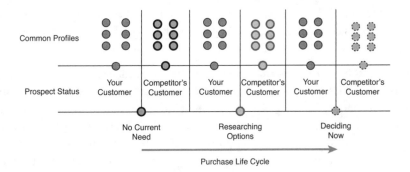

Figure 7.1 *Purchase life cycle prospect categorization*

This example is overly simplified for illustration purposes; however, the point remains that a small, representative group can be identified and used as the baseline to begin an effective influence marketing campaign. This chapter reviews a methodology for reverse engineering the influence path from the decision maker to those who influence their purchase decisions, by analyzing the conversations and profile data of the business's prospective audience.

Importance of Text Analytics to Reverse Engineering Influence

Reverse engineering the influence path is dependent on conducting the proper text analytics across social media channels. Scanning social commentary and identifying those involved in conversations is easy; gleaning real meaning from that content and the context of those relationships is difficult, which is the reason most social influence scoring platforms rely mostly on number of followers, volume of engagement, and common word usage as the basis for their services. For businesses attempting to do this on their own, sifting through terabytes of social media content isn't feasible or cost effective; junior staff don't have the necessary skills to interpret the data and senior staff don't have the time. As a result, monitoring and analyzing public conversations across social channels to garner meaning and insight into consumer behavior is an evolving science and a growing industry for software developers. The processing power required and linguistic interpretation algorithms needed are enormous and growing in complexity as we produce more and more social content in multiple languages, including new mobile-inspired shorthand. In addition, consumers and businesses alike are producing this data across multiple formats, including blog posts, comments, social network shares, images, and videos, which increases the challenges of defining context in communications. Conversation analysis software is evolving to scrape and analyze even more data, such as the comments on a blog, the titles of videos, and the alt tags set for images on the Web, much like search engines have been doing. Human communication is complex enough; adding new technological channels and the resulting language subsets adds even more intricacies to the process.

On the upside, consumers are more than willing to produce an unlimited amount of content, chat on public digital channels with family and friends, and freely share their personal profiles. This is the opportunity for marketers who can effectively deploy text analytics software to their advantage. Text analytics is the practice of deriving meaning from the written word. It can be used to connect the words posted by people within specific relationships and by contrasting them to the situations surrounding those involved. It can provide a framework from which marketers may build up context and insights from the dialogue.

Text Analytics

The practice of deriving meaning from the written word. For businesses today, text analytics is the process of acquiring and converting large volumes of text-based content into quantitative and meaningful insights that support marketing operations.

Delving into the intricacies of the programming and technologies required to develop and manage such software is beyond the scope of this book; that alone would require another book. However, marketers don't need to know the algorithms or coding to understand what the software must do to support the influence marketing methodology. The software(s) a business chooses to deploy must be able to

1. Identify the type of dialogue (original content, shared content, commentary on third party or the author's own content, etc.)

2. Identify the platform.

3. Parse the data to determine the subject matter, sentiment, intent, and attitude of the author and any historical context.

4. Interpret and provide grammatical analysis, natural language processing, computational linguistics.

5. Determine semantic orientation of data to segment the data and intent based on conjecture, opinion, beliefs stated as fact, and so on.

6. Identify the various people communicating across multiple social channels around specific themes.

7. Identify the publicly available personal profiles of those involved in these discussions and connect that data to determine relationships between people (people who work at the same company, family members, members of a social community, frequent commenters on a blog, etc.) or upload and match third-party profile data.

8. Create and save specific groups of people according to common topics of interest or conversations.

In essence, this model requires a form of artificial intelligence that demands more than just data; it requires relationships, definitions, and processes to be appended to data. Current social influence scoring platforms are criticized for this very reason; they provide neither the context of the conversations scored nor the relationships between the chosen influencers and their followers. Marketers must use ontology to properly configure our influence marketing methodology, which uses text analytic software to collect the necessary conversations, sort them hierarchically, and derive meaning from the results. Ontology is a philosophical concept borrowed by computer scientists to describe structural frameworks of organized data and the manipulation of that data to derive insight and meaning from the linear data collected, tagged, and archived. For our purposes, ontology can be used to understand the consumer's intent and frame of mind when producing and sharing the words they choose to post in social media channels or exchange in social conversations.

Ontology

A philosophical concept borrowed by computer scientists to describe structural frameworks of organized data, and the manipulation of that data to derive insights and meaning.

Without ontology, influence marketing in the post-digital era cannot be effective. As outlined in previous chapters, brand communications—including influencer recommendations—have been disrupted by the technology and social channels embraced by the public. The resulting dynamic between brand and consumers has shifted, from one of inherent trust in advertising and word-of-mouth marketing, to a distrust of any message issued by the brand or its paid influencers. In its place, trust is imbued in collective voices within a community of peers. Text analytics and natural language processing have become necessary to determine the sentiment of the online discourse around a brand and the consumer's hidden meaning.

Such processes provide the translation required to understand consumer intent, trend analysis, and the groupthink that impacts their purchase decisions.

Natural Language Processing (NLP)

The ability of a computer program to interpret or understand written text as it's spoken.

A systematic framework must be established to effectively reverse engineer the influence path from decision maker to the business along social media channels, which can rarely—if ever—be short cut. A step-by-step process, as outlined in Table 7.1, must be adhered to to collect the necessary conversation data and chart the relationships between people, networks, and data to create effective communication and influence marketing campaigns. The more detailed and documented the process, the easier it becomes to adjust the model based on real-time results. In addition, a well-documented influence path allows for improved success milestones and measurement. Let's summarize the steps required in reverse engineering influence.

Table 7.1 Reverse Engineering the Influence Path

1	Identify the purchase life cycle stages.	Identify the stages that consumers go through toward a final purchase decision.
2	Establish linguistic maps.	Create contextual maps made up of combinations of keywords specific to thought process and online discourse around a product by individuals at the different stages of the purchase life cycle.
3	Identify conversations and people active in each stage.	Capture the profiles identified by the linguistics mapping engaged in decision-making social discussions. Append their social graphs and the micro-influencers who are most likely to impact those decisions.
4	Chart key-stakeholder relationships and micro-influencers.	Chart the relationships between the decision maker in each pre-purchase stage and the identified micro-influencers.
5	Identify situational factors.	Uncover the situational factors that impact the decision-making process of the consumer and sway the conversations among their social graphs.

Identifying the Purchase Life Cycle

Keeping in mind that our methodology's goal is to impact the purchase decision instead of simply increasing brand recognition, no influence can be exerted without first understanding where the prospect aligns within the purchase life cycle. No matter how valuable an offer is or how clever the call-to-action is, an influencer's recommendation to buy will not produce the desired result. As illustrated in Figure 7.2, the prospect must be well defined if an advocate's recommendation is to be actionable. The motivations to purchase a product are vastly different for someone with no current need than for someone with a need. Similarly, converting sales opportunities through peer recommendations is less likely when the customer is not in the market for the solution, is employed by the competitor, or is a customer of the competitor. Yet, even the latter should not be ignored when identified. The future of influence marketing can see customers across the entire purchase life cycle targeted and influenced to move from awareness to nurturing, from nurturing to consideration, from consideration to purchase, or from purchaser to advocate.

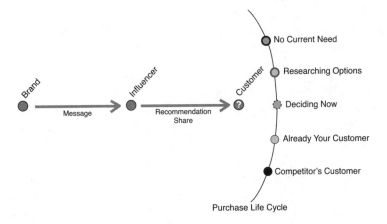

Figure 7.2   *Matching influence marketing to the purchase life cycle*

Table 7.2 identifies three general stages of the purchase life cycle that apply to most businesses. However, each business must identify its own life cycle. These stages are dictated by the psychological and logistical factors that drive the customer from identifying a need or desire to making a choice to purchase the product or service as outlined in Chapter 6, "The Consumer Decision-Making Process."

Table 7.2 Typical Prepurchase Life Cycle Stages

Stage	Description
No Current Need	There are two options in this stage: The consumer is aware of your product but has no current need or the consumer isn't aware of your product and doesn't know she has a need, such as with a startup introducing a new product.
Researching Options	The consumer has identified a need or desire for a product or service and is actively seeking information with which to make a purchase decision.
Deciding Now	The consumer has gathered all the information she requires to justify a purchase decision and is currently analyzing the data collected.

The next section looks at adding sample customer profiles to each of these stages; however, the social monitoring and text analytics software may identify some customers who potentially don't fit into any of these stages. These are consumers who could buy the business's products and services but are either already a customer or a competitor's customer. We must create subcategories for these prospects because the message or tactic required to exert influence on their decision-making process is unique when compared to those who have never purchased before. That is why we included "Already Your Customer" and "Competitor's Customer" as two additional options in the prospect's life cycle in Figure 7.2.

Identifying the prepurchase stages and where the target customers are when receiving an influencer's message is necessary for targeting strategies discussed in the next chapter. Impacting a purchase decision requires influence with different context and possibly shared by different people. Consider the scenario of a cellular subscriber who receives recommendations across his social channels for a competitive provider's service soon after signing a contract with his current provider. While the recommended service might, in fact, be a better option for the consumer, he is not in the right prepurchase stage for that recommendation to be effective. Now consider that same recommendation received by someone whose service contract with another provider has ended and who is actively searching for options. Obviously, the recommendation will have a higher success rate with the latter.

Does this mean that the prospect who just signed a contract with a competitor should not be influenced? Should he not also be targeted by influence marketing campaigns? That prospect might still become a customer in the short term (if offered a trade-in option, a buyout contract, etc.) or in the long term (when a buyout option becomes worthwhile or when his contract expires). In either case, this person is a potential revenue source for the business, but the nature of the influence required to convert him is markedly different. One is short-term, the other a long-term conversion opportunity; so a one-size-fits-all influencer scoring or influence marketing campaign cannot work.

As the cellular provider, consider how a social media-broadcast message is received by a current subscriber who is near the end of his contract versus someone subscribed with a competitor, but also at the end of his contract. Technically, each is at the same stage of the purchase life cycle, but the context and nature of the influence message (to renew a contract or convert to another provider) are different. The cellular provider's marketing team could easily—and with less investment—find active, high-profile people engaging on social media around terms related to mobile devices and cellular services. But without this critical data point, the customer acquisition ratio will be dramatically lower. As a result, before any serious consideration of influence marketing campaigns can be entertained, the marketing team must first understand and be able to track prospects to a point in the purchase life cycle.

Creating Linguistic Maps

Once the purchase life cycle stages have been determined, linguistic maps must be built around each stage. Linguistic maps provide contextual insights into the prospect's decision-making process or purchase intent by analyzing sets of words or phrases used in combination or specific sequence and within a specific period of time. Creating these maps can be a science of its own but often requires simple trial and error using social media monitoring applications like Marketwire's Sysomos or Mantis's PulseAnalytics. Most social influence services use some form of text analytics in their programs but for those seeking to manage this process independently, there are dedicated solutions available that include products like Coveo, Lexalytics, or Smartlogic. The process outlined allows text analytic software to scan the Web and social media sites to determine who might be prospects that can be influenced but also which stage of the purchase life cycle they may be in, who they're engaged with, and the conversion opportunity.

Linguistic Maps

Using text analytics and natural language processing through social media monitoring platforms to identify specific words and phrases used in combination or in specific patterns that indicate a predisposition toward purchasing (or not) a product or service based on where the customer is in the purchase life cycle.

As illustrated in Figure 7.3, linguistic maps are based on relationships between words and/or phrases. Using the cellular provider case study from the previous section as an example, the main keyword searched by the marketing team in social conversations to identify prospects might be the word "mobile." The linguistics map search would include associated secondary words such as "cancellation" and "contract" when used in combination with the primary search term. The theory is that this combination of words represents the conversation of a person who is an existing or prospective customer attempting to get out of her contract and thus, an active prospect for the influence marketing effort. Additional business rules are added to the query to further define where this customer is in the life cycle and the nature of the opportunity. For example, the greater use of one brand name such as AT&T over Verizon might indicate that the people involved in this discussion, or the author of the specific post, are AT&T customers. This is where a little trial and error comes into play, until specific patterns are identified.

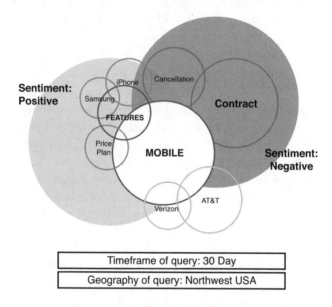

Figure 7.3 *Visualization of a sample linguistics map*

Additional supporting keywords or groups of keywords are chosen to highlight the prospect's needs or challenges. For example, searching for connected words like "price plan" and "features," with specific weighting on each, might provide insight into what specific issues they are having (if any) that preceded their desire to cancel their contract.

Further, subsearches (illustrated as additional circles in Figure 7.3) might not represent a specific word at all but groups of words. For example, the "features" query might be comprised of a combination of words used in varying frequencies such as "speed" >50%, "social networking" > 25%, and "keyboard" >15%. These advanced subsearches might be better served as secondary or tertiary rounds of queries when the business is seeking to further define or fine-tune initial results and assumptions. Advanced search parameters might also include grammatical and textual cues such as the use of "my contract" or "my AT&T" along with the word "contract" to identify whose current customer is looking to get out of her cellular contract.

Adding sentiment analysis to the query provides another layer of detail to better profile where the prospect falls within the purchase life cycle and what's driving her decision-making processes. For example, in this scenario "contract" and "cancellation" were filtered for negative sentiment along with brand mentions of AT&T. Within this same linguistic map, the marketing team can search for positive mentions of pricing plans and specific features, along with brand mentions of Verizon. Such an analysis may identify a prospect seeking to leave AT&T, for example, in favor of Verizon and what factors are driving that decision-making process.

Finally, the map illustrates the volume or specific combinations of words used during a specified period of time and, if appropriate, within a specific geography. In this sample, we look at specific combinations of words and context shared within a 30-day period in order to determine if this person is to be considered a prospect within a targeted sales geography.

We've outlined a simple example here to better illustrate how, with an accepted margin of error, a search of the social conversations can identify individuals as potential prospects in the Researching Options stage and a current customer, as an example, of AT&T. Further, the analysis provides some context around the reason the customer is looking to get out of his current contract. The customer profile along with the search parameters and insights can be saved to the purchase life cycle bucket "conversion" and "existing (or competitive) customer." Once set, additional profile data can be pulled and analyzed from publicly available data (online bios, for example), internal social Customer Relationship Management programs, accounting software, or acquired third-party data to display a more accurate profile of the prospect. For example, we might be able to determine the prospect's sex, age, employment, marital status, blog topic, and so on. Like the content scanned and collected across social channels, the additional profile data is information readily available to businesses and often provided directly by the customers themselves. It's a matter of understanding how to use the available data.

This profiled individual, along with the others captured in the same analysis, becomes the basis for this life cycle stage's profile, which we listed earlier in this chapter. The purchase life cycle stages are phases a consumer progesses through when discovering the need for—and the rationale to buy—a product or service.

These maps might be generated on assumptions or on real customer analysis conducted through other solutions. The scenario outlined describes a *planned* linguistics map and search where the business felt comfortable enough with its customer's life cycle, its customer's profiles, and the keywords and engagements that represent the customer's purchase decision-making patterns. However, this program can be used in reverse, meaning wide parameter searches could be set to monitor the full conversation their audience is engaged in, analyze those posts, and, based on the patterns that evolve, select and set the target customer profiles. For example, a query of "main keywords" that looks for combinations of some or all the brand names that offer cellular services can be analyzed and compared to other defined parameters such as geography, sentiment, or specific product features. Analyzing the weighting and frequency of specific brand names across various conversations—and contrasting those to fixed keyword searches—can provide insights and prospect profiles that could not be assumed prior.

In either case, the linguistics mapping process is a new reality for marketers seeking to exert influence over decision makers. It should also be noted that this map is a live, evolving entity that must be managed on an ongoing basis. We discuss this in greater length in the next chapter, but for now, as a point of reference, the parameters that go into the search queues must be updated and modified based on initial and ongoing results or other community, product, or business changes that may impact how prospects make purchase decisions.

Charting Relationships

To illustrate the importance of linquistics mapping and charting relationships, consider the case study of a client, a wireless telecommunications provider for whom we conducted a similar program. The linguistics map query identified words and patterns in the audience's conversation that isolated one common prospect profile as 25- to 40-year-old professional men who were unsatisfied with Outlook email synchronization with their mobile phones, searching for a new phone and/ or providers, and each flagged with an overall negative sentiment. Focusing on the conversations the sample prospects were having, we identified that the majority of those they were engaged with (where the cost of phones and phone plans were discussed in conjunction with the email sync feature) were other professional men and women, most of whom were co-workers. We determined that the micro-influencers in this scenario were work colleagues instead of the mass media, popular social celebrities, tech writers, or family members. We knew we had to encourage those micro-influencers to recommend our client's phone to their colleagues so we created a referral program targeting those micro-influencer profiles, which was promoted through tech bloggers and news outlets that this audience was known to read.

Now, let's break down this process. With the linguistic maps completed for each stage of the purchase life cycle, we can delve deeper into the social profiles of those engaged in the conversations. At this point we can look at the specific individuals contributing the content picked up by the linguistics map. The focus of this phase is

- Identify the profile of the decision maker.
- Who is in their social circles?
- Who, within that social circle, is engaging the prospect on the topic?
  - The relationships of those engaged.
  - The context of those discussions.

Identifying who the target decision maker is can be a challenge if you don't have concise parameters defined. Clearly articulating the touch-points that your business and products have with its customers—and the customer's challenges solved by your offering—into the linguistics map search parameters aids efforts to identify the actual decision maker. Once again, text analytics becomes critical to the successful execution of this phase of the program.

Once the decision maker has been defined, his social profile can be obtained and appended with any existing or third-party data available. Mapping that user's social graph is the next step and is the simplest endeavor throughout this process. There are a variety of social software solutions such as Sysomos, Nimble, oneQube, Traackr, LiveFyre or Appinions that help track the prospect's registered contacts (friends, followers, etc.) and those they engage with (blogs they comment on, people they exchange tweets with, etc.). This group forms the prospect's global social graph and the universe of people who might be analyzed to determine relationship and contextual references that impact the decision-making process around specific search terms.

With this larger social graph charted around the decision maker, we can focus on who the micro-influencers are at specific prepurchase life cycle stages in specific situations. Remember, micro-influencers are those people with more personal and contextual relationships around specific topics and conversations who are more likely to impact the other's purchase making decisions. For example, as illustrated in Figure 7.4, by overlaying the prospect's social graph over the linguistics map, we can determine the geofenced communities we introduced in Chapter 5, "Situational Influence: A New Model for a New Era," and those more closely engaged with the prospect at the time of a purchase decision—the micro-influencers. Social monitoring software could filter the prospect's conversations by "Considering Options" (the life cycle stage) and a "linguistic map" (specific topics), which highlight the micro-influencers who interact with the prospective customer at that stage across different issues.

When combined, these data sets can chart the relationships between those engaged in specific conversations and subconversations by topic and by life cycle stage. Scraping or downloading the social profiles of those involved in the conversations provides the necessary data points to define relationships between decision maker and micro-influencer. For example, Facebook profiles often contain data such as "In a relationship with...," Works for...," and provides information about your sex, age, and so on. To augment this data, the use of natural language processing when scanning the actual conversations to identify patterns can provide insight into familial relationships with an acceptable margin of error. Software can pick up comments such as "see you at work" or "is this on our corporate plan?" and define the relationship between those individuals as coworkers. Finally, third-party data can be applied to profiles. Other commentary, such as those collected via comments and blog subscriptions, can be appended to provide even greater certainty around relationship definition. With this process completed, we can begin to tag those who are family members, coworkers, media contacts, friends, employees, competitors' employees, and so on.

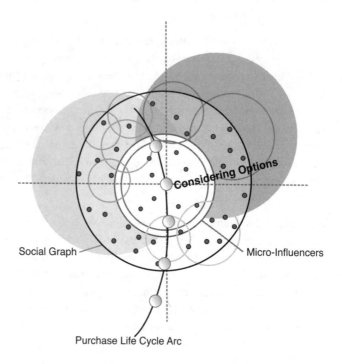

Figure 7.4 *Social graph-linguistics map overlay*

By mapping the relationships among those involved in product or brand discussions at a particular purchase stage, we can better predict which micro-influencers might best exert influence over the decision-making process based on those connections and lessons learned from past conversations.

Micro-influencers are not necessarily those people who a decision maker speaks with the most often or those in their closed family circles but those whose relationships are most relevant at specific decision-making points. Both macro- and micro-influencers can play a role in converting prospects to buyers, but charting these relationships within the target customer profile provides a framework to execute the influence marketing campaigns to achieve that success.

"Relationships continually evolve due to changing variables, such as interests and current events," offers Matt Hixson from Tellagence, a new, groundbreaking software that analyzes the changes in human behavior based on the content and context of social engagement. "Uncertainty and interdependency of individuals and groups can cause additional complexity." The steps outlined within this section of the methodology can be used to define the impact of groups or specific combinations of micro-influencers on the choice to purchase or not. However, that will be reserved for a more advanced campaign configuration. While important, we can't rely solely on the demarcation of relationships between micro-influencers and prospective customers. We must identify, using natural language processing, the situational influences that can accelerate or disrupt this influence as well.

Identifying Situational Factors

The final phase in reverse engineering the influence path is a look at what situational factors impact the context of the communication between the macro-influencers and the consumer's social graph or the micro-influencer and the decision maker. In the next chapter we also consider how to predict the changes in situational factors and plan influence marketing campaigns accordingly, but for now we look at how text analytics can help identify the current situations.

Remember that in Chapters 5 and 6 we described how situational factors are external stimuli that impact a consumer's decision-making process. These can include social, political, economic, and geographic factors that individually or in combination impact how a macro- or micro-influencer's recommendation is acted upon. Each industry and the businesses within it can be impacted by one or more situational factors, so the first step here is to understand which impacts your audience. For the purposes of this chapter, we identify situational factors that impact the decision-making process. In future chapters, we also consider how situational factors impact the path a consumer takes along the purchase life cycle, from brand awareness to consideration and from consideration to conversion.

It is worthwhile to note here that the possible situational factors that impact purchase stages are less discernible—and sometimes not relevant—for products and services with short purchase cycles such as stationery, DVDs, music, and so on. This process can be more easily defined—and more impactful—for products with longer term purchase cycles, such as raw materials, financial services, and real estate. In either case, this is an important step in the reverse engineering methodology.

Analysis of the conversations among the profiled audience, between the business and consumers, as well as in the posts and content they generate, helps identify which factors impact which groups. Technically, identifying situational factors can be performed without the aid of technology, especially for smaller businesses; however, this approach is problematic because the analysis can become tainted with human interpretation and bias. Text analytics is once again useful, in particular natural language processing. Most social media monitoring software analyzes the sentiment of conversations, but for influence marketing, this is only one small part. "The right text analytics technology will avoid the chances that situational factors are determined by the bias of the marketer," says Brian Vickery, president of Mantis Technology Group. "Further, there are many factors that might impact perception of a brand but not the decision-making process of a consumer and that's where natural language processing, in conjunction with audience segmentation and relationship mapping, is critical."

Until now, the analysis has been focused on specific conversations and relationships. For this phase of the reverse engineering methodology, we must take the profiled decision maker and the identified micro-influencer at specific junctions along the purchase life cycle and expand our search across all their conversations. Let's break down an example for reference. Keeping with our cellular provider and mobile device theme, let's look at a case where the goal is to influence a competitor's customers near the end of their contract term. The product features impacting their decisions to leave their current provider are identified in the linguistics map along with who within their social graph would be considered a micro-influencer. Now, we expand the search beyond this data set and add filters to include all the conversations occurring among the larger social graph of the prospective customer. As with the linguistics mapping process detailed earlier, there are two possible approaches: Predefine your search criteria based on anecdotal or existing knowledge to confirm perceptions of the situational factors impacting that audience, or scan for patterns to identify what they may be.

If a search were conducted between 2007 and 2009, when the United States was suffering the worst part of economic recession, the results would surely have demonstrated that economic factors were impacting the decision making of the mobile provider's prospective customers. The presidential election that occurred during that same period propelled other cultural, social, and religious factors that were impactful on some industries such as travel, the media, or hospitality, but would not have had an impact on the purchase of mobile phones. Situational factors may surround an entire social graph, but their impact on the purchase decision is not universal. And where they are, the impact can be further accelerated or diminished by other factors such as geography. For example, mobile providers' prospects in Detroit, the heart of the United States' automobile industry that was almost obliterated during this time period, would have seen the economic situational factor impact them with greater severity than, say, prospects in New York City or Los Angeles.

Frankly, many monitoring software platforms can analyze sentiment around global situational factors, but we need to go one step further. Is that fear of spending due to economic factors between 2007 and 2009 impacting the purchase decision of all products equally, in all geographies? How would the prospect's reluctance to spend money impact a consumer considering leaving his current cellular service provider, if at all? Natural language processing would be deployed to identify patterns in conversations around a target group, a set of products, or where the consumer is in the purchase life cycle to help answer that question. This final data set provides even greater context around decision making at specific times and in specific geographies that will support the creation of more responsive influence marketing campaigns, discussed in the next chapter.

What has to be achieved in this stage is an understanding of the current cultural, social, economic, and political biases (to name just a few) of the audience that is being profiled. During a recession, how does the lack of disposable income impact the purchase choices for specific products in different geographies? Similarly, during a presidential election period, how do political rhetoric and debate impact the consumer's decision-making process? Be it for confirmation or predictive search, such analysis is required to determine how—if at all—external situational factors impact the decision-making processes of specific groups of people. The key for analytics is to look beyond the specific product conversation to the nature and tone of all the conversations the target group displays.

Managing Influence Paths Through Social Customer Relationship Management Software

Now that we've developed a baseline profile of target customers, and the people and factors that impact their purchase decisions at different purchase stages, we need to consider how we apply the model to the wider audience in the short and long term. In the next chapter we discuss predicting these models, but we must first discuss how a business can apply the lessons learned here to proactively and reactively manage an influence program using this blueprint.

We must understand what we've done: By reverse engineering the influence path from decision maker to the influencer and the various factors that impact it, we've identified a path(s) that a recommendation or brand message can traverse from the macro-influencer to the micro-influencer that has an improved chance at generating the desired action with the right consumer at the right time. However, this path is simply a blueprint based on a profiled target group. Applying it to the larger audience in real-time creates a new set of challenges.

The solution to this challenge can be found in a new breed of social software being introduced into the market such as Nimble, an advanced customer relationship management software that combines contact management, unified communications, activity management, and social listening into a sales and marketing workflow that enables businesses to translate social contacts into actionable and measurable engagement. Such tools are critical to the success of the influence marketing methodology outlined in this book because they can apply the target audience profiles acquired against the business's entire contact database to generate campaign lists for influence targeting. Outbound campaigns, including trigger-based communications, can be configured to engage based on a match to the contact's profile, whom they're connected to inside the organization and out, or how closely their tracked conversations match the linguistic maps created.

"As businesspeople and marketers, we continue to live in isolated silos," states Jon Ferrara, CEO of Nimble. "The demands to engage with customers across multiple, disparate channels have only served to hinder communications, not enable them." This is the reason that Ferrara, who founded Goldmine, the first fully integrated CRM solution, invented Nimble. Where most social software platforms attempt to aggregate multiple social conversations into one screen, Nimble combines social conversations with contact profiles and traditional communication channels such as email, and applies marketing workflow and predictive analytics to the data. The methodology we outline in this book can become taxing on a business's resources if a social software such as Nimble is not deployed.

In addition, solutions such as these can be configured to proactively create, when synced with a monitoring application like Sysomos or PulseAnalytics, the sales funnel by seeking social personas that meet the criteria set in the linguistics map or newly imported contacts entered directly into the CRM. Based on the data input or the context of the social conversation, it can determine where in the purchase life cycle every new contact is and automatically assigns the contact to an influence campaign.

Finally, since the program tracks outbound marketing activity across online and offline channels, real-time responses to influence marketing efforts can be measured and the results appended in real time. For example, the combined social monitoring solution can help identify changes in communication patterns that would indicate a shift in situational factors or a movement along the purchase life cycle. In other cases, tracking a purchase transaction in the Social CRM's activity management or contact profile, and comparing it to the influence marketing campaign the contact has been engaged in, provides real-time measures of success or failure that aid in managing future engagements and improving the return on investment.

References

Obitko, M. 2007. *Translations between Ontologies in Multi-Agent Systems.* Ph.D. dissertation, Czech Technical University in Prague.

8

Managing Social Influence Paths

We start this chapter with this marketing advice: *Reach the right person with the right message at the right time.* Solid advice offered in many marketing books, so why include it in this one? Aside from the fact it bears repeating, the concept has been given renewed importance in social media and influence marketing. Since the advent of database marketing, marketers have been professing a shift in focus from the "reach and frequency" strategy of the mass-media advertising days to the more modern "connections and relationships" model enabled by technology and digital platforms. Today, as influence marketing becomes more popular, it seems that marketers are reverting to the reach and frequency concept. Specifically, we're referring to the practice of measuring a person's influence in social media by their number of followers and online interactions around specific topics. We're not criticizing marketers or technology providers for taking an old approach; the practice of influence marketing is still in its infancy, and few understand how to connect the concept of influence to financial transactions—or if it's even possible. However, influence marketing must progress forward if it's to succeed at impacting the business's bottom line. It must move beyond its reliance on volume and frequency of engagement to context and relationships.

Influence, as a marketing discipline, was formalized by public relations experts such as Daniel Edelman, who connected the visibility of celebrity with an increase in brand awareness. As referenced in Chapter 2, "Influence and the Human Psyche," Edelman was a pioneer in identifying and monetizing the power of an influencer over the public's perception of a brand by attempting to match celebrity with influence. This was the first stage of influence marketing, the assertion of mass influence through celebrity endorsement. For example, when the California wine industry turned to Edelman in 1966 to promote its products nationwide, he chose celebrity Vincent Price as its national spokesman. The choice was seen as a genius move by the media and marketing professionals, not because of Price's popularity but due to the new channels that his popularity provided access to. That same year, Price was booked to appear on *The Tonight Show*, the wildly popular late-night television program, which extended the wine industry's reach to a new channel and an even wider audience.

This practice continues today, as evidenced by the massive Accenture billboards erected in airports across the world that feature golf legend Tiger Woods. Even with Woods' very public troubles, his recognition is being used to elevate the awareness of certain brands, albeit less frequently. Supermodels, the go-to spokespeople for fashion and beauty products in the 1980s, were replaced by television and movie celebrities in the mid-1990s because the public saw them as more relatable. Moving into the 2000s, marketers, realizing the power of peer-to-peer recommendations, continued their move away from celebrities. One of the best examples of this shift is The Dove Campaign for Real Beauty, which was a marketing/public relations campaign that used everyday women in advertising designed to celebrate the natural physical variation embodied by all women.

Web 2.0 technologies introduced a disruptive force in brand-consumer communications, which changed the nature of influence for marketers and brands. Referencing Malcolm Gladwell's *The Tipping Point*, Jonny Bentwood at Edelman Public Relations confirmed the shift in how influence was now seen and measured in his article "The Influence Tipping Point"[1] in November 2012 in which he states, "We are at a wonderful tipping point in the business of influence analytics. For the first time ever, sociology and technology are colliding enabling us to identify the influence type of an individual by the patterns of their online behavior."

Arguably, the second stage in influence marketing's evolution, or the focus on identifying and scoring the influence of people engaged in social media channels, was ushered in by the development of social media-based influence scoring platforms such as PeerIndex and Kred. Azeem Azhar, president and CEO of social influence scoring platform PeerIndex, in an interview for this book stated "our current hypothesis is that people persuade each other to do things and buy things, and that people influence each other" more than celebrities. Aware that peer-to-peer and brand-to-customer communications were shifting to digital channels—and the disruptive factors that would make brand messages more difficult to target— these companies built technology based on the reach and amplification marketing model: Identify who has the biggest audience and engaged following across social channels and you identify who holds the greatest opportunity to influence other people.

Until now, influence marketing has been centered around the people exerting influence and their power to amplify a message to a large audience; in other words, brand amplification. A person's influence score, the size of his or her audience, and their advocacy of a brand on social channels has, for the most part, only been connected to purchase decisions anecdotally.

Influenced by David Ogilvy, the man many call The Father of Advertising, we believe that brand amplification does not provide the measurement and proof that a business's executive demands, nor the results clients expect. Ogilvy built his reputation and success on the principle that the function of advertising is to sell and that successful advertising for any product is based on information about its consumer.[2]

This principle has been the guiding sentiment in our efforts to move influence marketing from a promotional vehicle to a measurable sales acquisition program. Demands by marketing and business executives are pushing the practice of influence marketing towards its third evolution. Since Chapter 5, "Situational Influence: A New Model for a New Era," we've been setting the stage for what we believe is the next stage, a shift in focus from "reach and frequency" to "connections and relationships." Further, the expectation will be that influence-based marketing efforts will measurably impact the decision-making process of consumers at various stages of the purchase life cycle and be judged by the direct purchase results, not the size of the influencer's amplification. Referencing the influence paths we reverse-engineered in the last chapter, this chapter will continue to build the blueprint for this third phase by demonstrating how we can identify—and connect—the macro- and micro-influencer combinations that are most likely to impact those purchase decisions.

Emotional Contagions

We can convert influence marketing from brand to sales conversion when we understand the impact of local, personal connections over global, impersonal connections. A prime example was illustrated in the December 2012 Telenor Group study that sought to uncover who influenced a customer's mobile phone decisions. The Telenor Group is a global mobile operator boasting close to 150 million mobile subscribers, so it's clear why understanding the relationship between influence and purchase decisions is important; a 1% increase in sales for a company this size is a sizable impact on the business's revenue. Telenor Group's customer analysis discovered that if exactly one of its customer's friends had an iPhone, the chance that its customer would buy an iPhone was 14 times higher than if none of her friends owned one.[3] It confirmed the previously anecdotal belief that the likelihood of someone buying an iPhone is proportional to the number of people in a person's network who also had iPhones.

The concept of "emotional contagion," which references the public's tendency to "catch and spread" the feeling and associated behavior of those they're in close proximity to[4] has become an important aspect of influence marketing. The theory of emotional contagion among peers allows marketers to develop better predictive behavioral models. For example, if one or more of your friends has an iPhone, the likelihood that you'll buy an iPhone is 2X the baseline. If two or more of your friends have an iPhone, it is 5X the baseline, and so on.

Emotional Contagion

> The public's tendency to "catch and spread" the feeling and resulting behavior of those with whom they're in close contact.

By mapping the connections between the decision maker and his inner circle at different life cycle stages, a marketer can leverage the social and demographic properties of the group to design communications that transfer emotional contagion across members. Emotional marketing and messaging are important considerations in influence marketing, and especially when engaging micro-influencers. Negative events and sentiment, for example, elicit stronger and more immediate emotional and behavioral responses than those deemed positive or even neutral by those engaged in a conversation. This is a principle understood all too well by political strategists who often use negative "smear campaigns" to galvanize support around a candidate who is not generating an emotional connection with his or her constituents. Similarly, the energy exemplified in the communication has been shown to be directly proportional to the viral effect of the emotional contagion among the community.[5] In other words, the level of enthusiasm, passion, or emotion perceived in the public commentary of an influencer has a direct impact on how often an audience will share that message with their peers.

In our model, the micro-influencers surrounding the decision maker are most impacted by the emotional contagion described. Since micro-influencers are influenced by their macro counterparts, the strategy of choosing—and engaging—macro-influencers who can create emotional contagion with smaller groups is critical.

Rethinking Macro-Influencers

The last few chapters discussed the importance of micro-influencers and how they impact the decision making of prospective customers. Where do the macro-influencers play into this methodology? Are they even necessary? Why not simply engage the micro-influencers directly? Certainly, this is an option, but as with the decision maker, connecting to the many smaller groups of micro-influencers across the purchase life cycle is difficult, time-consuming, and costly. The purpose of reengineering the influence paths in Chapter 7, "Reversing the Social Influence

Model," was to identify the nature and makeup of the groups that have the greatest direct impact over the purchase decision. That information allows us to now reengage the macro-influencers with a more targeted and measurable focus.

Earlier, we established that broad amplification by macro-influencers was not an effective tool to drive measurable sales conversions, yet here we are attempting to identify and solicit them; we've come full circle. Influence marketing is evolving to a stage where specific transactions and reactions can be—and must be—linked to the influencer's outreach. We've explained how to identify the micro-influencers needed to make that connection, but that does not mean macro-influencers are to be removed from the equation or devalued. In fact, their power and utility may finally be realized by those seeking measurable results.

The process identified for mapping the connections between decision makers and micro-influencers can be mimicked to identify the relationships between micro-influencers and macro-influencers. The key, however, is to not focus on the public scoring of the individuals but on the context of their connections and the strength of their relationships. It's the qualitative nature of these connections that enable marketers to better identify key macro-influencers who will drive the required conversations among micro-influencers.

As illustrated in Figure 8.1, the messages broadcast by macro-influencers may reach the prospect's social graph but not necessarily her inner circle of micro-influencers. We discovered how to identify the typical micro-influencers of target customer profiles at different stages of the life cycle. The next step is to identify which macro-influencers are most capable of influencing that specific community.

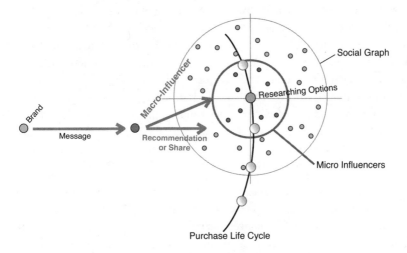

Figure 8.1   *Refocusing macro-influencers*

PeerIndex's Azeem Azhar stated, "There's no real way for companies today, at a large scale, to identify who are the nodes that are more likely to spread messages around given categories." Given that his business reportedly identifies who influences who, and on what topic, one might think he's discounting the value of his own firm, but the opposite is true. "The methodology [described in this book] is a thoughtful and intense consulting and research effort around a specific situation that a client or company might have. It's not a generalized solution. A generalized solution has to be done on a wider scale." Azhar is suggesting that his, and other similar social scoring services, provide a more broad service than the methodology we're presenting here. PeerIndex and similar offerings are platforms from which software solution providers (such as social CRMs) can acquire vast amounts of social engagement data, manipulate and analyze that data, and, by overlaying it with localized situational factors and transactional data, deliver a measurable influence marketing strategy.

He makes a good point; as more and more businesses attempt to acquire social intelligence from online data—and the influence marketing solutions based on it—providers must be able to store and analyze massive data sets, something most marketing teams and niche influence marketing tools don't have the capacity to do. Azhar sees his solution as the warehouse for that data and broader, generalized campaigns. In his own words, "if you're looking for the 7 people most important to me right now, PeerIndex isn't for you. If you're looking for the top 70,000, look to us. That's where PeerIndex is and where we're going."

Business brands seeking to drill down to a more finite and targeted influence marketing campaign, such as those presented in this book, can use social software services like Nimble's social software to absorb large data sets of people that tools like PeerIndex has flagged as influential on a particular subject matter. Next, they can overlay the personal and transactional data tracked internally to further define who their prospective decision makers are and which micro-influence communities are closest to them. This creates a multitiered ecosystem of interrelated solutions; top tier platforms scan conversations and profiles engaged in online conversations and feed it to mid-tier, niche solution providers, that append additional personal and transactional data sets to augment the data. They, in turn, allow marketing teams to self-manage responsive influence marketing campaigns on more local levels and measure activity back to bottom line impact.

These infrastructure and business relationships are already forming; Salesforce.com, Nimble, and Hootsuite are just some of the mid-tier solutions that are appending top tier social influence scoring data to a user's social profile within their applications. For the time being, the social influence scores appended to contacts' profiles are only actionable by human review and intuition, but as text analytic technology advances and becomes more affordable, this will change.

Social influence scoring platforms have a massive challenge to overcome: the sheer volume of social conversations and the variances in how that data can be interpreted based on channels, communities, and geographies; the relationships among people and the context of the conversations analyzed are nearly impossible for them to gauge. As a result, they represent context as general topics or areas of interests such as sports, technology, health, and so on. They're building a social graph of all the people engaged in social media, much like Google has done for content across websites. That is advantageous as long as we understand the limitations, we can focus on how to use them well. The general categorization of influence identified by these groups could be sufficient to determine which sub-communities they might impact.

Consider a micro-influence community found to have influence over a segment of a big box retailer's prospect base: college students and their parents. Based on the linguistic mapping process we described in Chapter 7, we learn that this group is comprised of sports enthusiasts with a specific focus on college football and financial aid. It's a niche audience with a high-return potential but requires more localized data to properly address and impact. Identifying the macro-influencers who have sway with these micro-communities is the opportunity for solutions such as PeerIndex and Kred. When managed properly, macro-influencers can insert the required content and information into the smaller communities that the retailer's marketing team and social CRM software can work on converting. Kred, for example, offers a consulting service that creates customized queries of the larger social graph, which can help better filter larger groups of individuals that may more closely match the profiles of the micro-influencers, including the removal of competitive brands and their employees or fake profiles. Further, they can provide additional customized analytics to remove people whose scores—and thus perceived influence—are artificially inflated because they cheated the system.

The macro-influencers identified in this process may not have a measurable impact on direct purchases at the store level, but they can insert the sufficient social proof and commentary among the micro-influencer's discussions. Using the methodology explored in this chapter, the marketing team can more easily connect macro- and micro-influencers to influence—and track—purchase decisions.

Mapping the Influence Paths

Managing and tracking the interconnected influence paths between a business and its prospects requires the assistance of technology, even for smaller firms. Luckily a growing number of software applications are being released to assist businesses of every size with this evolving industry. We introduce some of them in Chapter 10, "The Future of Influence Marketing;" however, for the purposes of this chapter we're focusing on two social CRM programs: Nimble and oneQube.

While it doesn't classify the solution as an "influence marketing platform," New York-based Internet Media Labs recently launched what we believe will be the future of influence marketing technology. oneQube, a social software and enterprise collaboration tool, looks at all the connections within a business's social graph (and beyond) and converts them into an actionable marketing database. In a nutshell, through a combination of natural language processing, user-defined queries, and manual categorization, the solution can "slice and dice" the conversation, profile, and relationship data points collected to highlight the most direct influence path from business brands to macro-influencers, from macro- to micro-influencers, and from micro-influencers to the decision makers.

The typical keyword searches performed by some platforms on channels like Twitter are too thin and too narrow to identify the key relationships in influence marketing, or to predict the most effective influence paths. oneQube found a solution to this challenge by initiating a "smart bot" that seeks, collects, and stores additional information about the people identified based on the initial linear keyword searches. oneQube's lead data scientist, Eric Weissman, calls it "the drill," because it drills down into the target's social and digital data across multiple digital sites to acquire extra information and context required for better marketing analysis.

Now imagine the power of a solution that uses a robot to find and analyze the full digital footprint of the author of a tweet found on Twitter. The smart bot searches for other networks and sites where the contact is engaged with others in open social conversations. It identifies whether the user has a blog or whether she guest blogs on other sites. It identifies whether the same user has profiles on other social networks such as Google+, Facebook, Quora, or LinkedIn and whether she is a member of any communities within those channels. Next, it determines whether the user participates in any other open forums or group discussions on association, business, or community websites. Along the way, the bot scans for content and sentiment within the conversations occurring on these sites, the subject matter of the communities, as well as the metadata and inbound links found within those websites and blogs. Essentially, it is mapping a contextual digital and social footprint around a single prospect.

As the bot identifies the contact's digital profiles, it collects any personal information the user includes, such as age, gender, email, address, or phone numbers. It seeks and tags information that might indicate employment status, current and past employers, and associated job titles. Subcontext is also analyzed to identify whether the contact is employed by a business, self-employed, or an affiliate marketer. By appending all this social data to a contact's profile in a social CRM we start to build a detailed view of the person's social graph, but this is not yet enough. If applicable, the scanning of the contact's profile can be programmed to include a customized linguistics map as described in Chapter 7, to pinpoint where a business's target customers are within the prepurchase life cycle.

To complete the profile, a two-pronged strategy is deployed to identify other people connected to the prospect in order to map the "waves" of impact and influence. First, the contact's connections are identified across the various social channels such as Google+ or Twitter, people who commented on the contact's blog, and so on. This includes the identification of key profile data points to determine/match the relationship this person has to the target profile, such as her employer, where she lives, and so on. The second part of this extended scan includes the use of text analytics to identify the subject matter and nature of the conversations that occur most frequently between the prospect and her social contacts.

While this scan is taking place—and depending on the nature of the campaign—the prospect's personal social graph is being filtered. This scan identifies those social profiles that belong to a unique person (not a business) or those with more than "X" interactions in "Y" number of days (X and Y determined based on the campaign's strategy). The result is a fine-tuned interconnected map of people based on subject, relationships, and context. The map continues to monitor and analyze the prospect's conversations, reach, and audience's reaction to the prospect's commentary. This methodology provides the foundation to monitor and manage influence paths among various social graphs.

The oneQube solution has already made great advances toward this methodology by including the "search and tagging" analysis and natural language processing required. "The systems that are used in influence marketing today are built on yesterday's methodologies," says oneQube's Weissman. "We see an opportunity to put something into the marketing industry that is based on tomorrow's methodologies and take features that exist in a lot of one-off applications (monitoring, engagement, collaboration) and apply the use of Internet robotics, artificial intelligence, and natural language processing to provide a solution that can achieve this."

Appinions (an influence marketing platform discussed in Chapter 10) expands the collection of data points one step further by acquiring select transcripts from traditional media sources such as newspapers, magazines, television, and/or radio broadcast. Appinions scans and appends the people and conversations or opinions expressed within those channels to a contact's profile. This answers the frequent criticism levied against social influence scoring platforms that their data is based solely in online engagements.

As of the publishing date of this book, we've not identified a single software program that naturally supports the methodology we're proposing, but certainly oneQube is very close. Based on the information shared with us, it's only a matter of time before oneQube achieves this goal. Similarly, Appinions is moving in the right direction by adding, among other innovative features, offline content to its data sets and advanced natural language processing. Further, by removing the public influence scoring layer, it has eliminated the issue of gamed social engagement by those seeking to artificially inflate their influence scores. Nimble is also moving its software in the right direction by offering a familiar communications interface that suggests sales, marketing, and customer service activity based on the social data collected and analyzed. Further, Nimble has synced email communications with social engagement activity for even greater micro-analysis of prospects and their social graphs.

With target profiles and life cycle stages as our baseline, the methodology outlined in this section establishes a foundation for active monitoring and updating of the influence paths between brands and the customers (and all points in between). This customized, interconnected social graph becomes a "living entity" from which marketers can also predict influence paths based on real-time response or by applying different situational factors that may interfere with the normal flow of communications. The next few sections explore some of these options.

Predicting Influence Paths

Once the target audience's social graphs have been mapped, we can start to analyze the live conversations occurring between specific groups of people to manage the influence paths and possibly predict where new paths may emerge or, based on different situational factors, how current paths may change.

Eric Weissman shared the story of an experiment he ran, which became one of the key knowledge sets that helped form oneQube's functionality. He created a program that would scan Twitter every 5 seconds to identify "trending topics" (keywords that receive the most mentions by Twitter users during a set period of time). In real-time, he compared the data with external situational factors to determine whether there was a consistent relationship between online dialogue and common external factors. He cross referenced the geography of those tweeting the trending keywords and mapped them against the current weather conditions and stock market activity in those cities at the moment the keywords were trending. His study identified specific subtrends forming within clusters of people and between different clusters, based on common changes in external situational factors.

What we're beginning to understand is that positive correlations exist between situational factors and the flow of social communication between people and among groups of people. Understanding what those situational factors are and how they impact a brand's influence paths is critical for businesses that want to use influence marketing as a measurable sales tool. As illustrated in Figure 8.2, even if a brand message hits the right customer, the situational and decision-making factors detailed in Chapter 5 and Chapter 6, "The Consumer Decision-Making Process," may result in an undesirable action by the recipient.

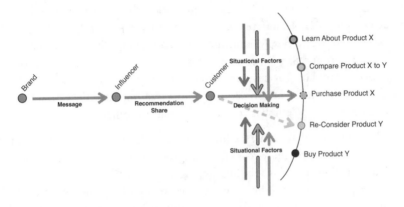

Figure 8.2 *Understanding situational factors*

It doesn't help that social networks and the digital space as a whole have become so convoluted, not just with people, content, and conversations, but with duplicate accounts across multiple platforms, fake profiles, bots, and brand accounts. The social web has become so unmanageable that most businesses and software just can't know which posts and users to prioritize, which query should go to which campaign for best resolution, and so on.

This is why the mapped social graph described above is so important; it creates contextual pathways between people that can be monitored and analyzed based on changing external stimuli. To illustrate this, let's look at a case study of a high-end fashion designer that sought to earn a greater market share across the United States. Using the linguistics map processing, the marketing agency monitored conversations over a 30-day period among people tagged in specific geolocations, including Los Angeles, San Diego, Dallas/Ft. Worth, Miami, New York City, San Francisco, and Chicago.

Using a combination of keyword search, sentiment analysis, and natural language processing, the agency identified 1,000 target customers in each city and, by extending the search to supporting social sites, created deeper profiles of each target prospect. Further, the agency mapped the prospect's extended social graphs to determine which people were within the prospect's micro-influencer communities based on context and frequency of communications around the target keywords. This influence map became the baseline for the marketing team's research. Each was siloed by its respective geography and a secondary analysis was performed to assess the economic, cultural, political, and social situational factors at play in each.

In each geographic grouping, the team determined distinct combinations of external factors. For example, different economic factors impacted the decision-making process in the Los Angeles, Miami, and New York groups than in the Dallas/Ft. Worth, Chicago, and San Diego communities. While decision makers in New York, Miami, and Los Angeles were found to be impacted by similar economic factors, they charted differently in cultural factors that impacted their brand perception and propensity to purchase one brand versus the other.

Over the course of six months, the brand launched three distinct blogger and media outreach campaigns across all the targeted markets. The content, theme, and calls to action embedded in the campaigns were similar in each effort. The marketing team monitored the conversations among each group separately to determine the impact of their efforts across different geographies. For example, did the conversation among those tagged in the "awareness" life cycle stage change to reflect they were considering the target brand? Did those in the "conversion" life cycle stage indicate they had purchased the product through their social channels? The changes or movement of the prospects from one stage to the next were then compared across geographies to understand how the various situational factors impacted the success or failure of various campaigns.

The resulting analysis provided insights into the impact that certain situational factors had on purchase decisions. Those lessons allowed monitoring software to be updated with additional data points that helped predict how certain communities would respond to different types of campaigns. Similarly, as the external stimuli changed within each of the subgroups, the marketing team could proactively change the tone or content of outbound communications to counter their effects and keep the influence path on track. This process allowed marketers to treat different micro-communities uniquely under the umbrella of one influence marketing strategy, effectively cutting through the localized situational factors and driving a measurable impact.

Purposeful Influence Marketing

Influence marketing for general branding and product awareness to large masses of people can be useful as a supporting strategy, but without a sales acquisition and conversion effort, results are hard to measure. There are two types of marketers (and related marketing strategies) in business: the performance marketer and the branding marketer. The performance marketer asks the question: "Did I generate sales?" This strategy seeks measurable responses and transactional data tied directly to specific marketing efforts both in the short- and long-term.

The brand marketer asks the question, "Did I increase our Net Promoter Score (NPS)?" or "Did I increase the positive sentiment associated with the brand?" NPS, created by Fred Reichheld, Bain & Company, and Satmetrix, is a measure of the loyalty and advocacy generated from positive customer relationships.[6] The creators of the NPS process suggest that there's a positive correlation between a high score and the sales/profit growth of a business. Yet critics argue that too many factors are at play in the long-term success of a brand to definitively attribute positive sentiment to specific sales growth.

Net Promoter Score

A measure of customer loyalty and advocacy (positive or negative) that is generated from the customer's perceived relationship and experience with a business.

Pundits have suggested that performance marketing seeks results in 30 days, whereas brand marketing looks for the results in 300 days; however this is a misrepresentation of the former. Performance marketing simply applies sales goals and metrics to the practice of marketing and advertising, which can be measured in the long-term as well as the short-term. In reality, both are required for a business to succeed. A combination of brand and performance marketing will be the most effective to ensure success. The influence marketing methodology presented here supports the use and measurement of both practices because it monitors and tracks all these data points to a single customer profile, which—when mapped to the life time value of a customer—highlights the overall impact on the business's bottom line.

But before we can speak about measurement, we must consider engagement strategies. Continuing with the fashion designer case study we started in the previous section, let's uncover how the marketing team identified where customers were within the purchase life cycle and how that data drove more strategic, sales-focused influence marketing campaigns. The linguistics mapping process identified three distinct opportunities common across all markets, which might impact the fashion brand's sales funnel and sales. Table 8.1 provides a summary of these groupings. *Note: For the purposes of this book, Brand X represents the fashion brand the marketing team was hired to promote; Brand Y and Brand Z are competitors.*

Table 8.1 Summary of Target Prospect Influence Marketing Opportunities

	Life Cycle Phase	Summary Description
1	Awareness	Frequent discussions with positive sentiment around high fashion related brands but with no mention of Brand X. Lack of keywords and phrases that would infer an immediate need or propensity to purchase.
2	Consideration	Frequent discussions around high fashion related brands, where positive sentiment is shown for competitive brands and negative sentiment toward Brand X. Weighting on words and phrases highlighted actions: comparison, information seeking, status seeking. (Note: This is just one of sentiment combinations used in search filters.)
3	Conversion	Frequent discussions around high fashion related brands, with generally positive sentiment around Brand X and competitive brands. Heavy weighting on words and phrases denoted to infer urgency in demand or purchase.

We can argue the importance of branding efforts, yet moving customers along the purchase life cycle from awareness to consideration and from consideration to conversion is the measurable effort that business executives look for. Referencing the data acquired, as summarized in Table 8.1, we summarize two of the performance-based influence marketing strategies deployed.

Building Awareness

The prospective customers segmented in the first category were selected because they posted commentary and/or engaged in online conversations across social channels that met specific criteria in the linguistics map search. The criteria selected was based on identifying people who were interested in high fashion but were not mentioning Brand X or the desire to purchase the product in the short term. A *simplified* version of the Boolean and linguistic map queries used follows.

Select social mentions:

- Where geography of author *equals* "Los Angeles" *or* "San Diego" *or* "Dallas/Ft. Worth" *or* "Miami" *or* "New York City" *or* "San Francisco" *or* "Chicago."
- Keywords *include* "Brand Y" or "Brand Z" and "Fashion" or "Retail."
- Keywords *do not include* "Brand X."
- Preference shown to commentary that *does not include* "Looking for" *or* "Buying" *or* "In market" *or* "Gala" *or* "Party."

The goal in this category was to drive awareness of Product X but also to track how many of these target customers could be moved to the "consideration" stage. As outlined previously, the extended social graphs of each target individual within each group were mapped. Among the New York and Miami subgroups, it was discovered that the micro-influencers were contacts tagged as family and friends within the social networks Twitter, Pinterest, and Facebook. The smart bot searching and indexing the prospects'—and their social graphs'—profiles also identified that the majority of those conversations were occurring through mobile devices and that the commentary on those networks were being posted via social plug-ins on fashion magazine websites and blogs.

To feed the micro-influencer community, the marketing team first looked for macro-influencers connected to fashion magazines and blogs versus those who simply had high social influence scores in "fashion." Second, because the majority of the conversations and posts originated via mobile devices, part of the content strategy seeded through the influencers included a newly created mobile app featuring daily video snippets of Brand X's fashion show with video commentary by selected macro-influencers.

This strategy was successful at increasing the awareness among micro-influencers because it was highly targeted in content, technology, and platform. The increased brand mentions among the micro community fueled increased brand mentions by prospects, which was measured by the context of their subsequent online conversations.

Competitor or Trend Disruption

The second group was associated with the "consideration" stage because their conversations included keywords—or multiple words used in specific combinations—that inferred they were comparing brands while speaking highly of the competitor's brand. Again, a *simplified* version of the Boolean and linguistic map query is shown here.

Select social mentions:

- Where geography of author *equals* "Los Angeles" *or* "San Diego" *or* "Dallas/Ft. Worth" *or* "Miami" *or* "New York City" *or* "San Francisco" *or* "Chicago."
- Keywords *include* "Brand Y" *and/or* "Brand Z" *and/or* "Brand Z" *and* "Fashion" *or* "Retail."
- Sentiment *equals* "*negative*" for "Brand X" *and* "positive" for "Brand Y" *or* "Brand Z."

- Primary preference shown to commentary that *includes* "Need it Now" *and/or* "gotta have" *and/or* "next month" and so on.

- Secondary preference shown to commentary that *includes* "Looking for" *and/or* "Buying" *and/or* "In market" *and/or* "Gala" *and/or* "Party."

- Preference shown where gender *equals* "female" versus "male" *or* "brand."

This campaign was a subcategory of those included in the "consideration" stage. It was designed to identify women speaking positively about the competition but negatively about Brand X. This filter was further segmented by the urgency of need as represented by the priority weighting on terms and phrases that referenced a time frame or desire to purchase. The goal was to seek a group of potential customers in the buying cycle but likely not purchasing Brand X.

The influence marketing efforts in this campaign were undertaken by a community management team tasked with strategically inserting themselves into the conversations occurring online to disrupt the competitors' influence paths. The team prepared a listing of articles, videos, and photography produced by the macro-influencers identified as influential over the prospect's micro-influencer. They inserted the content into online conversations, ensuring they identified themselves as brand representatives and attributed the macro-influencers who created the content. By manually highlighting the connection between positive brand sentiment and high-profile influencers to the micro-influencers, the community management team changed the tone of the conversation within this target community. They were able to convert 34% of those expressing negative brand sentiments to positive mentions. This campaign was an offensive strategy to convert sentiment and drive sales, yet from a defensive position, this methodology is required to offset any influence being exerted by competitors or brand detractors.

Adaptive Influence Marketing

The case study outlined in the previous section was a calculated, planned campaign. Using social CRM solutions such as Nimble or oneQube can provide the opportunity to create more responsive or adaptive campaigns. Be it through pre-defined workflows, trigger-based instruction to third-party software or manual monitoring of campaign results, these tools allow for real-time management of the brand's influence paths.

For example, managing prospects through the presales life cycle becomes possible via the processes enabled by these tools. The target audience profiles (explained in Chapter 7) become the checkpoint that social CRM software can continuously cross-reference against the profiles of existing customers and new prospects entering the sales funnel. A prospect tagged in the "awareness" stage, because his online conversation inferred no awareness of the brand or current need, requires a different strategy than someone in the "consideration" stage who is considering a purchase and comparing brands. The former requires a push toward brand awareness and convincing that the prospect needs such a product. The latter requires convincing the prospect that one brand is a better choice than the alternatives. Natural language processing can identify when the awareness-stage prospect's conversations change to indicate he is now considering a purchase.

Social CRMs can be configured to send out email or text alerts to specific individuals so that immediate or short-term action can be taken as the prospect's social conversations change. Alternatively, these changes may initiate trigger-based actions within the system that automatically update the prospect's status or category, thus automatically changing the influence path monitored or the campaigns they're included in.

In addition, social CRMs provide the ability to track and append activity occurring on other platforms and websites, which provide greater analysis of real-time response to these campaigns. For example, a target prospect group influenced to visit a customized landing page can be tracked with the actions taken: site visited, links clicked, information shared, downloads completed, time on site, purchase shared, and so on. The data tracked is appended to the contact's profile and contrasted to the campaign's workflow so that real-time results can be viewed. These stats show the effectiveness of specific campaigns, targeting specific people or groups in various channels and geographies. The net result is a clear view of the influence paths that are working and those that are not.

oneQube provides business users the option to launch smart bots that scan social channels looking for specific content in social posts or profile updates, within specific time periods and/or for specific people, that would indicate specific actions were taken by the target audience. For example, an influence campaign created for a recording label that asked followers to listen to a specific album or track on Spotify, would feature a oneQube smart bot that identifies how many Spotify users posted an "I'm listening to..." message within their status updates and social posts or, for those whose Spotify accounts are synced with networks such as Facebook, automatically updated their status. This social intelligence provides the ability to create predictive models of how recommendations are most likely to influence peers' actions.

One option we've explored is the inclusion of personal URLs (PURLs) into the influence marketing path for an international financial services firm. A PURL is a unique and personalized web address created for a specific recipient, such as http://bobsmith.yoursite.com. The web page that the PURL directs the recipient to can be customized with specific content and calls to action based on who referred the site, who received the link, or a combination of the two. For this project, the corporation tasked us to increase the sale of specific retirement funds; however, the company had no direct relationship with the end customer. Its products were sold by a channel of independent investment brokerages and brokers.

A list of investment brokers was acquired, based on the size of the clientele, the perceived authority of their firms, and other factors. We distributed an invitation to that list of brokers inviting them to visit a personalized web page that featured the new products and what benefit it would have for their clients and their business. Based on the broker's profile, including the types of products they've previously sold or inquired about, the content and product offerings were personalized to increase the likelihood that they would react to the promotion. Each site provided a viral function, allowing the broker an option to create an on-demand personalized video and PURL for their clients to use as a social sales tool. Each client's PURL site gave them the choice to request more information about the investment product, purchase the investment, and/or invite others to do the same. As the site was shared, the PURL, the personalized video, and the product offerings would dynamically update to better reflect the needs of those in the exchange. For example, the promotion changed based on factors including the sender's profile, the recipient's profile, the actions taken on the site, whether the prospect was an existing client or nonclient, the geography of the recipient, and the relationship between the parties involved. Further, because the content shared was adapting to real-time transactions and database profiling, we could watch the influence paths in action and see where blocks were occurring and where we needed to make adjustments in real time.

Combining the customer-centric influence marketing methodology outlined in this book within the structure of a social CRM solution such as oneQube or Nimble provides a powerful sales and marketing resource. In effect, the influence paths between your brand and the decision maker become adaptive, with real-time results directing manual or automatic shifts in campaign tactics or communities targeted.

Measuring Influence Marketing

Dissecting the influence paths among your audience's social graph also provides the opportunity for improved reporting and success measurement. The influence scoring platforms that gained popularity throughout 2012 have struggled to demonstrate success measures because they could not be tied to transactional data. Further, their scope and reach was too broad and general to show any impact they had on moving the prospect along the purchase life cycle. That's not to suggest they had no impact, only that measurement based on influenced sales was very difficult to report. It invokes the branding versus performance marketing argument discussed earlier in this chapter.

"Currently, influence platforms calculate their scores and metrics based largely on social media interactions simply due to the fact that this data is most widely available," offers Ferenc Huszar, lead data scientist at PeerIndex. "I agree that one of the main goals of influence marketing should be to close the gap between social influence and actual sales figures or profit. This is certainly the long-term vision, and we already have taken steps to deliver on this vision." He highlights the demand on this industry to connect marketing actions to transactional reactions.

PeerIndex recently introduced a program called PeerPerk, which offers product samples from businesses to people who the PeerIndex software shows are active in social channels and are perceived to be influential over a large group within a specific subject matter. These people are offered products to try before the general public has the opportunity to buy them. If they like what they were sent, they're asked to share their thoughts online to help build awareness of the new offering and (hopefully) impact the product's sales. Because the target influencers are driven to their corporate website to claim the perks, PeerIndex is able to track which influencers are interested in what products. Even if the visitor doesn't qualify for the perk (her score is not high enough, she's not living in the right geography, she's not considered influential in that subject matter), the person can still share the information about the perk with her social channels via tweets or Facebook shares. As a result, PeerIndex can track how many people were driven to its site, viewed the perk's details, claimed the perk, or reshared it. The measurement and metrics driven are based on the waves of amplification that the campaign and the chosen influencers push across their social graphs, which is an important metric in brand marketing. However, it does not measure the direct impact on the sales funnel, which is an important metric for performance marketing and, increasingly, one demanded by senior executives responsible for budget allocation.

Huszar shared a substantial obstacle in connecting these two: "Brands and businesses each have their data on sales, but they are naturally reluctant to share this with anyone else. These precious data are locked within those companies, who often do not have the analytical expertise to analyze any increase in sales in the context of social influence. Moreover, brands often run multiple promotional campaigns simultaneously, and it is hard to attribute any single purchase to one of these campaigns." He's correct; you cannot expect a third-party software program to be accountable to sales metrics if the brand does not share that data.

The financial services case study shared in the previous section is an example of how these integrated efforts can demonstrate bottom line measurement of influence campaigns. Because the program was integrated with a client database—and tracked back to the individual's recorded activity—both branding and performance measurements were able to be tracked and measured. The adaptive marketing technology allowed us to track which influencers within the community were driving the greatest awareness of the investment offerings, the most interaction and dialogue, and whose amplification drove the highest conversion rate.

This is one of the reasons we created this methodology and why we promote the use of social CRM and social collaboration tools for businesses. Platforms such as PeerIndex and Kred are excellent sources for gauging large volumes of social interactivity, but are most useful to performance marketers and business executives when that data is connected to the local, micro-analysis and segmentation possible in social CRM software. Within these tools, their macro-influencers become another data set linked to the customer's social graph that, along with the customer's transaction history, measures short-term and lifetime value. Understanding and segregating the short-term and lifetime value of a customer enables us to deploy the Four Ms of Influence Marketing, which is a core segment of any successful influence marketing campaign.

Endnotes

1. Bentwood, J. November 29, 2012. "The Influence Tipping Point." Edelman digital blog. http://www.edelman.com/post/the-influence-tipping-point/.

2. Ogilvy, D.. *Ogilvy on Advertising* (Vintage, 1985).

3. Telenor Group. December 2012. "iPhone Users Are Contagious." www.telenor.com/news-and-media/.../iphone-users-are-contagious/.

4. Hatfield, E., J. T. Cacioppo, and R. L. Rapson. 1993. "Emotional Contagion." *Current Directions in Psychological Science.*

5. Schoenewolf, G. 1990. "Emotional Contagion: Behavioral Induction in Individuals and Groups." *Modern Psychoanalysis.*

6. Reichheld, F. December 2003. "One Number You Need to Grow." *Harvard Business Review.*

9

The Four Ms of Influence Marketing

For more than 50 years, marketers have adhered to the Four Ps of marketing, as laid out by E. Jerome McCarthy:

- **Product**—Goods or services desired by a customer.
- **Price**—The determining factor of a company's success in marketing, since the price defines how many products are sold and whether the market is willing to sustain that price.
- **Promotion**—The umbrella under which all other marketing and promotional endeavors fall, including public relations, advertising, sales, and personal relationship selling.
- **Place**—The distribution channels and how easy it is for a potential customer to access your product or service.

Three other disciplines can also be added to the 4P mix—physical evidence, which relates to a physical storefront, signage, and branding; people, as in the company's employees and front-facing staff; and process, which aligns the marketing machine with the rest of the company. However, while these three additional disciplines are important, they generally don't make up the marketing mix as laid out by the Four Ps.

While the Four Ps have helped shape business success for companies for more than half a century, today's online-savvy businesses and influencer marketing campaigns are increasingly marginalizing the guiding principles behind the Four Ps. Now it's less about promotion and more about peer-to-peer or person-to-person; it's less about place and more about relevance and context. Without relevance to the audience and the context in which that relevance is presented, a message or campaign struggles to be heard, as we saw with the Four A's—audience, acceptance, application, and amplification—in Chapter 4, "The Current Influence Model and Social Scoring."

That doesn't mean the Four Ps will become irrelevant—far from it. Good marketing will always need strong strategy and tactic building, and any business that gets the mix of product, price, promotion, and place right will be rewarded with increased sales, customer acquisition, and loyalty. The difference now is that the consumer is more agile than ever before, and not in front of a TV screen where a marketing or advertising message could be continuously blared until the message was received. Digital consumers are the new *now*, and for brands and marketers to get in front of them, newer and more deeply integrated tactics and strategies are needed.

The Changing Nature of Predictive Influence

In Chapter 8, "Managing Social Influence Paths," we looked at the various disruptive factors that can occur around a campaign involving influencers. As you can see in Figure 9.1, from the moment a message leaves a brand's marketing team to the moment it creates an action by the customer—from downloading a white paper to signing up for a newsletter to making an actual purchase—it is highly probable that the message will be interrupted.

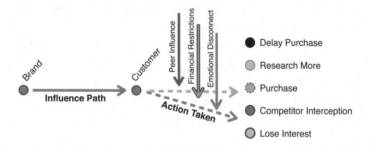

Figure 9.1   *Situational factors of the purchase decision*

Before social media and our ability to research and crowdsource information about a company, service, or product, this path would have been minimally disruptive. Fewer choices in front of a consumer mean fewer ways to say no. Today, however, brands no longer have the luxury of being able to monopolize a customer's attention on the TV or radio, or in a daily newspaper or print magazine. Connected consumers multitask between their smartphones and their social network connections, and use their iPads or similar devices to browse stores and ecommerce review sites. They're tapped into 10 or more networks and sites simultaneously, as well as email, and have an attention span of seconds—try getting your full-page advertisement in front of that customer!

Because of this attention deficit, consumers now rely on individuals and peers they follow and trust to help them make a purchase decision, versus a paid media campaign that may or may not be seen by them. This is why influence marketing has become such a key part of the business ecosystem today. Given the choice of several hundred thousand dollars spent on generic targeting versus the same amount on a fully integrated campaign where the audience will be already receptive to the influencer sharing your message, where do you think the smart businesses are spending their money?

However, as many brands have discovered, it's not as easy as it sounds to create, manage, and measure an influencer campaign and integrate it into your other marketing tactics. In 2011, American Express launched its Be Inspired campaign. This was the first time the company had used social media specifically for a campaign. Set up to benefit The Prince's Trust charity in the United Kingdom, American Express pledged to donate the equivalent of $0.80 to the trust for every Facebook update or tweet that shared where the person posting the update found inspiration. At a special Be Inspired workshop, actor Kevin Spacey and other celebrities launched the campaign to an eager press and attentive audience. However, despite the inclusion of Hollywood "influencers" and the ability for anyone sharing his or her own inspiration to be seen by millions, the campaign was classed a failure in many circles.

Andy Field, codirector of Forest Fringe, a company that offers a creative collaboration space for artists and audiences, called the campaign "crushingly unimaginative...a complete lie"[1] while Andrew Seward, development team lead of international SMS gateway company Esendex tweeted, "I was inspired to be more... <END OF MESSAGE – AMEX PR CHARITY LIMIT REACHED>".[2] What should have been a great example of corporate giving and social media citizen influence turned into negative sentiment and criticism of American Express. The reason: American Express capped the amount it was going to donate to The Prince's Trust to just under $250,000 but didn't make that clear to the people taking part in the campaign. This meant that people could still be sharing American Express with their friends when there was no further need to, and many people saw Be Inspired as a questionable marketing promotion instead of a charitable cause, leading to the negativity around it in certain circles.

This kind of disruptive force can throw a brand's message off course and is just one of the reasons influence marketing continues to be misunderstood. It's also why brands continue to suffer from poor return, even when working with platforms that profess to offer true relevancy amidst social scores. When something as fluid as influence of any kind is narrowed down to a score based on how active someone is on social media, the truth of the matter is poor results *should* be expected. While critics of traditional media and marketing may point to the lack of analytics available to measure results, these campaigns always had the right audience in mind due to premarket strategy, focus groups, intelligent analysis of the marketplace, and more. The problem with some of the social scoring and influence measurement platforms currently on the market is they often don't have the right target audience to start with, which is why brands need to adapt their thinking to the Four Ms of Influence Marketing principle.

Understanding the Four Ms

During the writing of this book, we asked fans of our Facebook page whether they had purchased any product given away as a free Klout Perk, Kred Reward, or similarly promoted influence campaign. As you can see in Figure 9.2, the response reinforced our view that trying to "buy" promotion through nontargeted influence is doomed to fail from the start.

Figure 9.2 *Free perks and rewards do not encourage the purchase decision.*

What really stood out for us was that not one single person took advantage of a perk or reward every time they were offered one. For brand managers, this statement—as well as the overall results—should sound alarm bells, since the cost of partnering with social scoring platforms isn't inexpensive, and it's clear that the action of making a purchase simply isn't happening. Yet, as we shared in the opening chapter of the book with the MV-1 case study, influence marketing does work and does result in purchasing, but like any other business discipline it needs focus, goals, and metrics. We call these the Four Ms of Influence Marketing:

- **Make**—Chapter 7, "Reversing the Social Influence Model," introduced the concept of reverse engineering influence. By using this model, brands can identify the exact moment a promotion or campaign tipped and who caused the ripple effect. This information allows you to "make" influencers by identifying the people who are truly responsible for the virality of a campaign, and actual actions taken, versus those identified as simple amplifiers of a campaign's message. Additionally, how people identify with each other in their social graphs allows you to determine whether you need to connect with macro-influencers or micro-influencers.

- **Manage**—Influence marketing is like any other marketing tactic: To truly succeed, it needs to be managed from before the campaign starts to after the campaign ends and beyond. Relationships need to be nurtured; messaging needs to be massaged; positioning needs to be scoped. When combined with the decision-making factors that occur when situations and relationships come into play, these various components make the management of the whole campaign easier to structure and adhere to for you and your team.

- **Monitor**—We've mentioned numerous times in this book how easy social media makes it to monitor the ongoing success of a campaign. With listening tools, search analytics, dedicated messaging, landing pages, and more, marketers and brand managers begin to understand who and what are offering the greatest return on their investment, where they need to adapt the brand message, and which influencers are actually influencing the decision process at any given time. Using our tactic of geofencing influence from the previous chapter ensures you only need to monitor those who have an effect on your bigger campaign, making more effective use of your own time and resources and the costs attached to those efforts.

- **Measure**—The single most important part of any campaign—apart from the execution—is the measurement of its success or failure. Unless marketers can dissect the various data points and metrics available to them to learn why Tactic A worked when Tactics B and C didn't, they won't be able to put these learnings into practice for future campaigns, and the success potential of these campaigns will be severely limited. There are two core metrics to measure in an influencer campaign, and we highlight the most important ones later in the chapter.

By implementing the Four Ms across each part of an influencer campaign, brands can start to exert their own influence on how successful that campaign is. The smart brands that use the Four Ms as an integral part of their overall strategy will always succeed more than the brands that are running one campaign at a time, with silos between the marketing team, the brand message, and the influencers they're trying to work with.

Making Influencers

The dictionary definition of influence is "a person who exerts influence...an effect or change produced by influence."[3] By using this definition, it's clear why influence marketing has become such a key marketing goal for brands: Connecting with someone who can influence his audience to take a certain action increases the likelihood of that campaign's success. A warm and captive audience is a lot easier to work with than a cold lead you have to nurture from the start. The problem facing brands is how to identify the type of influencers they *should* be working with versus who they're told they need to be working with.

Social scoring platforms can help, but they should be viewed as a high-level starting point, as opposed to a true indication of influence. The other core problem is brands are primarily using influence marketing for amplification; they feel the more buzz and awareness generated by an influence campaign, the greater the likelihood of a product being purchased. However, as our Facebook experiment (refer to Figure 9.2) highlights loud and clear, there's a big disconnect between a free perk and a purchase. This can primarily be tied to two key factors:

- Brands and social scoring platforms are not looking beyond short-term buzz with an influence campaign.
- Brands and social scoring platforms are not working together to take influence beyond amplification and into lead generation and return on investment.

This could be caused by the brand not truly understanding influence marketing; it could be that the brand is not setting expectations ahead of the campaign; or it could be that the social scoring platform is not educating its client about the nuances of influence marketing campaigns, and how these can transfer to dollar return. It could even be a mix of all three; when any new technology or business solution comes onto the market, it can take a while for it to find its true nature and where it can be most effective.

While word-of-mouth marketing has been around for years, social influence and—by definition—influence marketing is still a relatively new discipline. This is why it's so important to know where to start before you actually begin, and why the reverse engineering model needs to be an integral part of your overall strategy when it comes to the Make part of the influencer equation. The Make part can be attributed to two definitive sections, Identifying and Activating.

Identifying the Path of the Persona

In every influencer campaign, there are two core stages: the Trickle and the Ripple Phases, as identified in Figure 9.3.

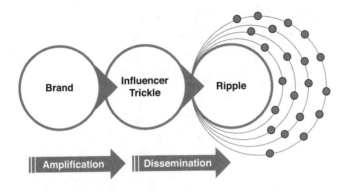

Figure 9.3   *The Trickle and Ripple Phases of influence marketing*

While influencers are used for their ability to impact a larger, more targeted audience, every campaign still needs to start in the Trickle Phase. This is where the message is first disseminated, and the direction the message takes from here determines whether it's successful. As we saw in Chapter 5, "Situational Influence: A New Model for a New Era," the path of a message isn't as simple as giving it to the influencer and letting her work her magic. The noise of the social web offers many distractions to overcome, and for a brand's message to be heard the optimum path and time must be ascertained. This is why we refer to this stage as the Trickle Phase—the uptake of a message starts slowly (or trickles out), with brands needing to work with influencers to identify key audience information:

- The time they'll be online
- The platforms they'll be on
- The people they'll be speaking with
- The topics they'll be speaking about
- The actions they'll be creating

To gather this information, brands need to create personas of the audience they're targeting—demographics, location, shopping patterns, technology used to access the Web, and other important information that allows them to tailor the right influencer and message to that audience. Chapter 4 highlighted some of these technologies, and the results from these platforms can help develop quick starting points from which to start building an influencer list and program. Chapter 5 provided the blueprint for segmenting these personas into the three key segments of the influencer circle, as shown in Figure 9.4: decision maker, micro-influencer, and extended community (followers, fans, listeners).

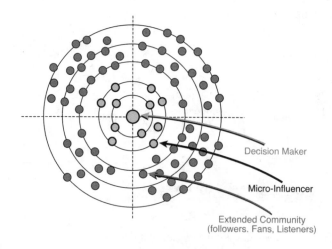

Decision Maker

Micro-Influencer

Extended Community
(followers. Fans, Listeners)

Figure 9.4 *The three segments of an influencer circle*

By segmenting influencers into definitive personas, and segregating which of their communities are most likely to react to your particular message, the potential for an influencer campaign to be successful moves from possible to probable. This moves the campaign from the Trickle Phase into the Ripple Phase—the influencer's community has picked up the brand's message and is now disseminating it through their own communities, essentially creating a ripple of brand awareness and promotional messaging.

Activating the Influencer

Once a brand has identified the core audience it's going after with each specific campaign, the next stage is to activate the influencer that's right for that message. This is a key component to the success of the campaign, and a reason why many campaigns utilized via social scoring platforms haven't shown a sizeable financial return on that campaign's investment. The influencer has been picked from a generic topic pool and engaged to spread a message he may have no contextual connection to.

Instead of identifying someone who has a connection to a topic, speaks with authority on that topic, and is relevant in that space, influence campaigns via social scoring platforms have been primarily based on amplification of the message via influencers with high follower numbers. However, as illustrated in Chapter 7, influence marketing is not about having the largest follower base or the loudest voice; it's about making the customer the influencer and working back from there, identifying the context behind their purchase decisions.

With that understanding, you can become far more effective at knowing how to activate the right influencer for your campaign. The first filter, as shown in Figure 9.5, is to identify which influencer is right for your campaign.

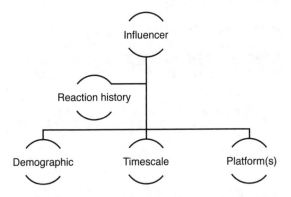

Figure 9.5   *The influencer filter, stage I*

Using this simplistic and high-level overview of what your campaign goals are allows you to immediately create a list of the influencer type needed for your goals. The specific filters in this stage offer the right starting point needed to ensure you pick the right people:

- **Demographic**—The age, sex, and locale of your audience play a key part in how your message needs to be crafted. A young, female Latina audience is very different from middle-aged, male Caucasians. A generic marketing outreach won't work here, which is why it's key to understand the demographic and pick the influencer most relevant to that audience.

- **Timescale**—Historically, influence campaigns have been used to engender a quick hit or build a level of short-term buzz for a brand, as part of a longer marketing campaign. The problem with this approach is it doesn't encourage true advocacy; nor does it allow secondary and tertiary influencers (the next level of influencer that can be activated as part of a crisis or to redirect a previously disrupted influence campaign like the examples in Chapter 5). To run a truly effective influencer campaign, it needs to be a constant part of your strategy, and the various parts of that campaign dictate which influencers are needed at each stage.

- **Platform(s)**—Social media is ubiquitous; there are several hundred popular networks and thousands of other, lesser-known sites that are no less effective when it comes to connecting with your audience.[4] Additionally, as you can see in Figure 9.6 from Pew Research[5] each platform has its own attraction to certain demographics, with sex, race, and income playing a large part in the popularity of each network.

Who Uses Social Networking Sites

% of internet users within each group who use social networking sites

All internet users (n=1,873)	69%
Men (n=886)	63
Women (n=987)	75*
Age	
18-29 (n=351)	92***
30-49 (n=524)	73**
50-64 (n=567)	57*
65+ (n=404)	38
Race/ethnicity	
White, Non-Hispanic (n=1,355)	68
Black, Non-Hispanic (n=217)	68
Hispanic (n=188)	72
Annual household income	
Less than $30,000/yr (n=469)	73*
$30,000-$49,999 (n=356)	66
$50,000-$74,999 (n=285)	66
$75,000+(n=501)	74**
Education level	
No high school diploma (n=129)	65
High school grad (n=535)	65
Some College (n=513)	73*
College + (n=692)	72*

Source: Pew Internet Civic Engagement Tracking Survey, July 16 – August 07, 2012. N=2,253 adults ages 18+. Interviews were conducted in English and Spanish and on landline and cell phones. Margin of error is +1/-3 percentage points.
* Statistically significant difference compared with others in the same grouping

Figure 9.6   *The demographics of social media*

Using Pew's analysis and combining it with your own internal audit based on your customer base, you can build a strong and targeted outreach to the right influencer for your next promotion. If your brand's audience is primarily women aged 30 to 49, then image curation site Pinterest would be a good starting point to consider, with 20% of female online users active on that platform. If your audience is primarily black or Hispanic with an income of more than $50,000 per year, a mobile-led influence campaign would be a better platform to use, due to that particular demographic's high adoption rate of using smartphones to browse social networks. This strategic approach to which platform you use is key for your success and the only way to guarantee that the influencer(s) you partner with are the ones that will relate to your target audience.

- **Reaction history**—For more than 30 years, the RICS Retail POS Software solution has been used by thousands of retailers across different verticals to manage loyalty programs, customer data from point-of-sale, purchase history, targeted marketing campaigns, and more.[6] By using RICS, retailers can be smarter at identifying which programs work, which channels are more effective than others, and what promotions are more likely to increase customer loyalty and retention, both in store and online. Using the same approach as RICS Software within influence marketing campaigns enables a brand to identify the tipping point when a customer makes a decision and/or takes an action based on the content of a certain influencer's message. These reactions can be something as simple as favoriting a tweet, liking a Facebook update, or commenting on a blog post or news article. More advanced history analysis can determine whether the reader downloaded a white paper and if she returned to make a purchase following that earlier action. Understanding the reaction history of your audience ensures your message is seeded at the right time and with the right influencer.

- **Influencer**—On November 12, 2012, leading technology news site TechCrunch published an article by Dr. Michael Wu, principal scientist at Lithium, a social software company that "...helps companies unlock the passion of their customers."[7] In the article, Wu posited one of the key problems with influence marketing as it currently stands—that brands are only trying to connect with elusive high-profile influencers instead of ones that are actually relevant to the consumer.[8] As we saw in Chapter 4, this leads to the gaming of social scoring platforms as people try to become influential in topics they may have no real expertise in to be noticed by brands running an influencer campaign. This sees brands partnering with the wrong influencers for their product, and subsequent lack of quality return on their investment. Utilizing the right influencer from the start is key; otherwise, the message is diluted. With many influence campaigns merely looking to create an initial buzz, this type of dilution can severely impact the future success of subsequent tactics in the overall campaign.

By using all the components identified here in stage one of our influencer filter, you can determine which influencer is perfect for your campaign, where to activate him, and where you would need secondary and tertiary influencers to either complement or replace your core influencer(s) for a specific campaign. In the next chapter, we highlight some of the tools that can help in this identification and creation process.

Managing the Influencer

For any marketing campaign to succeed—whether online or offline—every facet of it needs to be managed carefully. From the initial concept to the final execution and the metric-led reports after the event, campaigns can and do fall off track without proper management. The same goes with influence marketing campaigns: Without proper management the goals of the campaign simply won't be met, whether it's an impact campaign for short-term buzz or a longer campaign to drive continuous word-of-mouth actions and purchases.

Managing an influencer campaign is driven by the goals a brand sets for the campaign's duration and beyond, if an influencer relationship is to be continued for future outreach and promotions. The benefits of a continued relationship are numerous—established trust, knowledge of each other, a ready audience—but the biggest benefit is the increased likelihood of the switch from brand influencer to brand advocate. An influencer's main role is to share your brand's message with his audience, but that doesn't necessarily mean the influencer has your brand's best interests at heart.

Instead, the influencer may simply be promoting you for the financial reward, much like celebrities do when working with and promoting a brand they often have no emotional connection to. A brand advocate, on the other hand, is someone who not only promotes your brand but also shares, grows awareness of, and recommends it without any expectation of financial reward (although acknowledgment of and rewarding advocates for their loyalty helps cement the relationship even further). Continued management of the initial influencer relationship can help turn these respected authorities into your brand's advocates.

Each relationship needs to be managed differently to ensure the best possible outcome for the campaign. However, there are seven core steps to managing this relationship successfully that every brand should follow, as identified in Figure 9.7.

Each step is interconnected with the previous/next one and enables both brand and influencer to highlight any areas of concern as well as ensure the campaign has the requisite resources to be successful.

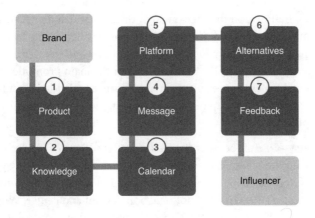

Figure 9.7   *The seven steps for influencer management*

1. **Product**—As important as the message of an influence marketing
    campaign is, the product is equally so. Trust is the ultimate currency
    of the social web. To solidify your brand's relationship with your cho-
    sen influencers, you need to ensure they have all the tools they need
    when it comes to your product as well as a product worth promoting.
    Provide training and in-depth overviews; offer your support network
    for questions they can't answer; be clear on the state of the product
    (beta or production); and have enough excess amounts of your prod-
    uct for the influencer's community to receive and test a sample if
    requested.

2. **Knowledge**—The ability to check information and facts with the
    click of a mouse has made consumers savvier than ever before. At
    every touch-point of a campaign, a brand's influencers need to show
    experience and knowledge of the product they're promoting. Provide
    worksheets, hands-on training, and fact sheets to ensure your chosen
    promotion partners—bloggers, celebrities, media outlets and/or online
    publications—have as much knowledge of the product as you or your
    employees do.

3. **Calendar**—Influence campaigns traditionally consist of short-term
    outreach and longer term marketing efforts by the brand, building on
    the buzz the influencer has created. Our preferred method is to culti-
    vate a longer-term vision and one that establishes the influencer as a
    core part of a brand's ongoing marketing efforts and team. However,
    whether a campaign is short-term or long-term, mapping out the
    content and promotion calendar for the campaign is crucial for its

success. Building on the precampaign research and audience targeting, determine the days and times each influencer will promote to which audience, as well as any follow-up promotion (tweets, status updates, secondary or tertiary blog posts to support the main promotion). The additional benefit to mapping out an influencer calendar is it allows you to prepare a backup plan for any disruptive elements during the campaign proper.

4. **Message**—One of the essential factors in the success of any influencer marketing campaign is the wording and execution of the message. Brands need to adapt their message to the influencer's natural tone while keeping the core promotional points front and center. Working with each influencer directly ensures a message that is on point as well as on target for that person's audience. Determine early what they are willing to say and any language they're unwilling to use and craft the promotion around that.

The key to successfully connecting with influencers and their community is often determined by this part of any outreach campaign. Read the influencer's blog—or watch, if he or she's a video blogger—and understand their topics of expertise. Use their blog archives and search function to identify if they've discussed anything similar to your brand's message before, and how they approached that. Monitor their social footprints elsewhere—Twitter, Facebook, LinkedIn, Google+, etc.—and get to know what they talk about and share. Building this awareness will help you shape the initial contact and increase the likelihood of working together.

5. **Platform**—Opponents of social media as a marketing tool often point to a lack of return on a certain platform as a reason not to use social media in your marketing campaign. What they often fail to see is the platform is not at fault but the strategy around participation on that platform. As we saw with the Pew Research data around social media demographics, certain platforms attract a larger female audience, while others attract a larger male one. The same goes for age, income, browsing preferences, and more. Use these insights to determine which platform will be your lead go-to-market one, and which ones will act as support networks around the bigger campaign.

6. **Alternatives**—Success within social media is built on the ability to adapt quickly to unforeseen market reactions. Even the most meticulously planned campaigns can receive a poor reception or a negative response from the target audience. Good marketers understand this and prepare for this possibility with several alternatives should they

be needed. These range from alternative influencers who are expert at responding to negativity and can help shift the balance of a campaign back to positive, to alternative promotions and landing pages if it becomes clear one particular message isn't working. By combining these alternatives with the campaign calendar, brands can ensure an ineffective promotion doesn't continue for too long.

7. **Feedback**—The success of focus groups in marketing—and their online groupthink equivalent—has helped brands fine-tune a product and promotional message before it hits the marketplace. Utilizing the same approach to an influencer campaign can not only help the brand make as strong a statement as possible when launching a new product, but also strengthen the relationship between brand and influencer. They're the ones who have built their audience and the trust from that audience. Therefore listening to what that influencer felt worked, what could have been different, and what other approaches could be used in future campaigns, needs to be a key part of the post-campaign analysis and dissection.

It should be noted that these seven steps previously relate to macro influencer marketing, although they can be adapted to the micro influencer. By using these seven clear steps throughout your campaign, the potential success of that campaign increases significantly and enables your business to be much more effective in all promotions across your audience's verticals.

Monitoring Influencer Campaigns

In October 2012, Robert C. Pozen, a senior lecturer at Harvard Business School, published an article in the *New York Times* titled "They Work Long Hours, but What About Results?"[9] In the piece, Pozen reflects on his time at a law firm and how people who were seen to put in long hours were presumed to be more effective than those who worked shorter hours. The truth of the matter, as Pozen highlights, is that effectiveness isn't measured by effort but by results. By focusing on results it allows for a much more structured framework to accomplish goals and meet targets. The same approach needs to be used when monitoring the efforts of an influencer campaign. Without knowing which influencer actually drove action and leads, and how much time, effort, and resources were required to make this happen, subsequent campaigns will lack any real results.

Each brand's goal with an influencer campaign will be different, but as you can see in Figure 9.8, there are three essential targets that every brand should be building their strategy around and monitoring how each campaign is progressing based on these goals.

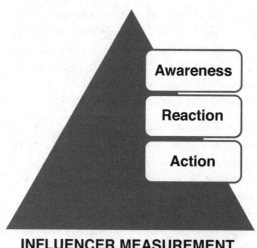

Figure 9.8 *Three essential influencer statistics to measure*

To ensure each goal is monitored effectively, brands need to determine the results they want from each one, either individually or collectively, and set up their chosen monitoring platform with each metric in mind. As a minimum requirement, these should include

1. Awareness

    - Blog posts about your campaign

    - Social shares and updates

    - News articles

    - Media interviews and/or pitches

    - Mentions of your company or product

2. Reaction

    - Visits to your company website or landing page

    - Newsletter subscribers increase

    - Increased traffic to offline properties

    - Increased search queries

    - Peer recommendation

    - Increased social followers

3. Action

- White paper download

- Seminar and/or webinar attendance

- Affiliate sign-up

- Purchase

These are just some of the basic results that each brand needs to monitor to ensure that a specific part of their campaign is working. Knowing which part of a program isn't working allows fast and effective adjustment to improve any weaker sections, including specific influencers and their messaging. Monitoring the campaign for these three results complement the final stage of the Four Ms of Influence Marketing—Measurement.

Measuring an Influence Marketing Campaign

While the other three components of the Four Ms—Make, Manage, and Monitor—are important, they're all rendered ineffective without the final piece of the equation: Measurement. A campaign can enjoy all the viral buzz a brand manager could ask for, with thousands of social shares and hundreds of blog posts and articles. But without measuring why that buzz happened and—more importantly—who created it, that same success will be difficult to replicate in future campaigns. In 1991, Silicon Valley pioneer Regis McKenna stated in his *Harvard Business Review* publication that, "Marketing is Everything, and everything is marketing."[10] In today's digital age, and with the increased use of influence as a key tactic in a brand's marketing strategy, McKenna's paper can easily be updated to "Measurement is everything, and everything is measurement."

Measurement is one of social media's key advantages over traditional marketing and advertising. Prior to social media's rise as an essential business solution, marketing campaigns were primarily through print, media including TV and radio, and direct mail. The use of flyers, posters, billboards, and print editorials were the staple method of promotion, often complemented with radio spots or television ads. The main problem with these methods is that it was difficult to pinpoint which ones were working and driving foot traffic to a brick and mortar store. If a business sent out 10,000 flyers, how could it guarantee its intended recipients saw all 10,000? Or if a radio spot played during a certain time of day based on that radio station's demographics, how could the brand be sure a certain percentage of that audience heard and acted on that ad? The answer to both questions is simple—they couldn't. If there was increased foot traffic to a location or more calls to a call center for a company's information brochure, more often than not the source of that referral was virtually impossible to identify. Social media changed that.

The ability to create extremely targeted campaigns, combined with platforms that measure which networks and content create the most return on investment, has made social media a key part of every smart business owner's toolset. This ability to measure business results is easily transferrable to measuring influencer results. The difference is in what, and who, you measure. Brands need to measure two core metrics in any influencer campaign. The first, as highlighted in Figure 9.9, is the brand metric.

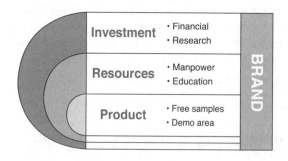

Figure 9.9   *Measuring the brand metric*

- **Investment**—The investment metric is the precampaign cost of researching which influencers are right for you by using our micro- and macro-influencer identification model from Chapter 7; how much it costs to set up the program; and using that as a barometer against how much return (financial or awareness) you experienced.

- **Resources**—The financial investment of an influencer campaign involves more than pure monetary costs. Resources such as manpower (how many employees are needed and how many hours they need to allocate to the campaign) and education (how much time you need to allocate to train each influencer on your product and company culture) also need to be measured and added to the bigger financial investment.

- **Product**—To encourage an influencer's audience to connect with your brand from a lead generation or purchase decision angle, free samples of your product need to be made available to the audience as well as the influencer. Test or demo areas may also need to be set up for more technical-led products or software. The cost to your company for the amount of products sent out, coupled with the hosting costs of the demo area online, need to be factored into the overall financial invest- ment of the campaign.

In addition to measuring the brand metric, the second key metric to track is the influencer metric, as shown in Figure 9.10.

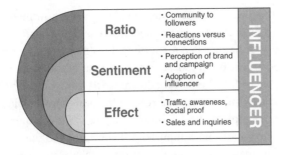

Figure 9.10   *Measuring the influencer metric*

- **Ratio**—The biggest problem many brands have when it comes to results from social scoring platforms is that the "influencer" targeted is simply another number in a database with a large following and an amplified voice online. This lack of differentiation is guaranteed to provide poor returns. Instead, the ratio of community to followers is key: A thriving, interactive community that reacts to an influencer is far more important than higher follower numbers. It's these qualitative reactions that provide a higher propensity of actions taken by the influencer's community. Measure how many reactions an influencer receives when sharing your message as a percentage of the influencer's overall following to extract a more exact return on that specific influencer. The Squeeze platform from Sequentia, which we look at in the next chapter, is perfect for this type of measurement.

- **Sentiment**—Every marketing campaign, whether online or offline, succeeds primarily for one main reason—the perception of that campaign and the buy-in of the audience. Using the same metrics to measure your influencer campaign allows you to understand the sentiment around the brand message, and how the target audience perceives both your brand and the campaign itself. It also allows you to quickly identify areas that upset a certain demographic and amend the message accordingly, or instigate a crisis communication response if needed. Additionally, you can see which influencer receives a favorable reaction and adoption, allowing you to increase awareness around him or her and helping to improve the perception of a less well-received influencer. Platforms like Sysomos (www.sysomos.com) and Sprout Social (www.sproutsocial.com) allow your organization's social media team to track these conversations and the sentiment around them.

- **Effect**—The most valuable barometer to showing whether an influencer campaign has worked is the effect it has on your brand. From a brand awareness point of view, measurement needs to include traffic generated to a website, microsite, or landing page; how many times your brand or product is mentioned online and how many people recognize your name when mentioned; how many new fans or followers you accrue on the social networks your brand is on; how many white papers or fact sheets were downloaded from your website; and how many new subscribers you receive to your company blog or newsletter. From a more dedicated business angle, it's much more straightforward—how many new inquiries did your inbound sales team receive; how many referrals did your direct sales team receive; and how many sales were directly attributed to your influencer's work with their community. Depending on your product or service, the purchase cycle of your customer may be a longer one than the duration of your campaign; include a plan to continue measuring the effect of the initial influence campaign on this purchase path.

While by no means exhaustive, both the brand metric and the influencer metric measurement examples are key parts of any kind of influencer campaign your brand partakes in. Each metric is a guideline to the core information that needs to be tracked in each example—your own brand's definition of additional metrics will be determined by the results you're looking to achieve. You may only be interested in awareness, in which case you'd place more emphasis on what platforms will show most return; what new platforms you can take advantage of; where your competitors are interacting online and how you can insert your brand into these conversations via your influencers. If you're more geared toward pure sales and lead generation, your outreach and subsequent measurement need to be focused more on potential ecommerce partnerships with peers and colleagues of your influencer; affiliate sales programs for your influencer's community; and strategic partnerships with other businesses in your industry who can benefit from increased exposure through your influencer while introducing you to their audience.

The Complementing Arc of Consumers and the Four Ms

In Chapter 6, "The Consumer Decision-Making Process," we identified when the consumer is ready to buy based on the language she uses when interacting online, as well as the relationship stage between that consumer and your brand. The situation the consumer finds herself in at a specific point in time, as highlighted in Chapter 5, solidifies the information available to a brand and how that brand reacts with a marketing message, from simple education and more details for someone not yet ready to buy, to product samples and sales help for someone ready to make a purchase.

Using this information to complement the Four Ms of Influence Marketing offers your brand a level of consumer intelligence previously unheard of and turns influence marketing from a potential marketing solution to an integral and actionable tactic. The gray areas that brands have previously encountered through the use of social scoring platforms as their influencer program partner dissolves and the metrics and tactics needed for successful campaigns are apparent and easily identified. Instead of wondering whether your brand should be involved in influence marketing, our model of making your customer the influencer coupled with the framework laid out in the previous four chapters, allows your business to answer one simple question instead: Where do we begin?

In the next chapter, we show you what technologies can help answer this question.

Endnotes

1. Andy Field Twitter status. September 9, 2011. https://twitter.com/andytfield/status/112141257039560706.

2. Andrew Seward Twitter status. September 9, 2011. https://twitter.com/MrAndrew/status/112143984243118080.

3. "Influence." The Free Dictionary by Farlex. http://www.thefreedictionary.com/Influencer.

4. "List of social networking websites." Wikipedia. http://en.wikipedia.org/wiki/List_of_social_networking_websites.

5. Brenner, J. February 14, 2013. "Pew Internet: Social Networking." Pew Internet & American Life Project. http://pewinternet.org/Commentary/2012/March/Pew-Internet-Social-Networking-full-detail.aspx.

6. "Customer Relationship Management (CRM)." RICS Software. http://www.ricssoftware.com/products/customerrelationshipmgmt.aspx.

7. "Our Company." Lithium. http://www.lithium.com/company/overview.

8. Wu, M. November 9, 2012. "The Problem with Measuring Digital Influence." Tech Crunch. http://techcrunch.com/2012/11/09/can-social-media-influence-really-be-measured/.

9. Pozen, R. October 6, 2012. "They Work Long Hours, but What About Results?" *New York Times*. http://www.nytimes.com/2012/10/07/business/measure-results-not-hours-to-improve-work-efficiency.html.

10. McKenna, R. January 1991. "Marketing Is Everything." *Harvard Business Review*. http://hbr.org/1991/01/marketing-is-everything/ar/1.

10

The Future of Influence Marketing

When dealing with people, let us remember we are not dealing with creatures of logic. We are dealing with creatures of emotion, creatures bustling with prejudices and motivated by pride and vanity.

—Dale Carnegie

When Dale Carnegie uttered these words, there was no Klout, Kred, PeerIndex, or any other social scoring platform. Yet his words highlight the very nature of social scoring's problem: No matter how good an algorithm is, the human psyche is too complex to be pigeonholed into bits and bytes. As we saw in Chapter 2, "Influence and the Human Psyche," psychologists have spent centuries trying to understand what makes the human mind tick. At what point does a wish or need change into intent and action? Where does logic make way for emotional purchasing? There are so many disruptive paths en route to any final decision being made that trying to gauge influence based on an algorithm defined score becomes almost impossible. Scores can certainly help shape opinion on who *may* be influential on a certain topic, but this is primarily looking at activity online, versus truly getting into the emotional mindset of the human behind the score.

While many social scoring platforms access different datasets across multiple platforms to calculate an influencer's score, the truth of the matter is the majority of the information still comes from Twitter. The other major networks often make it difficult for a scoring platform's search software to index them: Facebook is essentially a closed-off walled garden; Google+ conversations are often only shared with a select private group of people; and LinkedIn Group discussions are public only if the moderator allows them to be. Other networks like YouTube do offer a public data feed (views and likes, for example), but these don't necessarily tie into the influence of the video channel owner.

Niche networks like Quora (www.quora.com) and SlideShare (www.slideshare.net) are better examples of influence. Quora is a question and answer-type platform, where users ask questions about a certain topic. When someone answers, it's voted on for its validity to the question – the higher the amount of up votes someone receives, the more influential that person is viewed. SlideShare allows individuals and brands to upload presentations—PowerPoint, PDF, videos—which can then be shared, downloaded, or embedded on another website. The most popular presentations are highlighted on the SlideShare homepage and, like Quora, increase the perceived influence of the users who uploaded them.

However, while these two services can highlight popularity and authority, they still don't offer a comprehensive overview of a person's relevant influence. A large reason for this is because the communities on these platforms are consistently in flux; for example, questions on Quora are answered and the provider of the best answer moves elsewhere, or someone else provides a better answer a month after the topic essentially ended, opening up the topic again to a newer audience.

When we begin to understand the various nuances of the human mindset at a given time—mood, propensity to a message, family factors, peer pressure, financial impact, and more—and how that alters a person's positioning within a certain community of interest, then we can begin to understand where our influencer's message will have the biggest impact. Chapter 9, "The Four Ms of Influence Marketing," looked at how we can create influencers based on the information we already know about our audience. Information gained from following our models of reversing influence and predicting social model paths was discussed in Chapter 7, "Reversing the Social Influence Model," and Chapter 8, "Managing Social Influence Paths," respectively. Now that we have the relevant data, a key factor in how successful your campaign is lies in choosing the right platforms and technologies based on your goals, and which part of the Four Ms of Influence Marketing your current campaign is concentrating on: Making, Managing, Monitoring, or Measuring.

This chapter looks at the technologies that are moving the influence conversation beyond social scoring and into true contextual and actionable business intelligence and results. These are the technologies that most align with our new model for the future of influence marketing and can be interconnected through each segment of the Four Ms of Influence Marketing—Make, Manage, Monitor, and Measure. Which one(s) you use for your brand will be determined by where that platform sits in the Four Ms circle and the goal of your specific influence campaign—brand awareness and buzz, or message amplification for lead generation and purchases.

Tellagence

Located in Portland, Oregon, Tellagence (www.tellagence.com) is the creation of enterprise software veteran Matt Hixson and former Intel Business Intelligence

Analyst and data scientist Nitin Mayande. Tellagence's strength lies in predicting how information moves across communities, who the key influencers are that will drive that journey, and which relationships offer the biggest likelihood of amplifying that message to increase the reach of your brand or product, based on the passion that influencer has for your brand or industry. Tellagence measures different variables to achieve this data:

- Interests
- Number of participants in associated conversations and communities
- Depth of relationship
- Degrees of community involvement
- The changing flow of the relationships within the community

By combining this information, Tellagence can move the data beyond simple archived information (which is how most brands have previously built databases of personas for outreach campaigns) and instead offer predictive behavior analysis of how your brand will impact a certain community, based on the flow of information between the core influencer(s) and the secondary and tertiary tier of micro-influencers, as highlighted in Chapter 7.

As shown in Figure 10.1, this intelligence allows your brand to identify the targets you should be connecting with, based on the relevance of that target to your brand and audience, and the propensity for them to become an advocate for your brand, or encourage *their* community to become an advocate.

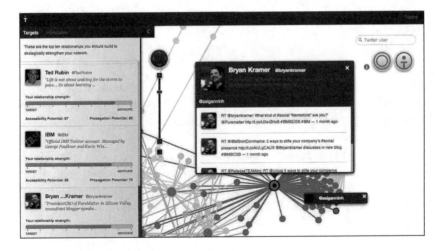

Figure 10.1   *Tellagence targets versus advocates*

By analyzing the conversations taking place on Twitter and between whom these conversations are taking place, Tellagence can recommend the most effective outreach for your influencer campaign. This sole concentration on Twitter allows Tellagence to provide deeper context into how communities on Twitter are connected, compared to scoring platforms using Twitter's API as a key part of a multiple network solution. This context ranges from how accessible the person is to potentially how far the message may spread when shared by that person and their community. The social graph of the relationships this particular influencer enjoys is displayed via a hub-and-spoke model, with nodes connecting the various communities based on relevance and context. These nodes identify who the core connections are for your particular message, as shown in Figure 10.2.

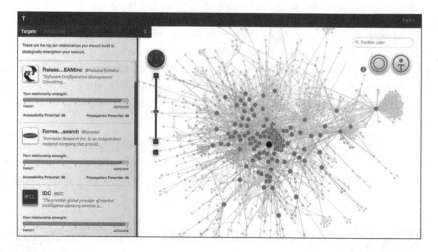

Figure 10.2   *Identifying the optimum influencer path*

Instead of the social scoring method of proffering clients the top 1,000 most influential people on automobiles based on Twitter activity, Tellagence filters out the noise of that activity and instead concentrates on true, genuine relationships that will help distribute your message to the largest audience—an audience truly invested in either your brand's message or the type of product you're bringing to market. This number can be as small as five key influencers; the strength of their relationship with their communities is the differentiator from other solutions that ensures your brand is at the center of the right kind of attention for your marketing promotions.

Analytics before, during, and after your campaign offer reports on the successes of your outreach.

- The growth of your brand
- The influence it wields in these new communities

- The increased advocacy around your brand
- Alerts when influencers and/or their community members are approaching advocate level
- The impact of your content and the communities now spreading your message

This data enables your brand to adapt on the fly to changing influence spheres and network fluxes—when one influencer reaches peak effectiveness, Tellagence identifies who the next layer of influencers are, and where they are in the advocacy chart for your brand. This intelligence empowers your brand manager to change the messaging and outreach as required, and ensure your campaign has the maximum potential for success due to the strongest advocates always being engaged.

Tellagence currently supports Twitter only; additional networks, including Facebook and Google+, are on the roadmap for future releases. Its core audience is enterprise marketers—Chief Marketing Officers, public relations teams, and advertising and sales professionals and agencies. It costs $750 per month per community, with up to 10 queries—how communities and their members are identified—per community.

- Four Ms application for Tellagence: Make, Monitor, and Measure

Appinions

Located in New York, Appinions (www.appinions.com) is steeped in science and education. Building on more than 10 years of Cornell University research, Appinions ignores the type of popularity metrics prevalent in social scoring platforms, and instead provides influence measurement based on its patented "contextual evidence of impact" algorithm as well as actions taken. Collating data from more than five million sources, including blogs, social networks, and online forums, as well as print media and news stories, Appinions's goal is simple: to provide the most robust influencer data of any solution provider. To attain this goal, Appinions takes a different approach to what and how it measures.

- The opinions that people express about topics and brands are key.
- They place as much importance on traditional media sources as they do online sources.
- Context is everything; without context, there is no metric to measure.
- The actions taken by a person are measured in credibility, as opposed to audience size and reactions.

This last component, in addition to the context of that action, is a core part of the Appinions approach and an area where the solution differs from many of the earlier influence vendors. By filtering the context of the conversations around a certain topic, and applying their search purely to those that are influencing the direction of that conversation, Appinions provides clear data on where your brand or product currently is when compared to a competing alternative.

This Influencer Gap model offers a clear visualization of where your brand currently stands and how much work needs to be carried out to increase your share of voice. In the example shown in Figure 10.3, we can see a distinct gap of 79 points between the mentions around the terms "big data" and "eCommerce." The gap is further broken down into the main networks where the conversation on these two topics is taking place:

- **Blogs**—The topic of eCommerce has a far larger influence reach and audience on blogs, with more than half its audience using blogs to discuss the topic.
- **News**—This is a closer metric, although eCommerce still enjoys a larger audience on news sites than big data.
- **Twitter**—This is where the metrics change drastically. Big data has more than two-thirds of its influence audience using Twitter as the discussion point, whereas eCommerce has less than one-third of its audience.

In addition to these metrics, the Influencer Gap also provides analysis on who's more influential on the topic in question, whose influence is increasing or decreasing, the credibility of that influencer with the topic's audience, the sentiment around that influencer, and the validity of the influencer's opinions. This allows a business to identify who can propagate its message the most effectively and who the business needs to introduce itself to. An additional benefit to these metrics is they can be used internally, so your brand can identify employees or key stakeholders within the organization, enabling you to use both internal and external influencers together to work on improving the Influencer Gap between your product or brand message and that of your competitor.

Appinions collates metrics from the three main areas of promotion in today's marketplace: earned media, paid media, and owned media. Each can be used individually or can be combined to complement the Appinions solution even further.

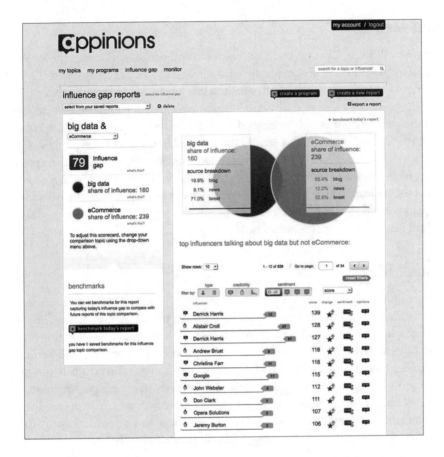

Figure 10.3 *Identifying the Influencer Gap*

Earned Media

As more consumers move from traditional media outlets to online resources for
their news and research needs, bloggers and influential publications have come
to the fore and introduced earned media into the equation. Whereas previously a
brand could expect a certain amount of print space or airtime through paid advertising, earned media offers no guarantees; your story truly has to resonate with the
publication, blogger, or influencer. Appinions's solution for earned media helps
reduce the process of connecting with these warm leads by minimizing the guesswork of who is most likely to partner with you, and who the most effective partners
are. The solution includes identifying and building influencer lists on the topics
most relevant to your brand; biographical, social, and linked profile information on
each influencer; measurement of the campaign and reports of which influencer is
driving the buzz around your brand; and identification of local influencers to grow
awareness for company events in the local community.

Paid Media

As we will see in Chapter 11, "The Business of Influence Marketing," the long-term goal of an influencer program is to build customer loyalty and passionate advocates for your brand. The most effective path to this loyalty lies in the mix of earned and owned media, as part of your brand's ongoing relationship building and customer understanding initiatives. To engender this future loyalty, paid media is a key tactic in ensuring your brand is seen in the right publications at the right time, from news sites to blogs and online media productions. Appinions's paid media product identifies the blogs and publications where your message is most likely to be shared; increases the return on investment for ad campaigns based on relevance to audience and the likelihood of clickthroughs; and targets influencers to partake in paid placement or sponsored content partnerships.

Owned Media

According to research by the Content Marketing Institute, 55% of business-to-consumer marketers plan to increase their budget for content marketing, or owned media, in 2013,[1] while 31% will continue with the same financial commitment to content marketing as was allocated in the previous 12 months. These findings highlight the continued growth of owned media—content and channels your brand controls versus paid or earned media and third-party partnerships. Appinions helps a brand grow the influence of its own content with targeted opportunities on influential publications for guest posts and webinars, and helps identify topics that resonate with readers to grow your traffic audience and authority.

Appinions is clear in its objectives on how to move the influence conversation forward. Appinions has no plans to offer a consumer dashboard along the lines of Klout and similar scoring platforms; its goal is to work with brands as a consultancy and educational resource and ensure the influencers identified and targeted are the ones that can drive the most effective results over each campaign.

A typical price point for Appinions is $60,000 per year, for the platform, data and included services including analytics and reports.

- Four Ms application for Appinions: Make, Manage, Monitor, and Measure

Traackr

The biggest problem with current influence measurement is that several of the better-known platforms purely measure influence by amplification and popularity metrics; if someone is active enough online and has a large following, then that person is influential. The flaw in this approach is it ignores key factors such as relevance, context, trust, and how a message resonates with that "influencer's" audience. San Francisco-based Traackr (www.traackr.com) offers a solution for enterprise users that provides metrics and data that popularity-based influence scoring can miss.

Traackr's algorithm, as shown in Figure 10.4, is based on three Rs: Reach (the size of the influencer's audience); Resonance (how effectively that audience is engaged by the influencer); and Relevance (how that audience is contextually connected to your brand's message or product). The combination of these three core metrics enables Traackr to work with brands to implement influencer programs that increase the potential for brand advocacy, more effective influencer identification, and results that impact your organization's bottom line, providing a quantifiable solution across your next campaign.

Figure 10.4   *Identifying the influencers*

Bottom Line Impact

Influencer campaigns have traditionally been about increasing awareness and short-term buzz around a brand. While this helps grow an audience, it doesn't necessarily translate into sales. However, as illustrated with MV-1 in Chapter 1, "Logic and Reason (or How We Learned to Love Influence Marketing)," and Lebanon Ford in Chapter 3, "The Rise of Social Media," influence can be at the forefront of an organization's lead generation and customer acquisition strategy. Traackr's technology enables brands to implement this approach by tailoring search results based on your brand's goals and identifying the ideal influencer based on relevance to your brand through the influencer's content. Traackr applies its 3R model of Reach, Relevance, and Resonance, and provides a full overview of where they're active online. By targeting the networks where your customers are, and which influencers are active there, and then providing the most relevant content for this targeted audience, the potential to turn an influencer outreach into financial return and new customers is exponentially higher.

Increased Potential for Advocacy

As we see in the next chapter, the desired end result of any influencer campaign should be to create brand advocates that will promote your message for you organically as part of their natural everyday conversation. Traackr's algorithm increases the potential for turning influencers or their audience into advocates by deciphering how they present themselves online as well as how they contribute to the bigger discussion, allowing your message to be tailored specifically for that person; tracking sentiment around that person as well as how your message is being received; analyzing the influencer's content to increase your relevance to them; and measuring the outcome of your campaign as well as track the most influential people for your brand and how they affect your online mentions and brand perception. When combined, these metrics will help you create a campaign that connects on all the emotional and logical touch-points that turn someone's intent to buy or take action into a purchase and advocate for your message.

Faster Influencer Identification

As brands become more active in experimenting with influencer programs, the biggest roadblock to effective uptake is the time it takes to accurately identify the right influencer for your brand. While social scoring platforms can offer an early indication of who these people may be, they're often limiting when it comes to more in-depth information on how relevant each influencer is for you. This lack of information adds to the resources needed by brands to carry out effective research and filtering of the influencer in question and results in the program being cancelled before it begins. Traackr overcomes this issue by running live searches for the influencers in your niche and providing instant and relevant results; regularly updating the influencer database to include new influencers and identify those who are dropping in relevance; and providing an analysis of why a particular influencer should be part of your program. This solution has reduced the identification process by weeks and months, allowing brands to begin a campaign faster and more effectively.

Actionable Insights

Like any campaign, an influencer program needs strong insights and analytics to provide validation of the campaign, or highlight weak points for improvement and adjustment. Traackr's insights filter the noise from the millions of conversations happening at any given time online and provide the actionable information you need to move your campaign forward. This includes only monitoring the conversations relevant to your campaign; early identification of what topics your influencer is currently trending for, allowing you to optimize your own content; and filtering out the less relevant people and publications for your brand and concentrating on connecting with and engaging the most contextual (see Figure 10.5).

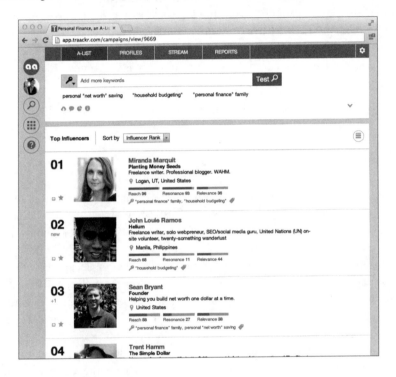

Figure 10.5 *Identifying the most contextual influencers*

Traackr's solution is built around its clients' audience, budget, and resources and enables influence programs for business owners across multiple industries, customer size, and revenue.

Traackr Features

Offering a comprehensive and customizable solution for enterprise, Traackr's technology utilizes its PeopleSearch engine to provide brands and agencies an in-depth suite of tools from which to build their influencer program.

- Instant search
- Geotargeting

- Dynamic influencer lists
- Influencer profiles
- Real-time listening
- Analytics and sentiment analysis
- Three Rs—Reach, Resonance, Relevance—scoring algorithm

This approach to identifying influence and those that drive true context to these conversations and relationships positions Traackr as a leader in the future of influence marketing. Traackr starts at $1,795 per month for its enterprise solution, and includes an account level dedicated keyword advice service, ensuring the most optimum searches are enabled. Its core business use is for companies in the technology, finance and healthcare sectors.

- Four Ms application for Traackr: Make, Manage, Monitor, and Measure

TrendSpottr

Canadian company TrendSpottr (www.trendspottr.com) is interesting in the influence space in that its product isn't sold as a dedicated influence platform; however, the applications that TrendSpottr can be used in make it a valuable component to add to any of the solutions highlighted in this chapter. While we've primarily been talking about influence marketing from a campaign level angle, and how to identify the purchase point of a customer and reverse engineer the path to the influential factor in that decision, this is based on a proactive and reactive model: Identify the end result and track the initiation point. TrendSpottr differs by using data streams and metrics based on frequency, velocity, acceleration of message, and its amplification to predict the next trend in viral content, and allocating a trending score for which content is most likely to go viral, with 100 being the highest potential, as shown in Figure 10.6.

This allows TrendSpottr's technology to accurately predict which content or media has the most potential to become the next Gangnam Style level of hit.[2] TrendSpottr's technology can predict these kinds of viral successes hours and days before the content achieves mainstream visibility. For a brand engaged in an influencer campaign, this level of predictability offers two opportunities: to position your content as influential and identify individuals or media channels to partner with to place your content in front of the biggest audience possible.

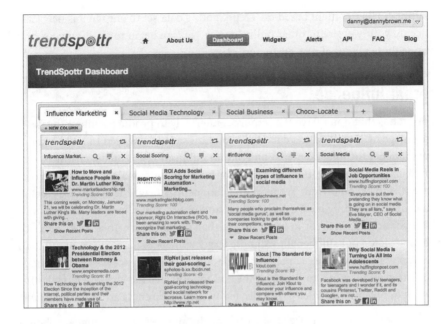

Figure 10.6   *Predicting viral content and influence*

Internal Influence

As already discussed, the short-term goal of an influence program is to gain traction and buzz around your brand or product. This leads to the longer relationship that comes from the advocacy and loyalty of customers that successful influence campaigns create. Part of this advocacy comes from the content your brand shares with these new customers. This can range from educational articles and blog posts to best practices, tips, and advice, as well as showing thought leadership in the space. When your customers see you leading the way in relation to their preferences and needs, your brand becomes influential to them and the potential for their advocacy increases.

With Trendspottr's predictive analysis identifying the kind of content that is set to go viral, in turn influencing others to take an action—watch, share, download, buy—around that particular article or media, brands have the opportunity to produce content of their own to take advantage of the impending online searches and conversations around this content, or buy ad space on connected sites or media platforms. Because the content is yet to go viral, any media a brand produces becomes the equivalent of an early adopter. For your brand, less of an audience around the still-to-be-viral effect means new consumers of the viral content looking for more information will find your message at the forefront of any search results, driving traffic to your content or landing page. With your marketing team crafting further content based on TrendSpottr's data set to engage this new traffic once on your website or other online portal, you can begin to position your brand as one these potential new customers can value.

External Influence

For brands that don't have the resources internally to produce content to take advantage of TrendSpottr's data, their solution can also be used to build external influence, using paid media on relevant publications or media channels. On YouTube, for example, this can help your brand identify which videos have the potential to become viral. TrendSpotter can identify new videos that are creating buzz online but only have a couple thousand views. This allows your brand to buy ad space on the video for less investment than buying space on a video with millions of views, but still benefit from the larger audience share. Smart brand marketers can craft ads that are contextually relevant to the audience watching the video and offer a strong call-to-action at the end to influence the viewer's next destination (your website or sales page), driving massive awareness around your brand.

TrendSpottr can also be used to identify media and news stories that are about to go viral, allowing you to mobilize your external core, secondary and tertiary influencers to produce content around a sound bite, picture, or other media. A perfect example of the effectiveness of TrendSpottr's value in this approach happened in November 2012, with the viral popularity of a photograph that showed President Obama striking a pose with Olympic gymnast McKayla Maroney.[3] The image was released to the general public on November 17 and was picked up immediately by TrendSpottr's algorithms. The company sent alerts out to its customers predicting Extreme Virality, including the prediction that there would be more than 4,000 tweets on Twitter within the space of five hours. This accurate prediction allowed TrendSpottr's customers to optimize their own content and social ad spend to include versions of this image, which resulted in exponential shares and click-throughs for their campaigns, generating positive return on investment and brand awareness.

In addition to the marketing benefits of TrendSpottr, its platform is ideal for crisis communications (spotting negative news stories before they break and allowing brands and organizations to create a proactive response) as well as financial organizations looking to find the next big event in the stock market. Nonprofits and government agencies also use TrendSpottr to identify the people and channels creating buzz and movement around the topics that are important to donors and constituents. This multivertical solution makes TrendSpottr an invaluable component in the next evolution of influence and advocacy.

The TrendSpottr Dashboard—allowing brands to curate topic streams around trending content, hashtags, sources and phrases—costs $99 per month per user, with unlimited searches. TrendSpottr alerts—which enables brands to be alerted instantly on monitored topics that are showing potential to go viral—start at $10 per month for one alert, rising to $75 per month for 10 alerts. There is also a custom pricing model for brands needing more than 10 alerts.

- Four Ms application for TrendSpottr: Make and Monitor

Squeeze

Throughout this book we've shared examples of using social media and, by association, influence marketing as a lead generation channel. Awareness and positive sentiment are wonderful metrics for the social community team, but end-of-year results don't include these types of metrics when it comes to the financial success of a business. Knowing which of your social media strategies and tactics offered the most return on your investment is key to continued success in the space, and this is where Squeeze should be a required addition to your influencer programs.

A software solution built by Toronto-based digital agency Sequentia Environics, Squeeze (www.getsqueeze.com) tracks the actions taken around any content shared across the social web. These actions measure how successful specific influencers, content, and platforms are at spreading your message, and which ones need more work. Using Squeeze's own URL shortener, you can allocate a specific tracking link for each network to the same piece of content. This URL is unique to each network and will show you which platform is the most effective at encouraging clickthroughs to your content. As you can see in Figure 10.7, for this particular campaign to drive traffic to a blog post, Twitter offered the most return, followed by Facebook and then Google+. This indicates that Twitter should be the lead platform when looking to replicate this kind of campaign.

While the primary function of Squeeze is to measure the effectiveness of content sharing on various platforms, the software can also be used as a complementary solution for your brand's influence campaigns. When you've identified which influencers you're going to be working with by using the platforms from earlier in this chapter, Squeeze can then be used to create multiple versions of the same link for different influencers. If your campaign uses multiple touch-points for your influencers—for example, one influencer on Twitter, three influencers on blogs, two influencers on Google+, ten influencers on Facebook, and four influencers on YouTube—you would create a unique Squeeze link for each influencer to use on his preferred network. In addition to the link shortener, Squeeze also enables you to create a landing page and embed a tracking script into the page for each call-to-action you have on there. This could be a digital download, a video message, a newsletter signup or a physical purchase. Each action taken on the page can be tracked by further Squeeze links, as evidenced in Figure 10.8.

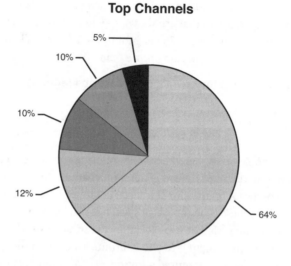

Top Channels

- Twitter
- Facebook
- Facebook Page Danny
- GooglePlus
- Linkedin

Figure 10.7 *Optimizing your content outreach across platforms*

Squeeze Link	Offer	Channel	Campaign	Theme	Squeeze Date	Clicks	Leads
▲ Campaign: Blog traffic							
http://sqz.co/t3R2Xwn	Spin Sucks blog post on new social channels	Facebook	Blog traffic	Social curation	16/01/2013	7	0
http://sqz.co/Ot93MkX	Spin Sucks blog post on new social channels	Linkedin	Blog traffic	Social curation	16/01/2013	9	0
http://sqz.co/r3QMx79	Spin Sucks blog post on new social channels	Twitter	Blog traffic	Social curation	16/01/2013	41	0
http://sqz.co/k3NMo94	Spin Sucks blog post on new social channels	GooglePlus	Blog traffic	Social curation	16/01/2013	4	0
http://sqz.co/Qs4f7Y2	Spin Sucks blog post on new social channels	Facebook Page Danny	Blog traffic	Social curation	16/01/2013	9	0

Figure 10.8 *Tracking action and reactions of influencer traffic*

By combining website tracking with which particular influencer's message is providing traction, Squeeze can advise you of multiple metrics:

- Which platform drove the most traffic
- Which influencer caused the most reaction

- What action was taken onsite
- Which influencer sent the most qualified leads versus nonparticipatory visitors
- Which call-to-action drove the most clicks
- How many visitors returned from a download to make a purchase
- Which influencer message created the most long-tail traffic

The ability to highlight the content and message driving physical sales versus simple brand awareness and buzz enables brands to truly understand which influencer partnership is creating the most value based on their goals. While an influence campaign's success metric may be the volume of sales in the first quarter of a financial year, for the second quarter it may be buzz volume and web traffic. Squeeze filters each influencer based on these metrics and ensures each influence campaign uses the most effective resource every time.

As we go to print, Squeeze is in public beta and free to use. Its core audience is brand managers, agencies and businesses looking to provide measurement and return on investment from digital campaigns.

- Four Ms application for Squeeze: Measure

oneQube

Created by Robert Moore of New York-based digital media company Internet Media Labs, oneQube (www.oneqube.com) is a software solution built to facilitate and engender more effective Twitter engagement. This factors in several key areas:

- Managing followers
- Engaging with followers
- Creating effective Twitter lists
- Identifying relevant connections, topics, and communities
- Understanding the demographics of your followers
- The digital footprint of your Twitter followers elsewhere online

While oneQube is primarily a Twitter management platform, it also provides a strong solution for identifying and connecting with influencers in your brand's industry as well as highlights potential advocates in your existing network.

The oneQube Twitter Influencer Connector

The key to any successful influence campaign is connecting with the right influencers for your brand. As illustrated with the other platforms highlighted in this chapter, this can be through topic, industry, and relevance between an influencer, the influencer's audience, and your brand. By drilling down to the connectors who already have a common interest with your brand, the potential of a campaign's success increases exponentially. With oneQube, your brand is much more effective at using Twitter as an influencer channel and identifying the connections you already have that either share common traits or the opportunity to partner with to communicate your message to their followers. As you can see from Figure 10.9, in addition to Twitter, oneQube also provides external information—if the connection is a business or individual, website address, email address, contact form, physical location, and other social links. This overview, coupled with oneQube's search and identification options for Twitter, provides a bigger picture of how relevant a connection is for your outreach and how likely they are to respond to your outreach.

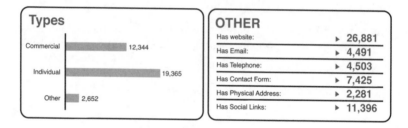

Figure 10.9   *oneQube's external data set*

The strongest relationships—personal and business—are often the ones that begin with a shared interest. With business relationships, this shared interest increases the likelihood of common ground when working together on a project. This, in turn, leads to a greater rate of success for that project. Social media marketing is no different, particularly when it comes to working with influencers. Paid media may increase your short-term buzz and awareness, but connect with an influencer who is genuinely interested in what your brand has to offer and she will ensure your message is shared in full with her community, and will share that message more than once. This is where the advocacy cycle begins and where the real value of influence marketing becomes apparent. oneQube makes finding the connections with these common interests more manageable and effective.

Filtering Your Twitter Followers

To identify which Twitter followers have an engaged community and which ones offer the potential to influence that community on your brand's behalf, oneQube dissects your followers into key components.

- **Trending words**—This collates your followers into segments based on the keywords in their bios, and shows the most-used words to offer a snapshot of the makeup of your following.

- **Gender**—A simple breakdown of the male-to-female ratio of your followers, as well as how many people follow them on average, as well as how many Twitter Lists they're on—a good indicator of a person's potential influence strength.

- **Top 5 time zones**—Offering the five most populated locations of your Twitter followers, enabling you to determine where a campaign may be most effective if you have a nationally available product.

- **Follower buckets**—A grouping based on follower count as well as the type of followers someone has. While we are no fans of higher numbers equating higher influence, for Reach and Amplification purposes a high number does suggest an influencer opportunity.

- **Type**—This filters accounts based on personal use or commercial use and can help with identifying which type of user will engage more with a certain message.

- **Followers last tweeted**—The problem with many follower counts across all social networks is they are skewed with dead and inactive accounts. This metric shows the last time a Twitter account was used, enabling your brand to delete inactive accounts and remove from data lists.

- **Other**—If a Twitter user provides further information with his account, oneQube can access this data, including website address, email, other social profiles, and contact details. This can help build a brand's influence profile and viability for different campaigns, based on what platform is being targeted and how active a potential influencer is on that network.

These components not only allow better filtering of a Twitter account's following, but is key when it comes to utilizing oneQube's search option for finding your influencers and advocates.

Using oneQube Search to Find Influencer Opportunities

As an example of how a brand can find followers relevant to the audience the brand wants to connect with, we use Danny's Twitter account in the oneQube search dashboard and select the following filters:

- Last tweeted in the past month
- English as the main language

- Females only
- Eastern Standard Time as the time zone
- Had a website
- Had other social profiles
- Had email and contact form on their site

From a starting point of more than 34,000 followers, oneQube filtered out the nonrelevant connections and narrowed the search result to a mere 106 followers, as shown in Figure 10.10.

Figure 10.10 *Identifying contextual influencers with oneQube*

Using oneQube's Trending Words option as well as Location and Follower Numbers, a brand could instantly find the most relevant 10 or 20 influencers who share a connection as well as fit that brand's goal. A list can then be created within the oneQube dashboard to allow a brand manager to monitor how active these influencers are, how responsive their community is, and the key topics that excite the influencer as well as their community. This enables a stronger outreach strategy and increases the effectiveness of a brand's communication with that influencer.

Identifying Who Influences the Influencer

As we showed in Chapter 8, it's not just core influencers who impact someone's decision. While macro-influencers amplify a message, micro-influencers are the most likely to create an action from their audience. These micro-influencers can also influence the influencer—or the people who influence the person you want to connect with for your brand's influence campaign. This opens up an alternative strategy to build an influencer outreach campaign: If a brand can begin a dialogue with the individuals who cause identified influencers to take action, the propensity of a connection to the target influencer is increased. oneQube can help identify these micro-influencers with its DRILL solution, as shown in Figure 10.11.

Figure 10.11 *Identifying the micro-influencers with oneQube DRILL*

Using social media influencer Amber MacArthur, who we met in Chapter 3, as a reference point, oneQube identifies the nine people Amber has tweeted the most. Of these nine, users @SarahLane and @KonnektNow are the two she converses with the most. This suggests these are two people whose opinion Amber trusts implicitly, making them ideal connections to strike up a conversation with. By connecting with these micro-influencers of Amber, the opportunity to connect with Amber increases. Additionally, because Amber connects with these two Twitter users and the other seven as identified by oneQube's DRILL, the potential is also there for these connections of Amber to become influencers for your brand as well, since there are clearly shared interests between the target influencer—Amber MacArthur—and those she converses with the most.

Hashtag Tracking

One of Twitter's advantages over other networks is the ability to isolate conversations using hashtags. Using the # symbol in front of a keyword shows only tweets with that keyword when using Twitter search. With oneQube's hashtag tracking solution, brands can monitor five different hashtags. As shown in Figure 10.12 and Figure 10.13, by providing certain influencers with specific hashtags to use when sharing their content, brand managers can measure how successful an influencer is at spreading a message, and which community members are resharing that content, increasing the opportunity to turn that person into an advocate for that brand. oneQube also identifies other Twitter chats relevant to the hashtag being monitored, offering further opportunities to connect with different audiences that are interested in the topic being discussed with the current hashtag.

Figure 10.12   *Measuring influencer effectiveness with hashtag tracking*

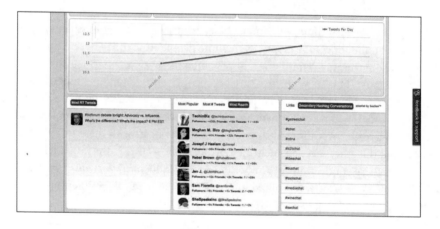

Figure 10.13   *Identifying potential influencers and complementary Twitter chats*

By utilizing oneQube's Twitter management software, the effectiveness of running an influencer campaign across Twitter is hugely increased and allows brand managers to identify and connect with the kind of influencers that have the potential to become advocates as well as increase the likelihood of their micro-influencers becoming advocates too.

oneQube's pricing starts at $9.99 per month and includes the Social Relationship Manager dashboard, searchable social database, unlimited list creation, 24/7 tracking of one hashtag and multiple Direct Messaging functionality. A community manager account costs $29.99 per month for up to five hashtags. Enterprise solutions with multiple accounts and hashtags cost approximately $2,500 per month.

- Four Ms application for oneQube: Make, Manage, Monitor, Measurement

The Future of Influence Is Fluid

This chapter highlighted just six platforms out of the hundreds providing influence identification and measurement services today. While other platforms offer solutions that can be applied to our new influence model of the Four Ms and reverse engineering, the six showcased in this chapter are the ones that align the most with what we see as influence marketing's true value—an important part of a marketing strategy for lead generation and customer acquisition, and turning influencers into advocates. For a business in the social media space, these six companies offer the most potential for not only influencer campaign success in the short-term, but longer term relationship building and customer cultivation.

By understanding who the influencers around your brand are today, and where the next generation of influencers are in relation to your ongoing brand recognition and loyalty building process, the strength of connection between your brand and your customer will continue to grow. This growth will foster your original influencers and their communities to become your brand advocates while connecting you to the next wave of influencers. With this continuous fluidity between influence and advocate, your brand can share resources that focus on the needs of the biggest influencers on the longevity and success of any business—your customers.

Endnotes

1. Pulizzi, J. November 14, 2012. "2013 B2C Content Marketing Research: Benchmarks, Budgets, and Trends." www.contentmarketinginstitute. com/2012/11/2013-b2c-consumer-content-marketing/.

2. "PSY – Gangnam Style." YouTube movie. www.youtube.com/ watch?v=9bZkp7q19f0.

3. The White House's Photostream. Flickr.com. www.flickr.com/photos/ whitehouse/8191317327/.

11

The Business of Influence Marketing

From the days when a surplus of agriculture was exchanged for other necessities such as a tools, textiles, or earthenware, commerce has been a main driver of communities and economies. From individual neighbors swapping products, central locations of trade such as fairs and local markets were formed for greater convenience, efficiency, and reach. It was in these group exchanges—when vendors began to compete for attention—that the psychology and math of marketing began to take shape. Decorated stalls, innovative product displays, and signage were all experimented with for the single goal of attracting more customers. If the cost of attracting those new customers was higher than the revenue they generated, it was time to try something else.

From day one, marketing has been a business function: attracting more customers to purchase more products from your business than that of your competitors. As a business operation, marketing must operate—and be responsive to—business needs. A business has many interrelated needs, yet they all function to deliver one end result: Profit.

There's both a psychology and a science to effective marketing, which continues to fuel the debate over how it should be measured and judged. Building awareness and positive sentiment around a brand is difficult to measure, especially for performance marketers and business executives who like to see direct correlations between dollars invested and dollars returned. Yet, few will argue that awareness and positive sentiment impact the sale of a product, even if the exact amount is unknown. The wit expressed in a slogan or the creativity demonstrated in artwork may improve the emotional response consumers have to an advertisement, but if the costs of developing those campaigns were more expensive than the resulting impact on the business's bottom line, how effective were they really?

The fact that marketing budgets are typically the first to be cut in a recession or when a business fails to meet its target sales is a stark reality check on the need to measure the bottom-line success of marketing efforts. As the economy continues to struggle and marketing campaigns extend to the online channel, the science side of marketing is becoming a dominant factor in how campaigns are created and, ultimately, judged.

While influence as a formal marketing strategy, arguably, started with Daniel Edelman in the 1960s, the Internet and social media have created a renaissance of sorts for the discipline. The practice of influence marketing is evolving from a "fuzzy science" and as such, greater demands for measurement and accountability are being placed upon it. In Chapter 8, "Managing Social Influence Paths," we introduced the concept that influence marketing is moving into its third stage of evolution. No longer are businesses satisfied to rely on amplification as measurement of success for influence marketing campaigns, they're seeking metrics that tie actions to bottom-line results as they do with other business operations. Doing so requires a new methodology for identifying and managing influencers and a new measurement standard. In previous chapters we outlined our methodology for identification and management of influencers. Now we turn to the issue of measurement and integration with other business operations.

Connecting Influence to Sales Revenue

Before we can explore measurement, we need to summarize the growing connection between influence marketing and the sales function. Advances in our understanding of social influence and improvements in the supporting technologies have enabled the transformation of influence marketing. More marketers are beginning to reformulate their strategies to be able to link activity to transactional metrics and that's the first step. Mark Fidelman, managing director at Evolve!, a social business agency and author of the business marketing book *Socialized!*, shared this successful case study of an influence marketing campaign he conducted recently for a Business to Business (B2B) software company, which helps illustrate this trend.

Case Study

Challenge: Introduce a new product whose business and brand were so new, each had zero brand recognition among prospective customers or the audience at large.

Solution: An influence marketing campaign was chosen as a strategy to create an immediate impact on IT and marketing decision makers within their target audience of Global 5000 businesses. Using a variety of social influence scoring platforms and tools, they gathered a list of 1,000 people whose scores indicated they might have a large following with active conversations in the selected subject matter. Understanding that such lists are too general and based on potentially incomplete data, they developed a proprietary process to work that list down to a smaller group of 25 people they believed had real influence over the decision-making process of the target audience.

Fidelman chose a unique path to engage this audience. Instead of offering them a free product trial, he produced a Top 25 Influencers list for this space and published it in a top tier media site, which was successful at capturing the attention of each influencer listed. Their inclusion in this publicized list encouraged the influencers to reach out and start a conversation with the business.

Result: The relationships built from this engagement with a small group of influencers led to an exchange of information, which in turn resulted in direct product referrals being made to customers within the influencers' inner circles. Through direct introductions or referrals cited by the business's newly acquired customers, the campaign tracked over $350,000 in sales tied directly to these recommendations.

Such case studies will continue to capture the attention of executives as influence marketing matures. In fact, businesses will begin to attribute the effects of influence marketing on customer lifetime valuation to make better decisions around future customer acquisition strategies. Influence strategies will move beyond one-dimensional tactics toward full integration with the customer life cycle and moving prospects along that timeline.

Impact on Customer Lifetime Value

The word "campaign" should be removed from influence marketing efforts and measurement because it suggests a beginning and end when, in fact, influence marketing is conducted along the full customer life cycle. Similarly, the impact—and thus measurement—of influence marketing transcends the campaign and is linked to the entire customer life cycle. As a result, the study of customer life time value (CLV) becomes critical in our study of how influence marketing is merging with the rest of the business's operations.

Combining the efforts of performance and brand marketing with other business functions drives what is really the gold-standard in marketing measurement: customer lifetime value, which is a prediction of the net profit attributed to the entire future relationship a business has with a customer. Understanding CLV allows a marketing team to establish the budget it can allocate to acquisition campaigns, potential loss-leader offers, and the strategies that should be deployed to acquire high-yield customers.

The most basic calculation method for CLV is: (Average Value of a Sale) X (Number of Repeat Transactions) X (Average Retention Time in Months or Years for a Typical Customer). For an existing business, actual dollar amounts and statistics can be used; for startups, estimates are typically used based on industry or competitive statistics. To illustrate this, consider a music download service, whose average customer buys 30 songs per year at an average price of $1.50/each. Assuming the customer will purchase music from the age of 16 to 49, the calculation would look like this: ($1.50/avg. transaction) X (30 units/year) X (43 years) = $1,935.

Customer Lifetime Value (CLV)

A prediction of the value of future net profits earned from a specific customer.

As far as revenue is concerned, this is an adequate formula. However, it assumes that the costs of maintaining that customer are equal across all customers, which we know is not accurate. A common mistake marketers make in calculating CLV is basing it on total revenue or even gross margin. Depending on the type of business, its products, or the geographic distribution of its clients, maintaining happy customers is not a one-size-fits-all operation. For example, some customers require more support and more training, which impacts the profitability of selling to those customers.

In addition, maintaining customers' loyalty can add costs to certain subsegments. Depending on situational factors including competitive forces, some money has to be invested in keeping customers loyal for extended periods of time. Then there's the retention rate of customers; customers may die, move away, or be swayed by a competitor's promotions. Unless you average the cost of maintaining customers and average churn rates, a CLV measurement that does not account for the net profit earned per customer will report values that might be multiples of their actual value to the business. However, averaging out such costs is not an effective strategy for CLV calculations because it will hide areas of opportunity and risk.

Further, due to the complexity of calculations required, too often the CLV measurement does not take into account the Net Present Value (NVP) of the revenue earned. The most accurate CLV calculations are those that predict the *net profit* contributed by a customer based on the future value of the money to be earned. Instead of being a simple profitability figure, lifetime value is a complex set of numbers, some of which are under the business's control, and some of which depend on external factors.

A proper CLV calculation is the strongest and most accurate tool to measure marketing's contribution to the bottom line. Campaigns generated must be measured on how they positively or negatively impact the values in that equation. However, as Bain consultant Fred Reichheld demonstrated in his study, "The One Number You Need to Grow," the value of any one customer is not solely defined by what that person buys.[1] The act of referral in our socially connected marketplace can impact a business's revenues and profits in equal or greater quantities.

Thus, the phenomena surrounding influence marketing adds yet another factor to this calculation: the future value of customer referrals. For example, using the simple revenue CLV calculation previously described for the music download service, a customer who makes less than the average 30 purchases a year could potentially have a greater contribution to the business's profitability than someone who purchases more than the average 30 downloads per year. Consider someone who downloads only 10 songs per year, but each time uses a social share feature to announce his use of the download service to his audience. If that user is among the micro-influencer community of the target audience, his social shares will positively impact others to use that same service; thus, the user's value is greater than the sum of his purchases.

Think back to the Telenor Group study referenced in Chapter 8, the likelihood of a prospect buying an iPhone was 14 times greater if one of the person's friends also had an iPhone. Understanding the audience and who influences their purchase decisions, casts a new light on how CLV must be calculated. The referral effect of a macro- or micro-influencer who downloads 10 songs can have a greater impact on revenue than a noninfluencer who downloads 50 songs per year. This highlights the need to connect the resulting sales transaction of influence marketing campaigns to various audiences' segments and to the campaigns that drove them to make a purchase.

Influencers Versus Advocates

As the practice of influence marketing continues to evolve, we believe a distinction must be drawn between influencers and advocates. "Influencers" has been used as a common term to reference anyone mentioning a business brand across social networks via shares, ratings, reviews or blogs. Few strategists—or software companies serving this space—have drawn a clear distinction between influencers who are customers and those who are not. Certainly, few of the available applications in this space today treat these two groups differently when it comes to influence marketing tactics. Before we delve further into measurement, it's important to take a moment to explore why this distinction is being made.

Influencers are people who are typically noncustomer individuals or businesses incentivized to recommend a business brand or product. Advocates are existing customers who, based on a superior customer experience, voluntarily recommend the business brand or product. The differences are the customer versus the noncustomer and incentivized versus voluntary nature of the relationships. However, the comparison also highlights a strategic shift in how businesses build their sales funnels. Each leverages the power of referrals, but influence marketing attracts leads through general audience engagement and promotion, whereas advocate marketing focuses on improving relationships with existing customers. Analysis of customer advocacy has proven that the value of referrals from existing customers could be much greater than the direct spend of those same customers.[2] An infrequent, but extremely satisfied customer who is properly connected to potential high-value customers drives greater value than a frequent customer with no relationship or access to prospective customers.

Building and measuring strong relationships with well-networked customers has been proven in the offline marketing experiences of Business-to-Business industries for many years. One example is the medical industry, where pharmaceutical companies identify and engage macro-influencers (doctors and researchers who speak at medical conferences, publish articles in medical journals, and so on) to drive awareness and product sampling among micro-influencers (family doctors and other health-care practitioners). Assessing and measuring the referral impact of those customers (the doctors) across their networks (other doctors, patients, pharmacies, and so on) can demonstrate the added value that influence marketing drives to the CLV.

Marketers are beginning to understand the impact of this influence on the customer lifetime value; however, few track anything beyond the customer's willingness to refer. Interestingly, a customer's willingness to refer is the prime measurement of the Net Promoter Score (NPS), which has been proven to positively correlate to a business's overall success and profitability.[3] In fact, referred customers from businesses with a high NPS were both more profitable and loyal than normal customers, with referred customers having both a higher contribution margin and retention rate. This is a key insight. In the world of influence marketing, not all referrals are equal. Referrals from advocates drive a higher CLV than those from influencers.

This lesson does not suggest that new customer acquisition campaigns (via influencers) should not be undertaken. The famous "chicken or egg" question can be argued here, especially for new businesses: Referrals from existing satisfied customers are the most effective source of profitable customer acquisition, yet without generic customer acquisition strategies, where do those customers come from? In reality, a mix of both influence marketing and advocate marketing is required until a business reaches a critical mass that allows the strategic mix to shift from influencer to advocate campaigning.

Today, many advocate influence campaigns are seen as incentives to existing customers to introduce their friends to the brand they're already doing business with. Often the incentives are savings toward the current customer's bill or the promise of future upgrades to the service or product they're receiving. However, general influence marketing within your existing customer base can also prove to be inefficient and costly if you're not targeting the right customers. As stated earlier, not all referrals are equal. The goal of advocate marketing strategies—as with influence marketing strategies—is to identify the "right customers." Ideally, the right customer is every customer, or at least that's who they should be. In reality, customers—just like prospects—are not all equal.

Creating Brand Advocates

Until now, we have treated all influencers as one group, which was a necessity to more easily convey the influence marketing methodology we've presented. Now that we've explored the model fully, we can deal with customer advocates as a unique group. In addition, the macro- and micro-influencer case studies described to this point have dealt with the pre-purchase life cycle, which is only half of the full customer life cycle. A business prospers when pre- and post-purchase operations are properly synced and managed; and so a proper exploration of influence marketing would not be complete without explaining how it impacts the business's post-purchase operations.

Since a business's advocates are those who voluntarily and actively refer the business to their social graphs, knowing which customers are the right customers to target is really not a question of identification; it's a matter of *creating* brand advocates. Creating brand advocates requires a formal understanding of the customer life cycle.

The customer life cycle refers to the stages through which a customer progresses when considering, purchasing, and using products or services purchased. The life cycle also encompasses the associated marketing, sales, and service tactics the business engages in to push those customers toward a purchase decision. This is not a new concept; however, the manner in which customers engage with a business—and with each other—has necessitated a shift in the typical linear model of the life cycle.

Figure 11.1 represents a typical customer life cycle marketing process, where the purchase is the main customer engagement goal.

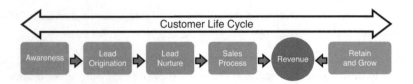

Figure 11.1   *Linear customer life cycle*

Many marketers—along with the sales and marketing software they use—focus on tracking, scoring, and even measuring the presale life cycle. The reason is no mystery: Customer acquisition costs can be very high. As customers become more connected through technology, marketing programs and software must evolve to include stronger customer development strategies. Yet, it's usually an independent practice appended to the program, not a core component of it.

There are three fundamental problems with this linear model:

1. The increase in customer acquisition attainable by strong customer development strategies is lost.

2. Placing revenue at the center of the model shifts focus away from the customer experience, which in fact decreases the business's total revenue generating possibilities.

3. Lifetime customer value and marketing effectiveness cannot be accurately measured or scored unless customer development strategy is set as an equal partner alongside customer acquisition in the methodology.

You can see the parallels with today's influence marketing strategies, which are designed to increase awareness of a product or business with the hope that it may lead to a sale at some point in the future. Today's popular influence marketing software programs deal with "awareness" and "lead origination" within the linear customer life cycle illustrated in Figure 11.1, which ignores the strategic value in the differences between prospect and customer referrals. This book has been dedicated to the strategies and methodologies that will drive influence marketing forward along the customer life cycle—to the point of purchase. However, there's another side to the life cycle that can drive even greater bottom line results for established businesses: existing customer development.

The life cycle is really a continuum, one that few businesses manage well end-to-end. It's a model where customer development strategies provide an equal balance to customer acquisition. In the future, influence marketing practices must integrate post-sale customer engagement, thus combining customer development with prospect development for maximum business growth. We've already discussed the prepurchase life cycle, but as illustrated in Figure 11.2, the second half of the cycle is just as important as the first.

Figure 11.2   *Customer life cycle continuum*

This marketing continuum is the basis for our customer experience management practice. It's based on the premise that customer relationships, when designed well, will facilitate a better customer experience and measurably impact the customer lifetime value. Managing (and measuring) influence marketing strategies that move the customer along the life cycle from awareness through the purchase toward advocacy creates a self-sustaining and highly potent ecosystem.

Figure 11.2 illustrates how the previous linear customer life cycle turns into a circular, self-propelling model for business growth. In this model, customer advocates drive the social proof and referrals that prospective customers are actively seeking through online channels. In fact, these advocates form the majority of micro-influencers in the smaller social communities that impact purchase decisions.

So how are advocates earned and why aren't all customers advocates? This is an important question for businesses who are seen to use influence marketing practices within their existing customer base. Technically, every customer can be an advocate; however, the value of that advocacy is different based on the life cycle stage that customer is in. Think of the customer relationship as a series of tasks that must be completed before the next task can be started. The following sections offer a brief summary of each stage of the customer life cycle continuum.

Awareness

Building awareness goes beyond introducing the business's product and services to a target audience. It must include the required audience research to identify the most receptive and potentially profitable customers. For established businesses this first stage can be driven by customer advocates identified in the last stage, because they often form the nucleus of micro-influence communities. For newer businesses, noncustomer macro-influencers are critical here because of the lack of existing customers. These macro-influencers support the broad distribution of brand messaging that will be consumed and converted in the upcoming stages between micro-influencers and decision makers.

Nurturing

Once the larger target audience is established, segmenting it by need, challenges, and opportunity is the next step. Building strong relationships within each segmented group is critical through personalized value-added content and information, which is driven by the target audience's micro-influencers. This is where the value of identifying and monitoring the relationships between the decision maker and her social graphs becomes so important. Understanding the context of those relationships will support and make the conversion more efficient and predictable.

Conversion

Aside from direct customer requests, monitoring the conversations among the target decision makers' micro-communities allows for the insertion of targeted calls to action to more effectively influence purchase decisions. Overlaying additional contact and situational factors collected in social CRMs supports this targeting process. It also ensures that the post-sale customer engagement team has the necessary historical data to better manage the relationship.

Satisfaction

This stage of the life cycle can range in time from weeks to months, depending on the industry and type of product. It's one of the most critical stages of the life cycle because it's where most of a business's churn happens. Activity here must support the customer's role transition from prospect to customer and ensure that the customer feels her decision to purchase from the business was justified. This requires a proper hand-off between the acquisition team (sales and marketing) to the customer care team (inside sales, customer service, and so on), which includes mapping the expectations set in the presales cycle to an onboarding program. After a period of engagement with the brand, if the customer's experience has been positive, the customer moves toward the loyalty stage.

Loyalty

Most businesses mistake loyal customers for advocates. A loyal customer is one who is satisfied that the product purchased or the service received delivers on the promise made during the sales pitch. The overall experience creates customers who are highly likely to repurchase. However, that does not mean they're highly likely to refer, at least not without direct solicitation to do so. Transitioning a customer from being loyal to being an advocate requires more than reward programs, incentives, and price breaks.

Loyal customers may offer a recommendation if asked by others in their social graphs, but they're less likely to do so when not asked. While desirable, such customers do not add any social proof of a business's value across social channels. Further, they're less likely to engage with macro-influencers and thus, less likely to act as micro-influencers in support of the prospect's decision making.

Advocacy

Only when the value of the customer-business relationship far exceeds the utility of the purchased product is an advocate created. An advocate's experience is so personal and exceeds expectations to the point that the advocate looks for any opportunity to share her love of the brand. These are the customers who post pictures of the products purchased, comment on the brand's social networks, and actively introduce the brand to others without solicitation. These are the type of customers who share the music they're listening to on social networks or select Share on Facebook and Twitter when checking in to their favorite business on FourSquare.

Advocates are motivated to act as connectors between the needs of those in their social graphs and the business's goals. In essence, they do the job of the natural language processing discussed earlier in this book; they read between the lines in the discussions occurring around them and insert the business's value proposition into the appropriate conversations.

True customer advocates are born from superior customer experiences, not incentivized engagement. They're the most impactful people in decision makers' micro-influence communities and require less management and cost than incentivized influencers. The key message here is that customer advocates are not earned in the same manner that influencers are encouraged. Advocates are earned rather than persuaded.

Understanding their role in the life cycle and identifying them in the influence path proves to be a cost-effective, high-yield practice. Further, understanding the progression of a customer along the life cycle helps set the metrics and milestones that assist in measuring the influence impact on the customer lifetime value calculation.

Case Study

To better illustrate how an influence marketing campaign can be created and measured among customer advocates, we present a case study featuring one of the largest cruise-vacation retailers in the world.

Challenge: The company's executives were not seeing the correlation between the awareness generated by their previous influence marketing efforts and the purchase of cruise vacation packages.

Solution: The marketing team turned to California-based Manumatix to create a solution that better engaged existing satisfied customers, and encourage them to drive and measure purchases from among their peers in social networks. Using Manumatix's Bamboo platform, they built an integrated online community that spanned their website, social networks and their customers' own websites (through embedded content).

The strategy was built on the theory that people are most influenced by their peers and more so by those peers with whom they have personal relationships. Existing customers, through these branded online communities, were invited to share travel-related content, recommend the brand, participate in customer-focused promotions, and engage in branded-games, activities they were often performing anyway. However, within these Bamboo-powered communities, customers were given points for the activity, which rewarded them with tiered, travel benefits.

As customers participated in the program, their activity was pushed to specific peer groups across their social graph. The application tracked direct and indirect activity generated by the advocates' peers, the profiles of those taking action, and attributed both the volume and dollar amount of the accumulated activity to the advocate that first made the referral. In addition, the application offered the advocates' peers who received the referral the option to purchase cruises directly from within the social application.

The solution replaced many disparate and isolated campaigns with a single customer advocacy community — integrating multiple Web and social networking platforms — and served as a full customer relationship management platform.

Result: Bamboo's solution and consulting team was able to provide a very accurate return on investment calculation because of the unique tracking features embedded in the Bamboo platform.

Because they offered in-line purchases within the advocates' referrals and tracked transactions beyond the initial influencer amplification, the travel was able to report on revenues-per-referral and cost savings-per-referral. The net results were $40,972 in cost savings/month and $99,000 in revenue/month.

Powered by platforms such as Bamboo—and driven by its ability to demonstrate a return on investment—such advocate programs are beginning to replace social scoring platforms as the main focus of influence marketing strategies. As we look forward, such case studies demonstrate the importance of customization in influence marketing practices and how they will become part of the entire customer life cycle.

Customizing Influence

Throughout this book, we've made reference to the distinction between platforms and processes. Specifically, we referenced current social influence scoring platforms as tools, which, when added to customer-focused methodologies and processes, can be better leveraged to measurably impact the customer's decision-making process. Used in isolation, such tools fail to deliver the customization or context required to connect broadcast marketing to specific sales goals.

Each industry, the businesses within them, and their customers have unique circumstances and situational factors that impact the brand's influence paths. The ability to self-manage what criteria makes a person influential within specific communities and for specific products must be considered, and influence marketing solutions will have to take this into account when developing future versions. Without this human interaction, one-size-fits-all scoring platforms limit the effectiveness of these campaigns. For example, Photoshop is a great tool for graphic designers, but using the tool does not make someone a great graphic artist. Photoshop is just a tool in the branding process; it does not dictate the process.

As our understanding of micro-influence in social conversations continues to expand, so too will the technologies that support those campaigns. Influence marketing strategy—and the software that supports it—will start becoming interwoven with most marketing, sales and customer service operations to create uniquely personalized campaigns.

We're already seeing signs of this in software programs such as Shoutlet, a social media marketing platform. Shoutlet was originally built by founder Jason Weaver for marketers to create, syndicate, and measure content across multiple social channels through a single dashboard. Its simple-to-use interface and powerful measurement toolset helped it gain traction among leading brands around the world.

As Shoutlet's team continued to monitor the engagement needs of its clients with its customers, they discovered that not all social relationships are equal. The nature of a person's relationship to one contact can be different from that of another, even if they're all engaged in the same social network. By extension, the context of the discussion and content shared in each relationship should be unique. What's relevant to one may be irrelevant to the other when it comes to impacting a person's decision to purchase from one brand versus another.

So Shoutlet created a new feature called Social Switchboard, which gives marketers the ability to better identify unique characteristics of people engaged in those online relationships and conversations. In turn, the platform allows for relevant content to be dynamically presented based on that identification. For example, if 5,000 people are targeted, content presented to nurture a prospect or convert a sale would not be received in the same way by each. As a result, this software now looks at the people engaged on the brand's website, online contests, and so on, and tracks their activity (what pages visited, what actions they've taken), appends additional profile data (for example, profile scrape from a social network profile), and then cross-references it with the campaign's user-defined profile rules. Based on this real-time analysis, the Switchboard inserts the appropriate social content into the right social interaction. "We're choosing to allow users to define their own influencer-identification criteria instead of allowing Klout and PeerIndex to do it for us," states Shoutlet's founder. "For the time being, we don't see those tools as providing the right context to properly inform our clients' campaigns."

The creation of Shoutlet's Switchboard is another indication that social influence is evolving past brand amplification and social influence scoring to merge with other business operations such as relationship management, customer life time value assestment and sales conversion.

Setting aside the need to measure influence against sales conversions for a moment, from a pure marketing amplification perspective, an individual's follower count and level of interaction with that audience does not make him influential over others. Knowledge of the nature of a person's relationship with those she's engaging, contrasted with the context of their discussion in different platforms and within different situations—at a minimum—is required to begin to leverage influence strategies. Not surprisingly, we're beginning to see more solutions like Appinions, oneQube, and Shoutlet's new Social Switchboard evolving to offer different ways to identify and act upon the context identified for unique customer groups.

The realization that a more in-depth understanding of a business's audience is required to manage influence campaigns is driving innovation in this industry. Instead of relying on social scoring platforms to dictate who is influential, marketers are demanding the option to personalize how influence marketing is defined in their unique communities, why it's relevant to their businesses, and how it impacts their bottom lines. For example, from a profiling perspective, the identification of influencers might be based on specific, industry-based contacts they have within LinkedIn versus their general following on Twitter. Similarly it might be based on the frequency and context of the brand's conversations with its audience on its blogs versus its customer engagements on Facebook; or some weighted combination of all of the above. The need to customize influence formulas based on the community circumstances, as they relate to the business needs, is forcing change in this industry.

Stop Scoring Influence, Start Creating Influence Paths

The year 2012 will certainly be remembered by many marketers as the year social scoring was "called out." Blog posts, articles, and conference presentations about social influence scoring platforms such as Klout were fodder for heated debate, criticisms, and rants. Aside from the common "influence cannot be measured by a numeric rank" protest, common criticisms include

- Inaccurate scores and faulty algorithms
- Lack of context represented in the scores
- Undefined relationships between influencers and followers
- No real connection to sales results
- Improper use of scores by HR and customer service departments
- Easily manipulated scores

The one common denominator that seems to have fuelled the debate is the practice of publicly scoring individuals on their social influence. A number from 1 to 100 is assigned to you by a mysterious third party—often without you knowing it—that infers something about you that may or may not be accurate. This score makes a statement about an individual's persona, experience, or status that may or may not be true; it is a number that may dictate how you're treated by brands or employers. That's a lot of power in a number. The level of vitriol surrounding influence platforms exists because people take exception to the score. They don't understand it. They want it to be higher; they don't agree or like what it represents. If these platforms did not publicly brand people in this way, they would have generated a small fraction of the negative publicity that was hurled at them these past two years and possibly gained wider acceptance from the marketing community.

Senior personnel at Kred and PeerIndex, two of the leading social influence scoring platforms today, during interviews for this book reiterated that influence marketing is still in its infancy with much room for growth. Each points to their efforts to further refine and improve the algorithms used to identify the influence of person X over person Y. Kred, for example, works diligently to identify and remove those seen as gaming their engagement to increase scores, or those found to be employees of competitor's brands when preparing influencer lists for brands.

Unfortunately, a lot of the conversational data produced through social channels such as Facebook, the world's largest social network, is not publicly available unless, of course, the public allows these firms access to personal data. Why would anyone allow them such access? For those people seeking to be recognized as social influencers and earn the perks and recognition that comes with it, there's only one reason: to increase their scores. Providing access to private social networks can earn a user the social status and improved customer service advertised as available to those with higher influence scores. Further, achieving higher scores by opening up our social networks to these platforms drives access to the perks that they, through their clients, make available. You see, publicly available scores are an integral part of the plan to gain more access to data. It's an effective tool to encourage greater usage through repeat visits and viral sharing—all of which are required to get more data.

Yet firms such as Appinions, which boasts its software's ability to accurately identify brand influencers for Fortune 500 clients, don't publicly display an influencer's rank. Partly because that number is variable based on the context of the assignment and partly, in the company's words, because "influence is not a game." If public scores were not available, the level of gamification and manipulation by enterprising individuals would decrease drastically and that cloud might be lifted from the industry.

The measurement of someone's influence across social channels is not a passing trend, but a marketing discipline that will continue to evolve. Influence marketing platforms will be well advised to rethink the practice of public scoring and focus on enabling brand managers more options to build and manage influence paths among their social graphs based on relationships and context, not scores.

Conclusion

Social media marketing—and the practice of influence marketing within it—still accounts for a relatively low percentage of the overall marketing budget. Influence marketing is no longer a curiosity but a growing communication channel connecting business with clients and in many cases, facilitating improved customer relationships. Yet the lack of proven sales metrics has kept budget allocation limited. This will change rapidly in the next 48 months.

Critics have called social media an enigma wrapped in a riddle in part because it's a relatively new communication channel but mainly because executives have failed to reconcile the efforts expended within this channel with measurable business success.

Ironically, within social media channels, marketers have been conditioned to resist "salesy" marketing speak in favor of starting discussions; to avoid advertising in favor of community building; and to provide value to the end consumer instead of broadcasting marketing messages. Is it any wonder they've struggled with efforts to influence online conversations toward sales? Public discourse about brands and consumer experiences with those brands continues to spread across an increasing number of social channels. As a result, the need to identify and engage influencers and advocates who can effectively sway purchase decisions will become an essential business skill set.

Almost since the introduction of social media marketing, business's online engagements have been plagued with questions of value and return on investment. A financial measurement of social media success has eluded most marketers, forcing many to invent calculations that imply a long-term benefit to positive sentiment, frequent social connections, and large numbers of highly engaged followers. Yet, at the end of the day, such success is anecdotal, and, not surprisingly, boards of directors and shareholders have an aversion to anecdotal measures of success. We're not arguing that such value does not exist, only that until such time as marketers can positively define the financial impact of their social marketing efforts, the required budgets to properly engage the business's audience across social media channels will remain elusive.

Building a case for influence marketing budgets mirrors the case that must be a made for social media marketing in general. Doing so requires marketers and business executives to comprehend the fact that social media is not a marketing tactic but a communication channel that builds customer lifetime value. Within that construct, social media plays four primary roles within the enterprise:

1. **Listening**—Customers, employees, media, vendors, and stakeholders are increasingly adopting social media for personal and professional discourse. Employing effective techniques and technologies to convert those conversations into lessons learned for product development teams, sales and marketing professions, and customer service teams will create the foundation for social media success.

2. **Building relationships**—Social media is not a one-way communication channel. In fact, it's not a two-way communication channel either. It's a multidimensional platform where social networks and tools are used to build relationships between the various stakeholders. It provides a channel for consumers to—directly and in real time—tell their favorite brands what they love and hate, and for those businesses to reply in kind with an acknowledgement of the value of that feedback.

3. **Magnification**—While building relationships with specific individuals and groups of customers across social channels, one cannot underestimate the magnification effect that it has on the wider audience, including competitors' customers. There's nothing new about the online conversations occurring between a business brand and its customers. They're the exact same discussions that were happening in person, on the phone, via fax, or by email before Web 2.0 technologies were first introduced, except that the world is now listening to every conversation. This magnification of customer experience can drive unlimited benefit for business if leveraged properly.

4. **Driving sales**—Arguably the most important of the four roles is to convert prospects into customers and customers into advocates, subsequently providing advocates the encouragement and tools to build social proof and a more qualified sales funnel. Swaying consumer attitudes and behavior is the culmination of all social media strategies and where a business can most easily identify the channel's impact on the customer lifetime value measurement. It is here that the evolving practice of influence marketing has the greatest opportunities.

Be it for prospective or existing customers, these four interrelated roles support one goal: to influence the consumer's decision-making process. Embracing this business reality is the first step in connecting social media marketing strategies to sales and next, toward proving its financial impact. If the methodology and technologies outlined in this book take hold within software companies and businesses, the science of influence marketing may become the tipping point in the debate over social media return on investment.

The value of a consumer's social graph—and the conversation dynamics within it—will grow in importance as technology provides more ways for those personal connections to be mapped, analyzed, and measured. New technologies, along with the influence marketing methodology outlined in this book, will renew the value of word-of-mouth in the post-digital age and change the way businesses invest in lead acquisition and customer development strategies. Yet, we must move beyond the marketers' fixation on building social influence scores and "influencer-as-a-job" practices toward the strategies that build and manage influence paths between brands, macro-influencers, micro-influencers, and decision makers. Many techno-logical and social challenges are still in the way, but given the trends we're seeing within large businesses and the new breed of influence marketing software coming to market, the outlook is promising.

Endnotes

1. Reichheld, F., Frederick, December 2003, "The One Number You Need to Grow," Harvard Business Review.

2. Kumar, V., Petersen, A., and R. P. Leone. October 2007. "How Valuable Is Word of Mouth?" Harvard Business Review.

3. Reichheld, F., Frederick, December 2003, "The One Number You Need to Grow," Harvard Business Review.

Index

U

V

W–Z

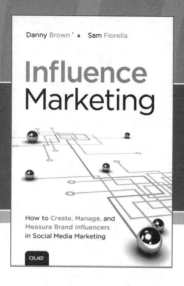

Influence Marketing

Danny Brown • Sam Fiorella

How to Create, Manage, and
Measure Brand Influencers
in Social Media Marketing

que

Safari
Books Online

FREE
Online Edition

Your purchase of *Influence Marketing* includes access to a free online edition for 45 days
through the **Safari Books Online** subscription service. Nearly every Que book is available
online through **Safari Books Online**, along with thousands of books and videos from
publishers such as Addison-Wesley Professional, Cisco Press, Exam Cram, IBM Press, O'Reilly
Media, Prentice Hall, and Sams.

Safari Books Online is a digital library providing searchable, on-demand access to thousands
of technology, digital media, and professional development books and videos from leading
publishers. With one monthly or yearly subscription price, you get unlimited access to learning
tools and information on topics including mobile app and software development, tips and tricks
on using your favorite gadgets, networking, project management, graphic design, and much
more.

Activate your FREE Online Edition at
informit.com/safarifree

STEP 1: Enter the coupon code: EDJCUWA.

STEP 2: New Safari users, complete the brief registration form.
Safari subscribers, just log in.

If you have difficulty registering on Safari or accessing the online edition,
please e-mail customer-service@safaribooksonline.com